Notes of a Plenipotentiary

D1600924

NOTES OF A

PLENIPOTENTIARY

RUSSIAN DIPLOMACY AND WAR

IN THE BALKANS,

1914–1917

G. N. Trubetskoi

Translated by Elizabeth Saika-Voivod

Edited by Borislav Chernev

Introduction by Eric Lohr

NIU PRESS / *DeKalb*

Northern Illinois University Press, DeKalb 60115
© 2016 by Northern Illinois University Press
All rights reserved
Printed in the United States of America
24 24 23 22 21 20 19 18 17 16   1 2 3 4 5

978-0-87580-726-3 (paper)
978-1-60909-186-6 (ebook)

Book design by Shaun Allshouse
Cover design by Yuni Dorr

Unless otherwise noted, all photos are from the translator's collection.

Library of Congress Cataloging-in-Publication Data:
Names: Trubetskoĭ, Grigoriĭ N. (Grigoriĭ Nikolaevich), kniazʹ,   1873–1930.
Title: Notes of a plenipotentiary : Russian diplomacy and war in the Balkans, 1914–1917
    / G.N. Trubetskoi ; translated by his granddaughter Elizabeth Saika-Voivod ; edited by
    Borislav Chernev ; introduction by Eric Lohr.
Description: DeKalb, IL : Northern Illinois University Press, 2015. | Includes
    bibliographical references and index.
Identifiers: LCCN 2015035591| ISBN 9780875807263 (paperback : alkaline paper) | ISBN
    9781609091866 (ebook)
Subjects: LCSH: Trubetskoiĭ, Grigoriĭ N. (Grigoriĭ Nikolaevich), kniazʹ, 1873–1930. | World
    War, 1914–1918—Diplomatic history. | World War, 1914-1918--Personal narratives,
    Russian. | Diplomats—Russia—Biography. | Russia—Foreign relations—1894–1917. |
    World War, 1914–1918—Balkan Peninsula. | World War, 1914–1918—Turkey. | BISAC:
    BIOGRAPHY & AUTOBIOGRAPHY / Personal Memoirs. | HISTORY / Europe / Russia
    & the Former Soviet Union. | HISTORY / Military / World War I.
Classification: LCC D621.R8 T78 2015 | DDC 940.3/224709496—dc23
LC record available at http://lccn.loc.gov/2015035591

Contents

РУССКИМЪ ВОИНАМЪ.

Г. Н. ТРУБЕЦКОЙ.
РУССКІЙ ПОСЛАННИКЪ ВЪ СЕРБІИ.

„Великая любовь и великій гнѣвъ дадутъ Россіи побѣду"
Трубецкой.

1. Official postcard with photograph of Trubetskoi. Printed text above reads "To Russian Soldiers." Printed and handwritten text below reads "Great Devotion and Great Anger Will Give Victory to Russia."

INTRODUCTION

Grigorii N. Trubetskoi was a unique and contradictory figure in the first three decades of the twentieth century. He was a leading liberal—and often scathing—critic of autocracy yet was perhaps most influential in pushing the regime toward an aggressive stand in the Balkans. Personally deeply religious and idealistic about his faith, he became the proponent of deep reforms of Orthodoxy and pragmatic solutions to the divisions between the church that remained in the Soviet Union under Patriarch Tikhon and the Orthodox in emigration. A prince in one of Russia's most exalted noble families, he spent his life working long hours as a civil servant and a writer.

His Career and Background

Grigorii Nikolaevich Trubetskoi was born in 1873 to one of Russia's oldest noble families, a family that traces its princely title to the twelfth-century Grand Prince of Lithuania Gediminas. Grigorii Nikolaevich had nine sisters and was the youngest of four renowned brothers. The eldest, Piotr Nikolaevich, was Marshal of the Nobility in Moscow. Sergei Nikolaevich was the rector of Moscow University, a prominent philosopher, and a popular professor. His funeral spurred large student demonstrations and proved to be an important event in the 1905 revolution. Evgenii Nikolaevich was also one of Russia's leading philosophers, a professor at Moscow University, and the editor of *Moskovskii ezhenedel'nik*, an important liberal weekly journal that published broadly on foreign affairs and other topics from 1906 to 1911.

Grigorii Nikolaevich studied in the department of history and philology, and in 1896 he defended his master's thesis on the Russian domestic situation on the eve of the emancipation of the serfs in 1861. He began his diplomatic career with a posting in Constantinople, where he served for nearly ten years. In 1901, he was promoted to the post of first secretary of the embassy in Constantinople. In 1906, Trubetskoi left his career to pursue scholarly work and public commentary on political matters, dedicating himself to work for "a free liberal Russia" and commenting extensively on Russian foreign policy. He contributed fifty-three articles to the liberal journal *Moskovskii ezhenedel'nik* (*Moscow Weekly*) between 1906 and 1911 and wrote an influential long article for the collection *Velikaia Rossiia* (*Great Russia*) on the tasks of Russian diplomacy and its great power interests.[*]

In this period he was both a liberal critic of the regime on questions of political freedom and domestic political reform, and also opposed the tsar's foreign policy on nationalistic grounds. Trubetskoi's critiques of imperial foreign policy were a nuanced mix of his attraction to pan-Slav ideas and his realist views on the best ways to maintain a balance of power and avoid war. On the whole, his influence probably made it more difficult for the tsar to compromise in the Balkans when Russian and Slav interests were threatened by Austria, and thus he may have—contrary to his intentions—contributed to one of the key causes of World War I.

In 1912, Trubetskoi returned to the foreign ministry. His close colleague and friend Foreign Minister Sergei Sazonov appointed him to head the Near Eastern Department of the Foreign Ministry, which was responsible for Balkan and Ottoman affairs. His influence on foreign policy during the following years was considerably greater than his title might suggest, in large part because of Sazonov's deep respect for Trubetskoi's opinions and expertise. Trubetskoi recalls in this memoir that he met with Foreign Minister Sazonov every day, several times a day, usually for relatively long discussions of a wide range of important matters before the minister.[†] In June 1914, the Russian representative in Serbia, N. G. Hartwig, died unexpectedly, and Trubetskoi was immediately appointed as his replacement. Trubetskoi's position thus put him at the center of Russian diplomacy during the crucial period of the Russian entry into the war, and his account of this period in this book is an important source for the study of the outbreak of the war.

Among other things, Trubetskoi recounts in this memoir how he drafted the proclamation on Poland and gives an interesting account of its origins. The predominant view of the proclamation is that it was a cynical expedient to bid for Polish loyalty in the war, but Trubetskoi claims that "Writing this proclamation gave me the greatest moral satisfaction of my

---

[*] For a full bibliography of his pre–World War I articles, see Sophie Schmitz, "Grigori N. Trubetzkoy: Politik und Völkerrecht, 1873–1930" (PhD diss., University of Vienna, 1971). This dissertation is reproduced in full with the permission of Sophie Schmitz at http://content.cdlib.org/view?docId=kt4g502159&doc.view=entire_text/.

[†] D. C. B. Lieven, *Russia and the Origins of the First World War* (New York: St. Martin's Press, 1983), 91; see also the obituary by B. E. Nol'de in P. B. Struve, *Pamiati Kn. Gr. N. Trubetskogo, Sbornik statei* (Paris: E. Siial'skoi, 1930).

life." He also provides a colorful account of opposition to the proclamation in the council of ministers. Trubetskoi discusses how he also wrote the appeal to the Ruthenians in Habsburg Galicia, noting that nobody liked both appeals (those who liked the Ruthenian appeal disliked the Polish appeal, and vice versa), but nobody knew that they had the same author. Trubetskoi's explanation testifies again to his rare combination of liberalism and imperial ambitions.

Trubetskoi is also a valuable source on the major historical problem of the entry of Turkey into the war. He seems to have been convinced that there was broad popular and elite support in Russia for conquest of the Straits and provides an inside view of his lobbying for making conquest of the Straits a strategic priority. Allied negotiations in early 1915 led to plans to occupy Constantinople, envisioning future control to go to Russia. In secret, G. N. Trubetskoi was named the future Russian commissar of the city. He provides interesting details about the agreements with Britain and France and his own preparations for the position.

The bulk of the narrative deals with Trubetskoi's diplomacy in the Balkans. It begins with his recollections of his role and the broader Russian diplomatic role in the complicated disputes in the Balkans in the years immediately preceding the war. He provides colorful descriptions of the major actors in the region, including the kings of Bulgaria and Rumania. He felt that, from the 1878 Treaty of San Stefano on, Russia had unduly favored Bulgaria at Serbia's expense. He details the rivalries between Bulgaria and Serbia and his attempts to mediate, especially over the question of Macedonia. There is a distinct theme in his memoirs of his attempting to counter the widespread view that he was partial to the Bulgarians over the Serbs.

Trubetskoi's wife came to join him in Serbia in 1915 and led a philanthropic effort to provide medical assistance to refugees and wounded soldiers. His depiction of the ravages of disease, hunger, and epidemic in Serbia bears poignant witness to the fact that Serbia's military and civilian death rates were the highest per capita of any country during World War I. In fall 1915, Trubetskoi accompanied the retreating Serbian army, which could not maintain a two-front war against Austria and Bulgaria. In 1916–1917, he served as head of the diplomatic chancery at the headquarters of the Russian army. In short, Trubetskoi was a key figure in several different ways during World War I. He was a rare example of an insider in the Russian regime with strong ties to the liberal opposition outside of it. His memoirs end with a scathing indictment of the tsar's decision to replace Sazonov with Boris Stürmer, giving the distinct concluding impression that this appointment marked the beginning of the end of professional Russian diplomacy. On the whole, his memoir provides a fascinating and revealing inside look at how Russian foreign policies were made at crucial points of the war.[*] Trubetskoi chronicles his involvement in Russian politics, diplomacy, and especially in religious matters during and after the revolutions of 1917 in a separate volume.[†]

Eric Lohr
Susan Carmel Lehrman Chair of Russian History and Culture
American University

---

[*] For additional information on G. N. Trubetskoi, see Schmitz, "Grigori N. Trubetzkoy"; Lieven, *Russia and the Origins,* 91–101; Struve, *Pamiati Kn. Gr. N. Trubetskogo.* Trubetskoi's archive is accessible online at Trubetskoi (Grigorii Nikolaevich), Papers, 1886–1989, Online Archive of California, at http://oca.org/history-archives.

Many of the original documents are held in the collection of the Gosudarstvennyi arkhiv Rossiiskoi Federatsii (GARF) in Moscow; others are held in the Archive of the Orthodox Church in America in Syosset, New York. See http://oca.org/history-archives. Some of his correspondence is available at Arkhiv vneshnei politiki Rossiiskoi Imperii (AVPRI), Moscow, f. 340 Kollektsiia 'dokumental'nykh materialov iz lichnykh arkhivov chinovnikov MID 1743–1933, op. 902 Trubetskoi, G.N. 1912–1914.

[†] Grigorii Nikolaevich Trubetskoi, *Gody smut i nadezhd,* 1917–1919 (Montreal: Napechatano Bratstvom I. Pochaevskago, 1981).

Translator's Preface

This translation into English of *Personal Notes of G. N. Trubetskoi, Plenipotentiary* is based primarily on Grigorii N. Trubetskoi's original intact manuscript in my possession. Passages from the 1983 Russian-language published edition of this translation have also been incorporated. This is, therefore, the most comprehensive version in English of my grandfather's memoirs pertaining to these turbulent years.

I would never have completed this opus without the professional and meticulous editing on the part of Dr. Borislav Chernev. Special thanks go to Susan Carmel Lehrman for her generous financial support and to Professor Eric Lohr for his introduction and encouragement. I am exceedingly grateful to Dr. Anatol Shmelev for suggesting that I publish with NIU Press.

We have retained foreign-language words and phrases as they appear in the original and provided an English-language translation. We have used the Library of Congress system of transliteration for Russian names and a modified Library of Congress system of transliteration for Bulgarian names. Serbian and Montenegrin names follow the standardized Latin spelling. The dates are Old Style (Julian calendar), which at the beginning of the twentieth century was thirteen days behind the New Style (Gregorian calendar). When both styles are given, the dates will be separated by a slash (e.g., December 6/19).

The endnotes are mine; the footnotes are my grandfather's with an occasional footnote by me clarifying some aspect of my translation. My footnotes are marked as such. My grandfather had his own transliteration of foreign names, and these are explained in the endnotes.

The spelling of "Rumania" was the prevalent one in 1914. However, Romania is also acceptable.

I would like to express my appreciation as well to Dr. Robert Grenier and Igor Saika-Voivod for their patient proofreading of my first drafts, to Mrs. Mirjana Pospielovsky for her help with the Serbian language, and to Dr. Maxim Golovkin for enhancing the original photographs included in this volume with such skill and patience. These photographs in my archive are from an album, a gift to Trubetskoi's wife, Princess Marie Trubetskaya, from the women of the Russian Red Cross Brigade in Serbia founded by her in 1914. They chronicle and complement my grandfather's memoirs.

Elizabeth Saika-Voivod

FOREWORD

The following excerpts from my memoirs pertain to the period just preceding this last war. At this point in time I was head of the Department for the Near East at the Ministry of Foreign Affairs. The position enabled me to follow international events very closely.

These reminiscences pertinent to this period were freshly written down by me before they could be overshadowed by subsequent events. I completed them in January of 1917—that is, just before the revolution. This reflects upon the evaluation of many facts. However, I prefer not to change anything in this narrative.

By G. N. Trubetskoi

1

DECLARATION OF WAR

In June 1914 I was offered a diplomatic posting in Persia. For family reasons, I requested time to consider the offer and went home for a holiday to my country estate at Vasil'evskoe.

Barely a few days passed before I received news that our representative in Belgrade, N. G. Hartwig, had died.[1] This was followed by a letter from Baron Schilling, director of the Ministry of Foreign Affairs. On behalf of Minister Sergei Sazonov he was offering me the post of minister to Serbia.[2] I telegraphed my acceptance and the very next day received a telegram from the same Schilling recalling me to St. Petersburg. Slightly perplexed by the urgent call, I cut short the holiday and left immediately. Everything became clear as I opened a newspaper on the train and read the text of the Austrian ultimatum to Serbia.

I arrived in St. Petersburg around July 13 and was swept up by the prevailing mood of heightened excitement. Little explanation was needed. The extreme harshness and categorical demands of the Austrian ultimatum to Serbia produced an unexpected explosive effect everywhere. This ultimatum was considered by everyone without exception, the government included, as a provocation to Russia over the head of Serbia.

The mood reflected an amazing unity of spirit that can only occur in times of serious catastrophes encompassing the vital interests and honor of a nation. Russia had to respond to the challenge that was now thrust upon her. No one wanted a war, but everyone understood that, if Austria did not refute its irreconcilable point of view, war was inevitable.

The Austrian ultimatum giving Serbia forty-eight hours to respond was handed to the Serbian government in Belgrade at six in the evening of July 10. Austria's intention had been to purposefully delay telegraphing the ultimatum to the European capitals. The Austrian ambassador in St. Petersburg communicated the contents of the text to the Russian Ministry of Foreign Affairs seventeen hours after it was received in Belgrade—that is, on the afternoon of July 11. On the following day the government issued a statement expressing grave concern over the recent events: Russia cannot remain indifferent to the conflict between Austria and Serbia. Simultaneously, the military were recalled from army camps to city barracks.

I shall not describe the day-by-day negotiations, which for the most part are already known from published documents. They serve to underline the fact that Russia, France, and England tried in every way to seek a peaceful solution, ready to appease Austria by smoothing over any standoff. When the answer of the Serbian government reached St. Petersburg, it surpassed our expectations with its moderate and conciliatory tone. It could make no other impression on objective people. This is demonstrated by the fact that even the Austrian ambassador in Paris, having acquainted himself with the Serbian reply in the French Ministry of Foreign Affairs, expressed surprise that the Austrian minister in Belgrade had not deemed it acceptable. Subsequently, I heard the following story from the Italian minister in Serbia, Baron Schvitti. He had gone to visit his Austrian colleague several hours before the Serbian reply had been delivered and found him already packing. "Why are you packing, if you haven't received a response yet?" Schvitti inquired. "How do you know this?" Baron Giesl countered in a trembling voice: "Have you seen any of the Serbs around?" He then explained that he had strict orders to depart if the Serbs had changed as much as a comma in the original set of demands.

At the time, of course, no one in St. Petersburg knew anything about this exchange. S. D. Sazonov, who lived in the country at Tsarskoe Selo, commuted daily to St. Petersburg, often in the company of Count Pourtalès, the German ambassador.[3] In the morning of the 15th, as they were taking the train together, the count expressed the view that the Serbian reply was not satisfactory. This was the first indication of the extreme seriousness of the situation, as it signified that Germany had no inclination to pressure Austria into accepting any kind of compromise. As a person, Pourtalès was a decent man, but unfortunately quite limited. He had no doubt that Russia would avoid an irrevocable decision and eventually yield. He remained optimistic longer than anyone and was convinced that things would not lead to war. His optimism was shared by the advisor to the German embassy, Litsius, who had recently departed from the capital. Such opinions underscored Germany's complete misconception of Russia.

German diplomats believed Russia to be on the brink of revolution. Any kind of international complications, therefore, no matter how unimportant, would provoke major upheavals within the Russian Empire. We already knew that the Germans were attempting to imbue the Turks with this very attitude. General Bernhardi's book [*Germany and the Next War*] shows that the Germans truly believed this, as all of the outlined strategic planning is predicated upon the inevitability of revolution in Russia in the event of war. Just before the Austrian ultimatum, strikes took place in St. Petersburg partly from lack of an effective police force. These disruptions established firmly in the mind of the German ambassador that Russia would not go to war.

In fairness, I must admit that Pourtalès, to the degree it depended upon him, tried to be conciliatory. At one point during this period he and Sazonov became overwrought during a conversation. Pourtalès was hard of hearing, so one had to raise one's voice when talking to him. This often irritated the already much stressed Sazonov, who later admitted to me that on this occasion he had shouted louder than he would have liked to. Pourtalès became offended and left. Later in the day, however, Pourtalès stopped by the office of his friend Neratov, assistant minister, explaining that he had overreacted earlier, that there should be no conflicts of a personal nature at such a time.[4] He subsequently paid a visit to Sazonov. They respected each other enormously.

The hopes of Pourtalès were dashed three days before the rupture. A decision was made to mobilize four Russian military districts in reaction to the almost total mobilization of Austrian troops and the bombardment of Belgrade. On July 16, Pourtalès visited Sazonov as always.

During this conversation, both men became quite excited; Pourtalès suddenly went to the window and, flinging both hands to his head, began to sob.

"My God, don't tell me that we shall be fighting each other! Our destiny was to walk hand in hand! We have so many political and dynastic connections, so many common interests serving to uphold the principles of monarchy and social order!"

"Why then do you allow yourself to be led by your damned ally—'Sacrée Alliée' [sacred ally]?" Sazonov interrupted hotly.

"It's too late now," Pourtalès murmured.

While there is little reason to doubt Pourtalès's sincerity, the subsequent course of events and published documents serve to establish that German involvement played a bigger role in the outbreak of the war than Austrian resolve.

Indeed, from the time of the Balkan crisis, the international authority of the Habsburg monarchy tottered, and this was felt inside the country to such an extent that in Vienna there was a saying, "Besser ein Ende mit Schrecken als Schrecken ohne Ende" [Better a horrible ending than horror without end].

As of November 1912, therefore, Vienna decided to restore authority by an active show of power toward Serbia by making demands of the Serbian government for definite guarantees. In case of a refusal, Austria would initiate a punitive expedition while assuring the powers that Austria was not seeking territorial gains.

This policy hoped to avoid Russian involvement. However, according to the proponents of the "Ein Ende mit Schrecken" theory, the possibility of Russian involvement must not deter Austria from clarifying the situation. This strategy was communicated in confidence to our ambassador in Paris, A. P. Izvolskii, by the Austrian financier Adler,[5] who arrived in Paris from Vienna at the end of November 1912.[6]

The realization of such a plan, however, was still a long way off. I doubt that the more responsible leadership of Austrian policy would have seen this policy through. It was the tragic demise of Archduke Franz Ferdinand and his wife at the hands of the Bosnian Serb Princip that contributed to the following events.

The circumstances of the murders astounded the Austrian imagination. There were anti-Serbian demonstrations and even pogroms in some areas. No doubt certain politicians in Vienna hoped that the death of the archduke would bring about a political unification and a consolidation of the monarchy, thus enabling the government to demonstrate its strength and thereby reinstate its failing credibility. Certainly, the support of Germany and, perhaps, the chivalrous sentiments of Emperor Wilhelm toward the heir to the Austrian throne, whom he had so recently visited, could not be overlooked.

I imagine this is how the governing circles in Vienna reasoned. Unfortunately, Austro-Hungarian Foreign Minister Count Berchtold was an unremarkable man, and it fell upon Count Forgách, head of the department, to actually manage all departmental affairs.

Compromised by certain fabricated documents hinting at Serbian involvement in domestic Austrian affairs, Count Forgách had been forced to leave the posting of Austro-Hungarian minister to Belgrade, accepting the lesser posting of Habsburg minister in Dresden. His resourcefulness and abilities were much appreciated by political leaders, however, and before long he found himself in Vienna. Obviously, he was annoyed with Serbia and harbored feelings of enmity. Conceited, full of intrigue, and of Jewish ancestry, he waited for his moment of revenge. That moment came with the murders in Sarajevo.

Essentially, Forgách did not develop a new plan, adopting instead the plan of 1912. He decided to use the accusations that had cost him his posting in Belgrade to substantiate the ultimatum to Serbia. Furthermore, by capitalizing on them he could prove to what extent he had been in the right the first time. He found an accomplice in the German ambassador to Vienna, Count Tschirschky.[7] This fellow at one time had been counselor to the German embassy in St. Petersburg, a position from which he was forced to resign because of some trivial social matter. He was now our fervent enemy.

Once, during a ball hosted by Grand Duke Vladimir Aleksandrovich, Tschirschky had invited a certain lady ahead of time for a dance. In the meantime, the grand duke chose to sit by her side. As the time came to take their position on the dance floor, Tschirschky approached his partner. The grand duke jokingly and with a tone of familiarity quipped—"qu'il n'a qu'à se promener" [He should take a hike].

This was too much for the vain diplomat! The next day he appeared before Grand Duchess Maria Pavlovna to voice his complaint to her as a "German princess" regarding the offensive treatment he had endured in her home. The grand duchess replied that she was not a "German princess" but a Russian grand duchess and showed Tschirschky the door. He departed from Russia, shaking the dust from his boots onto a country that failed to appreciate him. This trivial incident made of him an enemy of Russia.

I was assured in good faith that the ultimatum to Serbia was concocted jointly by Tschirschky and Forgách. Apparently the German government, after the publication of the ultimatum, felt compelled to announce publicly that it had no part in the wording of the ultimatum, becoming familiar with it along with everyone else. If this is true, it merely reinforces the impression that it was secondary administrators rather than the responsible leaders who had played a leading role in the road to war. The latter had seemingly allowed matters to slide out of control, owing to their limited abilities.

In any case, the danger of war was enhanced from the moment when Germany, recognizing that the ultimatum was not of its making, stressed that it could not permit Austria to retreat from its current stance, as that would be disparaging to its ally and ultimately to itself. In other words, the responsible governing circles now foolishly decided to back the initiative that secondary administrators had undertaken.

The ease with which all this came about emphasizes how widespread the conviction was in Germany that a European conflict was only a matter of time. The only conclusion was to bring to an end what was begun.

The key to the situation from the start lay in Berlin. The negotiations in Vienna merely echoed its mood. How remarkable that the declaration of war originated in Berlin, not in Vienna. Was it not equally remarkable that five days elapsed before Austria decided to follow through and do the same? During these five days, Count Berchtold made a point of exchanging pleasantries with our ambassador, showing him every courtesy at the Ministry of Foreign Affairs.[8] Our ambassador even began to think that Berchtold was definitely conveying the impression of backing off.

However, I am jumping ahead of myself.

From the moment when German diplomacy sanctioned the direction created by the Austrian ultimatum and the mobilization in Austria, events took their own course and talks became hopeless. Every day and every hour, even, we received updates on the growing military preparations in Germany. When the order was given to carry out mobilization in the four Russian military districts, our general staff fell into complete despair. The chief of staff explained that an impending general mobilization would inevitably result in conflicting train schedules, thereby delaying mobilization for up to ten days. Every hour had a sense of urgent expediency.

The fast pace with which Germany could mobilize gave it the advantage at the start of the war. Sazonov and other ministers fully understood this situation. He sent a most deferential note to the tsar requesting an audience for himself and Krivoshein, the minister of agriculture, for a personal report.[9]

The tsar received only Sazonov and asked him why he had wanted to bring Krivoshein along. The minister replied that, whereas he could clarify the international situation, Krivoshein was better informed about internal affairs and could therefore be more thorough.

"'I trust you, too!'" was the curt reply.

General Tatishchev, who was liaison to the court of the German emperor, was also in attendance.[10] The tsar had recalled him earlier with the intent of sending a personal letter to Kaiser Wilhelm and now delayed him until Sazonov's arrival so that Tatishchev be fully apprised.

Sazonov justified the reasons for the decision of the general staff in favor of general mobilization.

"Your Majesty knows that I have always done everything possible to preserve the peace. My conscience is clear of any kind of warmongering, and now, if I feel it my duty to insist on the urgency of general mobilization, then I do it only with the awareness of the historical responsibility that will fall upon you, if you decide not to pursue this course of action."

Sazonov referred to the amazing uplift that pervaded society, the army, and the general staff. Half measures would jeopardize this mood. In his opinion, there was virtually no chance for peace.

Urgent measures for the defense of the state needed to be undertaken. Impassioned and agitated, he presented the military, political, and even dynastic ramifications of this notion. For a long time the tsar resisted. It is well known that in the last days before the crisis, he maintained a lively correspondence by telegram with Kaiser Wilhelm. I had an occasion to see some of these telegrams, written in English in the hand of the empress. Seemingly, the tsar had partly dictated to her and partly had her translate the Russian text. This was the time when the empress was being blamed for trying in every way possible to dissuade the tsar from war. I, for one, heard from a very good source that the empress was disinclined to assert any kind of influence; she simply did not hide her fears because she knew that the reorganization of the Russian army that would allow it to regain the necessary fighting capacity would not be complete until 1917.

It is obvious that the tsar had quite a few burdensome moments before deciding on a responsible course of action. Earlier, he had received a letter of one sentence by mail that read, "Have fear of God. Mother." This letter left a singular impression. He thought of all the Russian mothers he would have to answer to for the death of their sons.

On the other hand, the tsar still endured the memory of the Treaty of Portsmouth.[11] His extreme love of peace, resulting in a magnanimous—yet to some extent sentimental—utopianism toward total disarmament, made him oversensitive to anything that could tarnish the honor of Russia. It is an irony of fate that it fell to the instigator of the Hague Conference on disarmament in 1898 to usher in the bloodiest conflict in the history of mankind.

Sazonov spoke for more than an hour. His impassioned plea was overpowering. In the end the tsar agreed to sign the decree for a general mobilization.

"You have convinced me, but this will be the most difficult day of my life," said the emperor as he left Sazonov.

Sazonov telephoned General Headquarters from Tsarskoe Selo as previously arranged.

The decree for general mobilization had already been drafted, and the tsar signed it right away. It was July 17. Previous orders for a partial mobilization were nullified. There was no confusion thanks to the speed with which the new orders were dispatched. The few incidents due to misunderstandings were easily rectified. The mobilization proceeded efficiently, with a speed surpassing general expectation.

During this time of crisis and the first month of the war, I remained the entire day and late into the night at the ministry. We were still hoping for a peaceful solution. The emotion we felt was akin to that feeling one gets when sitting by the bedside of someone who is gravely ill.

From the very start, hope for a resolution of the situation waned from day to day. The military preparations in Germany and Austria provoked great concern. That is why the decision for a general mobilization was received by all of us with a sigh of relief.

On July 18, Pourtalès was at the ministry as usual. The declaration of general mobilization had been posted in the streets. Late that evening, just when Sazonov had retired and we were about to leave, Pourtalès arrived, demanding an immediate meeting with the minister, who had to be woken up. Pourtalès left after two in the morning. I had involuntarily dozed off from nervous exhaustion. After his departure we learned that Pourtalès had presented Sazonov with an ultimatum demanding immediate demobilization. Sazonov had twelve hours, until noon the next day to respond. We worked throughout the night. We needed to apprise our representatives abroad of this new development by a circular telegram while simultaneously coordinating with the military authorities.

At 7:10 p.m. on the following day, not having received an answer, the German ambassador handed the minister a note stating that Germany was at war with Russia. The fact that the ambassador and his staff had neglected to erase words and phrases in parentheses from an earlier draft of the text is a reflection of their bewilderment and agitation.

That night the minister was once again roused from his sleep. The tsar received a cryptic telegram from Kaiser Wilhelm sent from Potsdam. It was undated, showing only the time: 10:00 p.m. Wilhelm expressed the hope that the Russians would not cross the border. The minister telephoned the German ambassador to determine how this telegram should be interpreted now that war had been declared. Count Pourtalès, awakened from sleep, replied that he did not know. Perhaps this telegram had been sent earlier and had been delayed along the way.

This concluded the first act of the historical drama. All those who were in Russia at that time will never forget those unique moments, that exuberance which pervaded the nation.

"Ernst und ruhig" [serious and calm] was the observation of the Austrian ambassador in a letter to his government that we had intercepted. All of us felt great emotion and pride for our country. That entire month was a sort of honeymoon, which passed by without any kind of conflict, disagreement, or differences of opinion between the different political parties, estates, and national groups. There was only one great Russia.

Immediately after the declaration of war, the tsar summoned the Council of Ministers and announced that it had always been his intention to become commander in chief of the armed forces in case of war. He was now soliciting their advice on how best to govern the country in his absence. One after the other, the ministers expressed views against his decision to take command. They were unanimous that he did not have the right to limit his responsibility only to military duties: he had to unite all of Russia. He should safeguard himself from the criticism that would inevitably follow in the wake of some possible military setback.

During these first days, allusions to the war of 1812 became commonplace. Krivoshein and Director of the Chancery Tvorzhevskii included verbatim a phrase from the manifesto signed by Alexander I in the draft of their own official manifesto. Even the tsar was moved. The ministers referred to the fact that Emperor Alexander, having heeded the advice of his entourage, left the army.

All ministers spoke heatedly and openly. The enormity of this moment compelled them to acknowledge their great responsibilities and to become one in spirit. Until this moment, the only thing they had in common had been the room in which they worked. Only Minister of War Sukhomlinov remained silent.[12]

"And what is your opinion?" asked the tsar.

"I concur with the opinion of my colleagues," he answered.

"You used to sing a different tune not so long ago," the tsar observed.

Sukhomlinov blushed, murmuring that the situation had since changed and that now he could not but agree with the general consensus.

As he brought the meeting to a close, the tsar thanked his ministers warmly for their candor and added that, although it was personally difficult to resist the desire he had harbored for so long, he was swayed by their arguments.

On July 20, Grand Duke Nikolai Nikolaevich was appointed commander in chief of all the military forces. It was a popular decision with the army and embraced by the nation. At this point the mood was such that no one wished to be so critical as to destroy this sense of unity.

The Austrians who remained in St. Petersburg presented a strange picture. That Austria delivered its declaration of war five days after Germany was common knowledge. The embassy staff was in a state of consternation. The expression of incontrollable sorrow on the face of Counselor to the Embassy Count Otto Czernin alone was enough to lessen my previous antipathy toward him caused by his uncompromising stance toward Russia. I even felt a gush of pity. Such an unexpected unraveling of events! Upon his arrival at the ministry for a meeting with Baron Schilling, he broke into tears. Later I heard that First Secretary to the Embassy Fürstenburg openly admitted to his Russian acquaintances that he feared there would not be any Austrian embassy in Petersburg after the war, only a small mission.

Each day, young men paraded off to war, accompanied by a general exaltation and pride.

Nothing interfered with the serene triumph of this moment.

There are two instances so vivid in my mind that I shall always consider them as the most fortunate of experiences. The first one is the tsar's glorious entrance into the Winter Palace on July 21. The palace was filled with officers of the Guard and from military garrisons around St. Petersburg, although some regiments had already left the capital. After the *Te Deum*, the tsar gave a short speech from the middle of the hall. The contents of the speech are commonly known. The impression of that moment is simply impossible to convey. The emperor spoke with such fervor that the vast Nikolaevskii Hall, where no one moved while every spoken word clearly reverberated, shook from the spontaneous hurrahs. The officers, many of whom had tears in their eyes, waved their caps and handkerchiefs. The enthusiasm was beyond description; what a true feeling of common unity! Their clamor was joined by loud hurrahs emanating from a crowd of one hundred thousand people who had flooded the Palace Square.

The second solemn historical moment was the session of the State Duma.[13] How to describe all of the emotional stirrings of that day? Deputies from every party and representatives from every corner of Russia took the podium in turns, endorsing the unity of mind and spirit that had permeated united Russia.

I met daily with two people who were very close to me, N. N. L'vov, member of the Duma, and P. B. Struve.[14] We shared with each other our hopes and anxieties. L'vov's oldest son had just joined the Preobrazhenskii Regimental Guard and could not wait to go. He was killed in the trenches within the first three months. I did not see L'vov at that time, but when I recall how lovingly he gazed at his firstborn son in soldier's uniform, I can only imagine the enormity of his grief.

All of us at the Ministry of Foreign Affairs found ourselves in a vortex during this initial period after the outbreak of hostilities. Our foremost preoccupation was whether England would declare war.

Whereas Germany had the upper hand in Europe in terms of military preparation, its political situation was quite difficult. German diplomacy was not without its failings. To some extent, this was a contributing cause for the war, for Berlin was incorrectly apprised of the situation. I have already mentioned Germany's mistaken assessment of Russia as a sort of China in dissolution. Another outcome of this deficient diplomacy was a disregard for France and its military. The result was the conviction that France could be defeated with one concerted strike. Such a plan had apparently been formulated in Germany quite a while ago. During the last days before the breakdown of relations, when Pourtalès had seemingly accepted the inevitability of war, Sazonov asked him, during one of their conversations, "Well, then, so you are attacking us?"

"I don't know what they will decide," Pourtalès answered, "but I suspect that our advance will begin on the Rhine, with an initial invasion of France."

The most fatal diplomatic error on the part of Germany was its assessment of English policy. The Germans overestimated the English domestic preoccupation with the Irish Question.[15] But most surprising of all was that, in their blindness, they failed to appreciate the main stimulus, which, in the past, always drew England into a war—the threat of Continental hegemony by a single power. Bismarck's *cauchemar de coalitions* [nightmare of coalitions] had not dashed Germany's hopes of breaking the enemy coalition. In the years leading up to the war, the main efforts of German diplomacy had been aimed at driving a wedge between the countries of the Entente, which kept each other informed of these German endeavors.

The Treaty of Portsmouth in 1905 brought about a rapprochement between Russia and England. This could have occurred even earlier had we met England's proposal halfway back in 1898. At that time, England sought to end its territorial expansion and strengthen its dominions instead. To that effect, an arrangement with Russia was desirable. In the archives of the Foreign Ministry there is a document, a note written up by British Ambassador in St. Petersburg O'Conor outlining a proposal for the division of the world into British and Russian spheres of influence.[16] Our sphere of influence would include the Straits with Constantinople and all of North China. England demanded the recognition of its interests in southern China, Arabia, the Persian Gulf, and so on. Had we concluded such an agreement with England, perhaps there would never have been a war with Japan, and history would have taken a different course. But, at that time, our appetite was great. We did not want to back away from our tea trade with Hankoi and Yangtse-kiang. Witte showed considerable dim-sightedness.[17] He opposed the treaty because it would have limited the activities of the Russo-Chinese bank. In his opinion, we had to consider the French capitalists, who had invested their money in this bank. Instead of entente then, there was increased political friction over Far Eastern policy. For its part, Germany tried to capitalize on this antagonism by urging us to undertake other risky ventures. The situation changed at the time of the Treaty of Portsmouth, when England realized that a weakening of Russia meant a stronger Germany in Europe.

The domestic upheavals leading up to the creation of the Duma affected foreign policy as well. Inevitably, Russia was forced to concentrate her attention on domestic affairs. The main thrust of foreign policy, therefore, was the preservation of peace. Thus, the path of bitter experience was directing us back to England's proposal of 1898. As of now, nothing stood in the way of entente between our governments.

France, pursuing the same path, had already concluded an entente with England in 1904, championed by the late King Edward VII of England. Count Lamsdorff, who was then the Russian foreign minister, understood well the need for entente with England.[18] His successors, Izvolskii and Sazonov, were determined to establish a close relationship with England.

Izvolskii successfully concluded an agreement in 1907. From that time on, there was a tripartite agreement on all political dilemmas, giving no peace to Germany. To turn this entente into a formal treaty was a burning issue for French and Russian leadership. Tradition and prejudice toward Russia, however, held the English back from a commitment, although England did conclude a tentative military convention with France. While keeping its options open, England agreed to have its military leadership draw up preliminary agreements for joint military action with the French military in case both countries found themselves at war with the same adversary.

In the spring of 1914, England agreed to a similar exchange of ideas between its Admiralty and Russia's. Sazonov found in Buchanan, the British ambassador to Petersburg, a counterpart in his own ardent desire for a treaty. Both men understood the need for careful diplomacy.

The Balkan crisis brought the two powers closer together. England was swayed by Russia's genuine and sincere desire for peace. Through daily dialogue in their search for peace, the political leaderships of England and Russia developed a mutual respect and trust for each other. They were brought even closer by German arrogance. In January 1913, Prince Heinrich of Prussia visited England. On behalf of Emperor Wilhelm, he inquired of King George what his position would be in the event of a war between Germany and Russia. King George replied that the decisive factor would be who the aggressor was. In any case, England might not remain neutral. The king relayed this conversation in confidence to the Russian ambassador.

At the time of the Balkan crisis, Russian public opinion criticized its Ministry of Foreign Affairs for its vacillation toward Germany. It did not comprehend that only a policy of caution could guarantee the support of England. England would never go to war over obstinacy on our part in the Balkans. If anything, England would be otherwise inclined if Russia's dignity and great power status were at stake, in which case Russia would have to respond to the challenge The Austrian ultimatum of 1914 created just such a situation.

Some person expressed in an article that, had Grey made it clear to Germany that England would become involved, the war itself could have been avoided altogether.[19] There is some truth to that in my opinion. Why indeed did Grey not do just that? It was for the following reasons. In England, foreign policy is definitely guided by public opinion and by Parliament. The conservative consciousness of the English at the time was incapable of grasping the idea of a treaty in principle. Decisions would then have to be made not only consistent with such a development but with the actual potential involvement of England in a war, a war that from the start was escalating to enormous proportions. It would take a remarkable leader to make such important decisions, and Grey just did not have what it takes. In fact, the absence of strong leadership in Europe, especially in Germany and Austria, was a major cause for the war.

There was no single authority to stem the tide. Instead, military preparations and growing nationalism formed the framework for the rapidly developing events.

The question of why England failed to stop the outbreak of war can also be explained by Grey's personality, which was a reflection of the specific political structure of the country. I personally never met him. My opinion of him is based on everyday affairs and dialogue with English diplomats from the time of the Balkan crisis. My impression of Grey as a political leader was that of a typical member of the British Liberal cabinet. His view of international events was subservient to the opinion and the justification of Parliament. For this very reason, he was reluctant to make decisions of consequence. Whenever a joint declaration of the Entente powers was under discussion, he insisted on clarifying certain clauses. His corrections resulted in continuing delays and, ultimately, a devaluation of the text itself.

It is no wonder then, that until the last minute neither we nor the French knew whether England would take our side. All depended on the growing mood of the English people.

Our ambassador in England, Count Benckendorff, outdid himself during these critical days with his sensitive and observant analysis of the situation.[20] We received telegrams from him three times a day in which he kept us apprised of social sentiment. He differentiated between the positive and the negative. During the first days, the *Times* printed an article sympathizing with the Slavs, which Count Benckendorff considered potentially damaging. The English were more inclined to sympathize with the situation in Europe than to become involved in a potentially dangerous adventure.

This leading diplomat had strength of character, self-discipline, and incredible will.*

England's entry into the war rested with the decision of Parliament. Excerpts of Grey's speech got through to us by way of the telegraph. Feverishly, we awaited each telegram. We speculated upon the possibilities. How characteristic of Grey that he never mentioned Russia by name in his speech. It indicated how remote to the British mind-set was the idea of an alliance with Russia and how chance circumstance brought about a decision of world importance.

Anyone other than the cautious Sazonov would have responded to the German ultimatum with lesser restraint, and British society would then have reacted negatively toward us.

Fortunately, this did not happen. England made the decision, and from that moment on, the Allies never doubted their superiority over Germany in resources and never lost faith in ultimate victory.

The war raised a whole series of questions that needed to be addressed. The first was the Polish Question. As everywhere else, mobilization in the Kingdom of Poland proceeded not only in a most orderly fashion but with enthusiasm. At the historic session of the Duma, the representative of Poland solemnly declared that the Polish people were united as one with the Russian people in the struggle against the age-old enemy. The Polish Question was both an international and a domestic one.

Already at the time of the Balkan crisis I had to draft a note for the tsar to be conveyed to him by the minister, outlining the necessity of changing our policy toward Poland. The premise was that a European conflict was inevitable. It was in our interests to create empathy for us not only among our own Poles but among Austrian Poles as well, whose support the German minority needed in order to obtain a majority in the Reichsrat.† Members of the Duma had written a similar letter to Chairman of the Council of Ministers Kokovtsev, who was well disposed to the contents of these two communications.[21] Unfortunately, Minister of Internal Affairs Maklakov was a procrastinator, who had the attitude of a provincial governor.[22] Thus, the

---

*   At the start of Russo-English diplomatic discussions, Tsar Nicholas decided to visit England for a few days on his way to France. All the appropriate social arrangements had already been organized as per protocol when Benckendorff's wife became very ill. This provoked some anxiety, of course. In fact, she passed away on the very day of the tsar's arrival. Benckendorff concealed the fact of her death and, covering her with ice, kept her body in a small room in the embassy. Each day, as the tsar inquired about her health, Benckendorff would sigh, look upward, and say: "Elle est toujour dans le même état, Sire" [She's still in the same state, Sire]. Eventually, noting his discomfort the tsar stopped asking. (Officially, Benckendorff's wife died just as the tsar's yacht left British shores.)

†   In the Russian text, Trubetskoi mistakenly refers to the Reichsrat as Reichstag. Tr.

whole thing was shoved aside and nothing was done for the Poles until the start of the war.

After the session of the Duma on July 26/August 8, the Polish Question was once again raised at the Council of Ministers, probably on Sazonov's initiative. In the last days of July he called me into his office. He told me that the Polish Question had come up at the Council of Ministers, and a proclamation should go out to the Poles giving them better prospects. I deduced from this conversation that the Polish Question had dominated the exchange of ideas. The proclamation was to include the unification of Polish lands, freedom of religion, language, and schools, and domestic autonomy. The minister added that the proclamation should be as solemn as possible and that it should be drawn up right away. I immediately formulated the proclamation and, taking it with me, went to the "France" hotel where I was to dine with my two trustworthy and closest friends, L'vov and Struve. I decided to share my secret with them in order to find out what they thought of this measure. They really liked the whole idea of a proclamation. We were overwhelmed by this unusual and new turn of events regarding issues for which previously there had been no solution. It was as if the first bombardment of the guns had condemned the old world to oblivion. A new world was about to be born and with it a new Russia.

We were aware of the prevailing and solemn historical moment. We truly believed that something new and better for everyone would come out of this. I inserted that idea into the proclamation. When I read it to Sazonov, he replied,

"Indeed, that is so."

Writing this proclamation gave me the greatest moral satisfaction of my life. What a rare joy it was to incorporate into an official document not only my own longtime yearning but the desire of so many Russian people, among them Chicherin, Solov'ev, and my late brother.[23]

Although not exactly a Polonophile, I was convinced that reconciliation with Poland was not a matter of conscience only. It was imperative for Russian political interests. To capture the hearts of the Polish people we needed slogans that would pierce their very core. What better appeal than the idea of national unity and freedom, all this brightened by the sight of a cross, the adored symbol of Polish Messianism.

The tsar gave his approval. Commander in Chief Nikolai Grand Duke Nikolaevich had just departed for Stavka [General Headquarters]. To precipitate matters, the minister of war requested that he append his signature to the document without explaining the contents for lack of time, adding that he had the tsar's endorsement. The grand duke replied that, in such a case, it was his duty to append his signature.

The proclamation initially provoked a strong yet varied reaction. The first person to see this document was a Pole, Count Wielopolski, whom Sazonov had invited to translate the text into Polish. When he read the proclamation, tears ran down his face, and he could not speak for a while. Strangely enough, this proclamation created an uproar in the Council of Ministers. Sazonov was criticized for not consulting with them; the proclamation would only create misguided hopes among the Polish people. Krivoshein was displeased, most probably because he considered the wording of all important government documents to be his personal responsibility.

Maklakov, whose reasoning was that of a compartmentalized, narrow-minded civil servant, protested that the proclamation should not be recognized, an opinion that unfortunately the administration upheld. Deputy Governor General von Essen, head of the civil administration in Warsaw, told a Polish delegation that this proclamation by the grand duke should be ignored.

The proclamation by the grand duke created a most favorable impression abroad. It served to eradicate prejudice and underlined the idealistic aspects of the war: the confirmation of people's rights and the right of small countries to defend themselves from oppression by the strong.

Even though the administration consciously ignored the proclamation, the latter kept Polish spirits up. When the tide began to turn against us, it was an asset.

Following the Polish proclamation I had to formulate an appeal to the Russian people in Red Ruthenia.[24] The well-known activist Dudyshkevich, who often used to visit me in the ministry, was an ardent supporter of such a proclamation, as was Count Vladimir Bobrinskii, who presented me with a rather long and overelaborate draft document. Those who did not like the Polish proclamation approved of the Russian one and vice versa. To my surprise, no one realized that the same person drafted both.

Each one was important. Slogans of equality were essential for a rapprochement with neutral countries of diverse populations. The government would have been accused of favoritism had it not approached the nations equally and with respect.

War having been declared, we now concentrated our efforts to determine which course of action the neutral countries would take, especially the Balkan states. In order to determine the actual situation, it was necessary to review the circumstances in the Balkans. The proclamation by the Grand

Duke Nikolai Nikolaevich to the Carpatho-Russians was translated into nine Slavic languages.

Proclamation to the Carpatho-Russians

I declare that it is not the first time that Russia has shed blood to free people from foreign domination and asks for nothing other than the return of rights and equality. To you, peoples of Austria-Hungary, she brings freedom and the realization of your national independence. The Austro-Hungarian rulers have sowed seeds of discord and enmity among you, for it is only by division that they are able to rule over you. Russia, on the other hand, has but one wish: may each one of you grow strong and profit, preserving that precious inheritance of your forefathers—language and faith. United in brotherhood, may you dwell in peace and harmony with your neighbors, respecting their autonomies.

Proclamation to the Poles

Poles! The hour has come when the precious desire of your fathers and grand-fathers can be attained. Half a century ago the living body of Poland was cut up into pieces, but not her soul. She lived with hope for the hour of resurrection of the Polish people, brotherly reconciliation with Great Russia. Russian forces carry with them the glorious news of this reconciliation. Let the borders that tear the Polish people into pieces be erased. Let them unite as one under the scepter of the tsar. Under this scepter Poland will be reborn, free in her faith, in language and self-government. Russia desires but one thing from you: the same regard for the rights of those with whom you are tied by history. Great Russia comes to you with open heart, extending to you a brotherly arm. Russia believes that the sword which defeated the foe at Grunwald has not yet rusted away. From the shores of the Pacific Ocean to the Northern Seas, Russian ranks are on the move. A ray of new life shines upon you. Let the sign of the Cross, a symbol of suffering and resurrection, shine in that light!

Воззваніе Верховнаго главнокомандующаго.

ПОЛЯКИ!

Пробилъ часъ, когда завѣтная мечта вашихъ отцовъ и дѣдовъ можетъ осуществиться.

Полтора вѣка тому назадъ живое тѣло Польши было растерзано на куски, но не умерла душа ея. Она жила надеждой, что наступитъ часъ воскресенія Польскаго народа, братскаго примиренія его съ Великой Россіей.

Русскія войска несутъ вамъ благую вѣсть этого примиренія.

Пусть сотрутся границы, разрѣзавшія на части Польскій народъ. Да возсоединится онъ во-едино подъ скипетромъ Русскаго Царя.

Подъ скипетромъ этимъ возродится Польша, свободная въ своей вѣрѣ, въ языкѣ, въ самоуправленіи.

Одного ждетъ отъ васъ Россія, — такого же уваженія къ правамъ тѣхъ народностей, съ которыми связала васъ исторія.

Съ открытымъ сердцемъ, съ братски протянутой рукой идетъ вамъ навстрѣчу Великая Россія. Она вѣритъ, что не заржавѣлъ мечъ, разившій врага при Гринвальдѣ.

Отъ береговъ Тихаго океана до Сѣверныхъ морей двинутся Русскія рати.

Заря новой жизни занимается для васъ.

Да возсіяетъ въ этой зарѣ знаменіе Креста, — символъ страданія и воскресенія народовъ.

Верховный главнокомандующій
генералъ-адъютантъ НИКОЛАЙ.

1 Августа 1914 года.

2. Official postcard of the Proclamation to the Poles with photograph of Grand Duke Nikolai Nikolaevich.

2

THE BALKAN QUESTION

I t is not my intention here to produce an in-depth documentary study
of the issues at hand. However, in order to establish the basis of my own
overview of the political situation in the Balkans as it stood at the start of
the war in 1914, I must unavoidably refer to past events.

One cannot say that Russia had a particularly straightforward or logical
policy in the Balkans. She wavered between utilitarian opportunism, a key-
stone of the foreign policy of any country, and ideology, which for the most
part took the upper hand.

Our political ideology itself was multifold. It was guided by two chief
tenets: the principle of religion, which dictated that Russia's destiny was to
preserve Orthodoxy in the Near East and to support unequivocally a nation
of the same faith, and the principle of nationality, which privileged Slavic
peoples. Neither principle was in fact applied consistently. More often than
not, there was an incongruous coexistence of various stimuli, often in the
most contradictory fashion.

Orthodoxy was the first and fundamental priority. It is tied to the ideal
of Moscow as the Third Rome, the successor of the fallen Byzantium. The
nationality principle, which emerged at the beginning of the nineteenth
century, became policy after the Crimean War. The incompatibility of the
two principles became evident during the Bulgarian-Greek church conflict,
when the Bulgarians sought to establish their own independent church,
against the opposition of the patriarchate of Constantinople. The row ended
with the unilateral proclamation of a separate Bulgarian Exarchate in 1870,
which was undoubtedly a violation of the canons of the Orthodox Church.
This led to a breakdown of relations between the Bulgarians and the patriarchate of Constantinople, which declared the new church schismatic. Our

diplomacy at this stage was to remain neutral. While maintaining a relationship with both parties, we gained the trust of neither.

Some six years later, our Slavophile policy drove Russia into a war with Turkey at great cost, intensified by a glaring lack of preparedness and command. As a result, at the Congress of Berlin in 1878 we were unable to uphold the peace terms that we forced Turkey to sign in the preliminary treaty of San Stefano.[1] Incidentally, there is no reason to regret this, as will become abundantly clear in due course.

It so happened that the initiators of the San Stefano treaty toyed with the idea of a "sea to sea" Bulgaria. This new Bulgaria was to include most of Macedonia and other territories, which at the Congress of Berlin were given to Serbia. Bulgaria became our favorite child; Serbia, the forgotten stepdaughter. Did this evaluation of the two states have any basis in their relative national and land rights? Was this in Russia's interests?

Curiously enough, the principal "creator" of San Stefano Bulgaria, Ignatiev, wrote in a letter in the late 1860s that the Serbs had a future as a nation-state.[2] In contrast, he was inclined to expect little from the Bulgarians. Evaluations can waver, of course, and people can be mistaken. Either way, I personally find it very difficult to grant either Serbia or Bulgaria exclusive rights to Macedonia. Having spent many years studying the question, I have been unable to find conclusive evidence in the heated scholarly dispute, our consular reports, or my personal travels in Macedonia.

The San Stefano agreement established definite national aspirations for Bulgaria and sanctioned them with the highest possible approval—that of Russia the Liberator. The Bulgarian people already had at their disposal a powerful weapon in the shape of the Exarchate, which they skillfully used to their advantage. It is well known that the sultan's *firman* [decree], which established the Exarchate, allowed it to expand its sovereignty to areas where a two-thirds majority in favor existed. In skilled hands this became a powerful weapon of propaganda.

Furthermore, the preacher and the teacher had the support of the *komitadji* [partisans]. The Bulgarian treasury was liberal with its purse when it came to sponsoring these efforts. By basing our policy on supporting Bulgaria, we left the Serbs in the lurch and presented Austria with the opportunity to occupy Bosnia-Herzegovina, also to the detriment of Serbia. My views of our policy are well known from the press, and I will not recount them here at great length.

A fatal conflict at that time between Bulgarian and Serbian interests in Macedonia served only to increase hostilities. We became disappointed with Bulgaria after it discarded the Russian protectorate. King Milan

Obrenović of Serbia had to seek support from Austria until his dynasty in Serbia was overthrown in 1903 and the pro-Russian Karađorđevići were established.[3]

From 1903 on, attempts for rapprochement between Serbia and Bulgaria were initially unsuccessful. The Young Turks' coup in 1908, however, and the chauvinist policy of the new Turkish leaders served to unify the Balkan countries against the common enemy.[4] This rapprochement could not have occurred without an involvement on the part of Russia, which had resumed its active policy in Europe and in the Balkans after the Russo-Japanese War.

The war between Italy and Turkey in 1911 gave the final nudge. The Balkan countries went from exchanges of ideas to negotiations, bringing about a détente. The agreement between Serbia and Bulgaria was concluded on February 29, 1912. Montenegro and Greece joined the two allies soon after.

Rumania, feeling itself slighted by the Congress of Berlin, remained on the sidelines insisting on the return of parts of Bessarabia it had lost to us at the Treaty of Paris in 1856.[5]

Eventually Rumania sided with the Triple Alliance and even concluded a military convention with our foes. As for the Balkans, Rumania showed cautious restraint. The intelligent King Carol did not trust King Ferdinand of Bulgaria. The Rumanians feared Bulgarian claims to the part of Dobrudja that they had received as compensation for the loss of Bessarabia. With their ingrained haughtiness, the Rumanians fancied themselves as Europe's avant-garde in the Balkans and were fond of saying they were a Carpathian rather than a Balkan state.

Time changes all. Eventually, Rumanian hostility to Russia waned along with Austrian prestige. That French charm, cultivated amid the educated, had the upper hand in Rumanian aristocratic circles, influencing subtly a more positive attitude toward Russia. France was indeed our ally.

For its part, Russian diplomacy did whatever it could to encourage this trend. Our General Headquarters made it a point to keep the situation under scrutiny to ensure Rumania's neutrality in case of a general European war.

The Balkan crisis finally undermined Austrian credibility in Bucharest. It predisposed Rumania toward Russia, despite the traditional hostility of Maiorescu's Conservative government.[6] Ion Brătianu, the leader of the opposition Liberal Party, assured our ambassador of a rapprochement with Russia should he ever come to power.[7] The feasibility of a possible alliance was interspersed with dynastic considerations flattering to the Rumanian ego. They wanted the eldest son of Crown Prince Carol to marry one of the daughters of the tsar.

Such was the desire of Princess Marie, the wife of the crown prince, whose origin led her to harbor English and Russian sympathies.[8] It is said that she had substantial influence on her somewhat insignificant husband.

Rumania's behavior during the Serbo-Bulgarian conflict alienated it from Austria, which openly favored Bulgaria and encouraged King Ferdinand's treacherous actions toward his ally. In contrast, Rumania did the right thing by professing reconciliation with Bulgaria and heeding our note of caution.

Rumania's sensible behavior was largely due to our influence; in exchange, we promised to support its reasonable demands for border rectifications in Sofia. Danev, intoxicated by easy successes, put a strain on relations between Bulgaria and Rumania by refusing to contemplate any concessions.[9] At the end of December 1912, the conflict between the two kingdoms was averted only thanks to our interference. Although not all of its aspirations were met, Rumania showed restraint and agreed to abide by the decisions of the Petersburg Conference regarding boundary adjustments.[10] Whenever the possibility of a rift arose between Bulgaria and her allies, Rumania did its part to preserve the peace.

Certain circles in Bulgaria and elsewhere have come to believe that we were hostile toward Bulgaria over the course of the Balkan crisis, eventually unleashing Rumania in order to prevent Sofia's territorial aggrandizement. These accusations are entirely unjustified. Throughout the crisis, we did everything to reconcile our allies. I mentioned earlier that in December of 1912, when Bulgarian intransigence almost drove Rumania to the brink of military action, we did not shy away from an ultimatum in order to prevent the escalation of the conflict.

The following circumstances led to the Rumanian involvement in the conflict between the Balkan allies. The quarrel between Serbia, Bulgaria, and Greece was becoming more acute every day. No side was completely in the right. Serbian forces occupied a part of Macedonia, which the 1912 agreement had assigned to Bulgaria. The Bulgarians were quite justified in their formal demand for the return of these lands. Serbia, however, did not accept the terms in principle, pointing to the changed circumstances.

At the beginning of the war, the allies had envisioned not so much outright territorial annexations as the creation of autonomous territories within the European provinces of the Ottoman Empire. As the situation turned for the better, both Serbia and Bulgaria made new claims. Serbia wanted a port on the Adriatic, which could only be achieved by dividing Albania between itself and Greece. Bulgaria wanted to occupy all of Thrace and even dreamed of taking Constantinople. Many lives were sacrificed at the siege of Çatalca, but the Ottoman capital was not taken.[11] Bulgaria, however, did get Thrace. Thus, the Balkan conflict lasted somewhat longer than the other allies wanted. Adrianople was taken, thanks to considerable Serbian assistance, especially with heavy artillery.[12] The Bulgarians even offered the Serbs remuneration for their participation. Nikola Pašić, the Serbian prime minister, however, refused this offer with great indignation, adding that the question of Serbian compensation would have to be settled in due course.[13] Later, the Bulgarians insisted that the Serbs were bound by a war convention to provide assistance without compensation. But does this not contradict their earlier offer of remuneration?

The differences between Serbia and Bulgaria stemmed from the fact that the outcome of the war was markedly different from the initial expectations at the time of the signing of the treaty of alliance. All Ottoman European provinces were up for grabs, Bulgaria had acquired Thrace, and Serbia had had to relinquish the Albanian coast, as Austrian and Italian pressure made a general European war a very real possibility. Pressured by Russia, Serbia accepted the status quo. However, this only strengthened its resolve to keep the Macedonian lands, where much Serbian blood had been spilt. This intransigence regrettably found a staunch supporter in our minister in Belgrade, the late N. G. Hartwig, who routinely ignored the Foreign Ministry's instructions to calm down the Serbs. A total Serbophile, the capable Hartwig often joined the Serbs in criticizing his own ministry, which made him extremely popular in Serbia. Although Hartwig often got carried away and acted without much regard to the means he was using, his actions were based on a correct, if admittedly exaggerated, premise. He did not trust the Bulgarians in their ambitions to dominate the Balkans and perhaps even conquer Constantinople. He regarded Bulgarian expansion as a threat to Russia's interests and wanted to create a balance of power by strengthening Serbia. To this end, he staunchly supported Serbian aspirations in Macedonia and the establishment of a direct connection with Greece.

I must reiterate that this premise was correct; even so, Russia and Hartwig himself had spent a significant amount of time brokering an agreement between Serbia and Bulgaria whereby both sides agreed to abide by Russian arbitration. Hence, it was unwise to encourage either side to break the agreement. Irritating those very countries we were trying to appease would place our honor and historical role in the Balkans under scrutiny. Furthermore, it would push Bulgaria into the open arms of Austria.

In light of these considerations, we began to perceive ourselves as a kind of tribunal with acknowledged rights of arbitration, in order to oversee a Serbo-Bulgarian agreement. We remained firm in our decision to make only minor adjustments to some points of demarcation, within the framework of the agreement itself. We aimed to adjust the northern border to Serbia's advantage, thereby establishing a common border between Serbia and Greece by way of Lake Prespa and Lake Okhrid. Bulgaria would thereby receive the entire uncontested zone with only negligible adjustments.

Friction between Bulgaria and Greece intensified the conflict. The only thing binding these two countries was a military convention. Nothing else existed that could bring about the possible delimitation of future borders. All attempts by Venizelos to come to an arrangement met with opposition in Sofia.[14]

Bulgarian attempts to take Salonika before the Greeks could arrive failed, but even so a Bulgarian military detachment was allowed to enter the city. In southern Macedonia, Bulgarian and Greek troops exchanged shots along the demarcation lines. There were even occasional skirmishes.

The result of this situation was a rapprochement between Greece and Serbia. Both sides worked out a political and a defensive war treaty that apparently remained unsigned. However, this mere formality could always be carried out at the last minute.

With the fading hopes for any kind of compromise, we declared to Serbia and Bulgaria our right to initiate arbitration, on the following conditions: (1) gradual demobilization of military forces to one-third or one-quarter of their wartime strength. We demanded this in order to ensure that neither side could violate our decision; and (2) concomitantly with our arbitration, Bulgaria and Greece would agree to settle their differences through the mediation of a third, mutually acceptable, party.

The suggestion to demand joint demobilization and disarmament came in secret from Bulgarian Prime Minister Geshov, who was replaced by Danev toward the end of the crisis. Danev was a difficult man to deal with; to make matters worse, he was unreliable and often changed his designs on the spur of the moment. He would agree to demobilization only on the condition that Bulgarian troops enter all disputed territories along with Serbian and Greek ones. Given the extreme volatility of the situation and the daily skirmishes between the allied troops, this suggestion was in bad faith, and we rejected it. Since time was not on our side, we acknowledged the futility of our proposal for demobilization and announced our intention to leave this open for discussion at the conference of Balkan leaders in St. Petersburg to which we were determined to invite Danev and Nikola Pašić. We also invited Venizelos so that he could come to an agreement with Danev about arbitration.

At first, Danev insisted on our making a decision within seven days as a prerequisite for his arrival. We refused to bind ourselves to such a deadline but reassured the Bulgarians it was not our intention to delay things unnecessarily. Danev deemed our reply unsatisfactory and withdrew from further negotiations. Sazonov told Minister Bobchev, who delivered this statement, that the Bulgarians were clearly determined to start a fratricidal war.

Prior to this exchange, Rumania declared it would resist any aggressor; this was done on the suggestion of Venizelos, if I am not mistaken. For our part, we approved of this declaration, as it promised to calm the tempers on both sides. When Bobchev on behalf of his government inquired about our reaction to the Rumanian statement, we told him in no uncertain terms that we would not lift a finger to defend Bulgaria if she attacked first.

These warnings seemed to have a sobering effect on the Bulgarians. Danev stated his words had been misinterpreted and he would travel to St. Petersburg. He had only inquired about a possible deadline rather than set a definitive one. At about this time, the growing chauvinism in Serbia preoccupied us as much as Bulgaria. Nikola Pašić assured us of his ability to assert control, however complicated that might seem. During the night of June 17, 1913, with only a few days remaining before the scheduled arrival of the prime ministers to St. Petersburg, Bulgaria launched a treacherous attack on Serbia and Greece.

A fair-minded study of the reasons that led Bulgaria to this suicidal decision shows things were not as straightforward as some people appear to think and cannot be reduced simply to King Ferdinand's treachery—even if his character traits played a role in subsequent events. Ferdinand had signed the treaty with Serbia with a cringe of heart as some clauses were aimed directly at Austria. A rather superstitious Catholic, Ferdinand harbored pro-Austrian sympathies, both cultural and political, and remained an Austrian at heart. His superstitious nature and cowardice were further compounded by vanity.

A Jesuit by nature, he was quite the actor as well, assuming myriad roles while posing in photographs and paintings. He once gave our former minister of foreign affairs, Count Lamsdorff, a portrait of himself in the guise of a medieval knight of Malta, which clearly reflected his effeminate and angry nature. He had his image printed on Bulgarian stamps. One stamp depicts Ferdinand in the ceremonial garb of a Byzantine emperor, with an elongated face resembling that of an ascetic on an icon. Another stamp portrays him in the uniform of an admiral of the Bulgarian fleet. Coincidently, there is a likeness to King Edward, a sailor and a sportsman.

Ferdinand had no love for his people. I can corroborate that he did not even bother to mask his contempt. The sloppiness and disorder of his subjects irritated him. Following a cabinet meeting, he would have all the windows opened in his palace. He encouraged his ministers to indulge in corrupt activities and bribery, blackmailing each one with compromising documents. Despite Bulgaria's economic achievements, the people feared and disliked him.

Ferdinand, in turn, was apprehensive of deceit or Bulgarian resentment.

His great antipathy toward Russia was mixed with anxious fear. He was convinced that we would bring about his end, expressing in no uncertain terms that Russia would depose him.

Perhaps he would suffer the fate of those hypochondriacs who end up suffering from the illness they are most afraid of. Such was the leader of Bulgaria.

Fear certainly is a bad advisor, and Ferdinand was surrounded by all sorts. He was fearful of an allied coalition with Rumania, of inciting the wrath of Russia. But most of all he feared the Macedonian party with its ambitious leaders. He sensed that they would stop at nothing to achieve their goals. Rather than relinquish any part of their territory to the Serbs, the Macedonians joined the military party headed by General Savov, who likewise stopped at nothing. Ultimately, it was phobia of these butchers and fear for his own life that did it. At the end of the Balkan crisis Ferdinand became neurotic, vacillating between decisions he hoped to avoid. It was Savov the adventurer and his Macedonians who coerced Ferdinand to sign the command to attack, thus influencing the somewhat irregular course of events in Bulgaria during the period preceding the Balkan crisis. The Macedonians in particular seem to have acquired a disproportionate influence on Bulgarian decision-making.

Russia cannot deny some responsibility for this extraordinary turn of events. I refer again to the Treaty of San Stefano. By consigning Serbia to oblivion, we recognized Bulgarian rights to Macedonia. There was really no basis for this extraordinary favoritism of Bulgaria.

From that moment, the Treaty of San Stefano in itself became a guiding light for Bulgarian policy right up to the Balkan War.

The vast majority of Macedonian Slavs were clay from which one could form either a Bulgarian or a Serb. The small urban and rural intelligentsia, however, favored Bulgaria. A number from this intelligentsia established itself in Bulgaria, creating in this way two homelands. Battling the Turks with gun and dagger in the Ottoman provinces, they were not averse to using the same methods in Bulgaria. That is why Ferdinand quite justifiably feared them. Bulgaria for the Macedonians was a means rather than an end in itself. From that point of view, the Bulgarian action of June 17 was quite explicable. Furthermore, their psyche matched the shortsightedness and folly of the grassroot Bulgarian at the time.

The country was intoxicated by its success in the war with Turkey. The egos of the ruling class of this small country were noticeably overinflated. The main thrust was to control Macedonia and establish hegemony in the Balkans. It irritated them that Russia stood firmly behind Bulgaria's allies, supporting the justifiable Rumanian claims as well. From this arose the concept that Russia stood in the way of Bulgaria's vested interests. As for the more ambitious, they dreamed of Constantinople.

At one point they came close to achieving this dream. We, of course, could not condone such ambitions, nor could we allow anyone the rights to Constantinople. It was our economic and military priority to keep the Straits free from any foreign domination replacing that of a weakened Turkey.

The Bulgarians knew this policy of ours very well. During some talks with them a few years before the war, we clearly stressed our rights to Constantinople and its hinterland, including Adrianople. It was the tsar, predisposed to Bulgaria, who ordered us to announce that Russia would not stand in the way of a Bulgarian annexation of Adrianople.

The issue of the Straits, however, was a completely different matter. In October 1912, when the Bulgarians reached Çatalca, we strongly suggested that they take advantage of the temporary Turkish confusion and conclude a favorable peace treaty. We took no definite stand regarding a temporary occupation of the Turkish capital by the Bulgarians. We kept a small division of marines in Sevastopol for such an occasion. Should circumstances warrant the decision, our ambassador in Constantinople was authorized to call on the Black Sea Fleet, waiting at anchor. In case the Bulgarians entered Constantinople, we would bring in the marines.

We wanted to avoid substantial international complications should Constantinople fall.

We were politically and militarily totally unprepared, which is why we tried in every way to curb the Bulgarian initiative to occupy Constantinople, where they would not have been allowed to remain in any case.

Be that as it may, the Bulgarians ignored our recommendations. The storming of Turkish fortifications proved useless, costing many lives. Constantinople was saved not so much by the bravery of its defenders as by an unexpected ally: cholera. I personally heard from the commander of the siege, General Radko-Dmitriev, that this strain of cholera moved swiftly, killing people within half an hour. Twenty-two thousand soldiers were stricken. Cholera was unfamiliar to the Bulgarian forces, and they panicked. According to Dmitriev, to take Constantinople under such circumstances was a hopeless task.

The autumn campaign of 1912 resulted in talks between the allies and Turkey in London.

The bone of contention was Adrianople. The Turks refused to cede it to Bulgaria, and the conflict resumed. Danev and Radko-Dmitriev arrived in St. Petersburg before the taking of Adrianople. The latter brought with him a letter from King Ferdinand, which sought the tsar's approval for a Bulgarian advance to the Sea of Marmara and the annexation of Rodosto to Bulgaria.[15]

In view of the tsar's predisposition to Bulgaria, this question really worried me. Before the audience of Radko-Dmitriev with the tsar, the foreign minister sent the tsar a memorandum outlining the subject at hand and noting the rather extreme claims on the part of Bulgaria.

It was at this time that Bobchev, the Bulgarian minister, came to see me in my office. He wanted to talk about Rodosto. I expressed to him, without any hesitation, my personal point of view: that should the Bulgarians enter Rodosto, we would not hesitate to take up arms against them. I told him:

"It is my conviction that you will not be given our approval. Otherwise I would not have remained in this office for more than half an hour."

My words had an obvious effect. Bobchev thanked me, adding that frankness was best in such matters. This way, there was no chance for false hopes.

Radko-Dmitriev was authorized to request the use of one or two warships in order to bombard the fortifications of Çatalca from the rear. The general's mission failed in every way, although personally he was greeted with great respect wherever he went. During his stay in St. Petersburg, Adrianople fell, on March 13, 1913, after a siege of 149 days. We speculated that Ferdinand sent Radko-Dmitriev to St. Petersburg with a delicate mission of this kind in order to compromise the integrity of this popular general so loyal to Russia.

Owing to the fact that I was personally involved in our relations with Bulgaria during the Balkan crisis, I cannot be entirely objective. However, I can honestly refute with a clear conscience those two central accusations leveled at us by Bulgarian Russophobes—that is, that we pitted Rumania against Bulgaria and that we, not wanting a strong Bulgaria, prevented it from taking Constantinople.

They justified the first accusation by pointing out that a military convention between Russia and Bulgaria obliged us to defend Bulgaria against Rumania. Such a convention had indeed been concluded at the time when Kuropatkin was minister of war.[16] This convention had been badly drafted, and certain clauses were found to be contradictory. Nonetheless, when Rumania intended to occupy the borderlands between Rumania and Bulgaria in December 1912, we recognized the potentially serious ramifications of this act and immediately communicated with our allies, the French, creating quite the consternation in Paris. The French expressed their obvious reluctance to be involved in a general European conflict. We stood our ground. Even now, except for a few in the inner circle, no one knows of these details. Certainly they are proof enough that Russia did not shirk her moral responsibilities to Bulgaria. What with the Bulgarian underhanded use of the convention, their rejection of our advice and warnings, their assuming that we would come to their aid against Rumania, we deemed it impossible to accept such an attitude. Quite obviously, any convention covering mutual acts of war is valid only when there is a common political agreement invoking such an act.

The Bulgarians as well as the other Slavs had become convinced they had all the rights and Russia all the responsibilities. Consequently, they accused our Ministry of Foreign Affairs of failing in its obligations to them and of advocating their interests. Unfortunately, these views were echoed by the press.

In a humorous feuilleton, Doroshevich wrote: "Russia is obligated to us."[17] "Poor ol' Russia, overwhelmed by countless responsibilities."

To expect that Russia would move against Rumania while Bulgaria itself made attempts to defeat Serbia and Greece serves to underline to what extent Sofia was blinded. There really was nothing we could do. Russia, by recognizing Bulgaria's rights in Macedonia, became the arbitrator of its disagreement with Serbia. That is an established fact. As for Greek ambitions, we only recognized their rights to Salonika with a small hinterland and nothing else. Russia's policy toward Constantinople certainly needed neither definition nor justification before Russians or objective Bulgarians alike. Therein lay the problem, as we could not expect objective reasoning from the Bulgarians. The Bulgarian people refused to acknowledge their mistakes. How much easier it was for them to simply place the blame elsewhere. After all, Russia was expected to always be there! This became an excuse for Russophobe agitation in Bulgaria. Manipulative and unscrupulous leaders like Genadiev, Radoslavov & Co. published an open letter to King Ferdinand in the press, accusing the Geshov-Danev government of being extreme Russophiles. They attributed all of Bulgaria's current problems to this factor. Their sympathies were on the side of Austria.

The writers of this letter were asked to form a government, which incidentally did not stop them from seeking aid from Russia, just as in his time Danev the Russophile considered a closer relationship with Austria. Austria did little to bring about an end to a war that now threatened to destroy Bulgaria. As for us, we did whatever we could to lessen a potential downfall for Bulgaria. Rumania stopped her forces in their march to Sofia on our insistence.

During the talks in Bucharest, our main effort was to curb Serbian and Greek claims. Regrettably, we were unable to secure Kavala for Bulgaria.[18] On this occasion, our French allies sided with the Germans, who in turn wanted Kavala for the Greeks. We ended up seconding Austria, which in fact was of little use. Austria was compromised to such an extent in the Balkans that no one listened to her.

Our efforts on behalf of the Bulgarians were unsuccessful in yet another matter. We insisted that Turkey return Adrianople, which it had occupied once again, to Bulgaria.

Everyone agreed in principle that Turkey did not have the right to single-handedly violate the conditions that recently had been set out between these same powers. Before long it became apparent that we would never reach a consensus on how to apply joint pressure on the Turks. Germany, maintaining the peace, began to side with the Turks. We, at one point, considered pressuring the Turks by taking the Black Sea port of Trebizond on our own.[19] However, after conferring with General Headquarters, it became obvious that we lacked sufficient means of transportation. Such an expedition would only weaken our forces. We also had to consider the possibility that Austria, capitalizing on our involvement in the Black Sea, would move to support the "oppressed" population of Bulgaria against the Serbs. Moreover, outraged over Bulgarian impropriety, Russian public opinion would never have agreed to any kind of sacrifice. We, of course, could never envisage such a turn of events. It is somewhat regrettable that we were unable to maintain our position as far as Adrianople was concerned. Bulgaria would have established a rapport with us. More important, it would have had a positive effect on the Turks. Ignoring the powers, they easily took back Adrianople. As the sole defender of Turkish interests, Germany was able to secure a big favor, as we shall see in due course. Thus it was that, at the Bucharest talks, there was no improvement in the relationship between Russia and Bulgaria. General Radko-Dmitriev was appointed minister plenipotentiary to St. Petersburg.

He was as much Russian as he was Bulgarian. As a man, there was no better person. He mistrusted the current government in power in Bulgaria. A. A. Savinskii was appointed as our minister plenipotentiary to Sofia. His goal was to remove the current government with the help of the opposition by means of financial pressure. Bulgaria needed a financial loan. Savinskii and his French colleague, Panafier, required a change in government as collateral. When the Bulgarians approached German banks instead, both ministers stated their willingness to take back their demand. It was, however, too late. The Bulgarian ministers apparently had time to secure a loan from German banks and conclude the matter. Savinskii kept close ties to the opposition to the end, ignoring their ineptitude and recalcitrance as an independent opposition party. This served to further damage his relationship with the government and Ferdinand, thereby weakening our influence in Sofia. At the same time, German influence was on the rise.

From the start of the Balkan crisis we tried in every way to settle our differences with Germany. In the spring of 1913, the tsar traveled to Berlin to attend the marriage of Kaiser Wilhelm's daughter. German society greeted him warmly, to his satisfaction. They obviously understood that, if the Balkan crisis did not ignite all of Europe, it was because of this peace-loving Russian ruler. This was the impression of all those who found themselves in Berlin at that time. The royal visit coincided with the strained relations between Greece and Bulgaria in the run-up to the Second Balkan War. As for the quite serious border clashes between Greek and Bulgarian forces, both monarchs agreed to send telegrams of caution to King Ferdinand, a kind of demonstration of friendship following a winter of tense expectations. In the autumn of that same year, Kokovtsev visited Berlin. He returned in the most optimistic mood following his discussions with the imperial chancellor.

Barely a few days passed before we received critical news from Constantinople: General Liman von Sanders was appointed commander of the Turkish army.[20] We were quite impressed with this information. Until then, German officers had been invited by the Turkish military as instructors only; they did not command any part of the army. Now, a German general became the de facto commander. He was accompanied by an entire staff of officers. Thus, a German protectorate was established in weak and underdeveloped Turkey. By taking control of the Baghdad Railroad, an artery of the utmost economic importance, the Germans gained control of the army. They were supreme.

In accordance with our policy of reconciliation, we decided to exhaust all possible means of resolving the conflict peacefully by initiating direct negotiations with Germany. With due consideration to German pride, we made it clear to Berlin that we could not permit a German general to take command of the ranks in Constantinople. Such a situation would undermine the equal status of other powers in Constantinople. The French and English supported our view. The diplomatic peace process became more complicated when this entire incident was exposed in the press.

At the beginning of January 1914, Kokovtsev called for a plenary session to seek a peaceful solution. We could not allow a German to command forces in Constantinople at any cost. England in particular was helpful in bringing about a peaceful solution between Germany and ourselves. The government in Berlin finally agreed that the German general should not command a force in Constantinople. The Germans, however, did appoint their own general to command a division in Scutari, located on the Asian shoreline of the Bosporus.[21] We decided to look the other way and stood by the previously achieved results.

We were far more successful in initiating reforms in Armenia. During the Balkan crisis, we managed to forestall revolts by promising the Armenians to bring about much-needed reforms once the immediate crisis was over. We certainly did not want to provoke reprisals by Turkey; neither did we want to be drawn into a war. Our interest was in keeping the Balkan crisis localized. Delegates of various political parties in Armenia often stopped by my office, including members of the revolutionary party called "Dashnak-sutiun." Members of this party, convicted of separatism and revolts against Russia just a few years ago, were now coming to us for support.

I give full credit to Count Vorontsov-Dashkov, the appointed deputy governor general for the Caucasus, with his intuitive grasp of the situation for the changes within Armenia.[22]

We did what we promised. At the appropriate time, we indicated to the Turks which reforms were needed in seven Armenian provinces and insisted on regulation by the European powers. We added that any delay in bringing about these reforms would likely provoke unrest in Armenia. Should any local disturbances arise along its borders, Russia could no longer remain passive. We invited all powers to a discussion of the proposed reforms.

Preliminary discussions rested directly with our embassy in Constantinople. The project for the reforms itself had been drawn up by our dragoman, A. N. Mandelshtam.[23] Before long, two opposing points of view emerged. An approval in principle by the Entente powers for the reforms and for European regulation was one view. In contrast, the Turkophile Triple Alliance wanted to whittle down the reforms and scrap the principle of European control altogether.

The key lay in Berlin. We began negotiations with the Germans to work out a possible compromise. We also kept discussions going with the Turks. The Germans tried to apply restraints to some of our conditions, but we still managed to achieve much for the Armenians. The framework for the reforms we had negotiated was signed by the grand vizier and by our chargé d'affaires in Constantinople. This act was significant in that it forced the Turks to recognize the special rights of Russia as a protector of the Armenians.

These latest developments in the Balkans as well as the increasing German activity in Constantinople compelled us to reexamine the status of our own military and naval forces in the Black Sea basin. Sazonov called a meeting, which included General Zhilinskii, the chief of the general staff, and M. N. Giers, our ambassador to Constantinople and head of the Ministry of the Navy.[24] Its main purpose was to strengthen the Black Sea Fleet and create a special force of marines. Zhilinskii was supportive of this idea. Quartermaster-General Danilov, who subsequently became an important player in the Stavka of Commander in Chief Grand Duke Nikolai Nikolaevich, took a negative approach. He firmly believed that Russia could acquire Constantinople and the Straits only as a result of a general European war, in which case our western front would prove decisive. In these circumstances, it would be a mistake to divert forces from the main European theater. At this time it was decided to reorganize our army, augmenting it significantly. Danilov considered the creation of a separate unit such as the marines to be pointless. Others insisted that we needed special forces if we were ever to make a move against Turkey. The decisions of this meeting were never implemented. They simply serve to demonstrate the prevailing political points of view on the eve of the general European war and as such are of some interest.

These exchanges of opinion had some outcome for the development of the Black Sea Fleet. The Ministry of Foreign Affairs applied pressure on the Ministry of the Navy. We had the support of the younger officers. The course of the war demonstrated how important our command of the sea was for our military operations against Turkey.

In the spring of 1914, when the tsar was in Livadia, a Turkish delegation led by Minister of the Interior Talaat-Bey had come to greet him.[25] Sazonov asked me to be there as well. Talaat-Bey was considered the principle figure in the Turkish government. At one point, before the coup by the Young Turk Party, he was an insignificant telegraph clerk in Salonika. On more than one occasion our consul general had even tipped him a Turkish lira. Here he was, by some quirk of fate, minister of the interior and one of the guiding lights in Turkey's destiny. It was amazing to behold this telegraph clerk of yesterday standing there with such calm dignity.

The arrival of the Turks in Livadia coincided with their strained relationship with the Greeks. Turkey did not accept the incorporation of some Aegean islands, especially Lemnos and Militene, by Greece. The committees of the Young Turk Party artificially propagated an anti-Greek sentiment among local people. In some coastal areas of Asia Minor near Smyrna, there were pogroms and killings. They were mustering support for increasing the navy. It was obvious that they were only awaiting the arrival of two dreadnoughts built for them in England in order to launch military action against Greece.

Talaat-Bey hoped to secure Russia's neutrality in a Greco-Turkish conflict. He presented a number of vague—yet at the same time enticing—proposals, even hinting at an alliance with Russia. He acknowledged the importance of the Straits to Russia. In his opinion, all that remained was to find a satisfactory solution. The tsar received Talaat-Bey in a special audience. The tsar told him that the relationship between Russia and Turkey depended entirely on the latter. We could conceivably have a friendly relationship with Turkey, but Russia would not tolerate the presence of another power in Constantinople. All in all, we were unimpressed with Talaat-Bey.

His proposals were not sincere, and his plans regarding Greece elicited little support. His hypocrisy became apparent a short while later, when, making his way to Bucharest from Livadia, he gave assurances of an agreement with Russia whereby the islands would revert to Turkey.

Such, then, was the situation in the Balkans at the time of our rift with Germany. Our primary concern was to thwart the delivery of the two warships purchased by the Turks from England, expected at any moment. They were appropriated by the British government. That provoked great consternation in Constantinople. During this time, the German vessel *Goeben* was sailing the Mediterranean. In the very first days of the war, my colleague V. N. Murav'ev stopped by my office and asked me:

"Does it not worry you that the *Goeben* could slip into the Straits?"

Now, that was a possibility that had not occurred to me. I made my way straight to the navy general staff to bring up this point. After an initial, rather low-key reaction, they became worried. They expedited a telegram to England requesting that all necessary precautions be taken not to allow this to happen. The English agreed. Admiral Traubridge telegraphed from Malta, "I cover Geben."*

It was on July 26, during the historical meeting in the State Duma that Neniukov, an aide to the commander of the navy general staff, found me and disclosed that the *Goeben* was making its way through the Straits.

When this unfortunate news was confirmed, our seamen became indignant with the British. We had warned them that the arrival of the *Goeben* would completely change the balance of power in the Black Sea. Our new warships were not yet ready. There was not a single ship that could compete with the *Goeben* in either speed or firepower. Although there was no real basis for this assumption, our sailors fully believed that the English had allowed this to happen. One cannot help but note that the instructions sent to the English admiral were somewhat vague and undefined. Apparently, the instructions were sent before the rift between Germany and England. Traubridge was given a court-martial, only to be vindicated and sent to an

---

* Trubetskoi's exact quote. Tr.

honorable exile in Serbia. I was to meet up with him later in Belgrade where he was sent to take charge of the mining of the Danube.

The arrival of the *Goeben* at Constantinople had fatal political ramifications, making Turkey's entry into the war on the side of our enemies a certainty. Ignoring the protests of the Entente powers, Turkey did not disarm the *Goeben*, acquiring it fictitiously from Germany instead. The Entente ambassadors still believed that Turkey would be afraid to move against us.

The behavior of the Porte toward foreign, especially Russian, visitors became more and more arrogant.[26] She unilaterally abrogated the capitulations and endeavored to arrest Russian citizens without any grounds, their businesses expropriated without restitution. Basically, this was German manipulation, as they brought goods and workers via Rumania and Bulgaria to arm Turkey more effectively. The English admiral, an instructor by invitation in the Turkish navy, tendered his resignation after he was completely marginalized. His protests and those of the Allied ambassadors fell on deaf ears. So it was that the Turks managed to increase their defenses in three and a half months.

In the spring of 1915, when the English launched an expedition to the Dardanelles, the English general commanding the Australian forces remarked upon the effective defenses mounted by the Germans in Gallipoli.

Although Turkey was arming and the Germans were gaining greater control, the lack of unanimity in the Turkish government kept alive the false hopes of the Allied ambassadors.

Minister of War Enver Pasha presented our military representative with a complete proposition: Turkey would move its forces to wherever Russia indicated.[27] In exchange, Turkey would receive all the Aegean islands that had been taken over by Greece and Italy and Thrace, while Bulgaria would be given Serbian Macedonia, and Greece would divide Albania with Serbia. Russia had only to agree to the abrogation of the capitulations. Enver was a bold adventurer very popular with the Young Turk Party. His plan was quite unreasonable, and we did not take him seriously. Nevertheless, we continued with the negotiations in order not to alienate him.

The policy of our general staff was to avoid a war with Turkey by any means and to put off the inevitable rift as long as possible. That the more efficient sections of the army in the Caucasus had been transferred to the western front, leaving behind a mere handful of soldiers, was reason enough for our negotiations at this point in time. Besides, as I have mentioned earlier, there were some differences of opinion in the Turkish government. In contrast to the easily swayable Enver Pasha, there were leaders intimidated by the possibilities of Turkey being drawn into the war. Prominent among them were Minister of the Navy Jamal-Bey and Grand Vizier Prince Sahid Khalim. Both remained somewhat irresolute. They lacked that determination needed in promoting a policy of caution through which Turkey could gain some concessions, thus guarding itself from the risk of war. They turned a blind eye to the obvious implications of the mounting of Turkish defenses by the Germans. Rarely did they acknowledge the precarious situation created by the increasing German presence.

In response to the rather fantastic plan for territorial expansion put forth by Enver, we offered Turkey economic freedom from the Germans, thus strengthening Turkey's independence. Sensible politicians like Fetkhi-Bey, their chargé d'affaires in St. Petersburg, were open to this line of reasoning. In exchange for a common agreement we would assist them in regaining control of the Baghdad Railroad. In conversations with me, Fetkhi-Bey expressed his personal concerns. To support the Germans would result in military conflicts and German domination of Turkey. On the other hand, wouldn't a victorious Russia become a threat to Turkey? What assurances could Russia give for the inviolability of Turkey's borders? I told him that in my opinion a defense alliance would guarantee that inviolability.

"Yes, but do you need the Straits?" he inquired.

I answered that, as far as our interests were concerned, a solution would be negotiable.

Turkey would remain untouched, and we would not encroach on her independence. Instead of chasing unrealistic dreams of expansion, Turkey would benefit. Fetkhi-Bey assured us in all sincerity that Turkey would never rashly enter into a war. Telegrams to his government cautioning against war with Russia and even exaggerating our military strength convinced us of his sincerity.

We were well acquainted with the intrigues of our enemies in Constantinople. From reading the telegrams by the Austrian ambassador we gathered that our enemies were unhappy with Turkey's wavering and had misgivings. Without the pressure of German gold, the Turks would certainly not have been able to conclude military preparations. When Fetkhi-Bey tried to convince me that Turkey would never be stupid enough to wage war on us, I cautioned him that the Germans, taking advantage of Turkish indecision, would make full use of the *Goeben*, flying a Turkish flag under German command, to force the issue. Indeed, one did not need to be a prophet to foresee such a turn of events. Nevertheless, when the *Goeben* returned to Constantinople after its treacherous raid, the grand vizier was shocked. The official Turkish version was that we were the first to open fire on their ships.

I attribute German success in fortifying Constantinople to the Bulgarians and Rumanians allowing supplies and men to pass through their territories. When the Germans declared war, we sent a telegram to Sofia on July 20, if I am not mistaken, to ascertain Bulgaria's position. To have done so was of the utmost importance. We explained that the conflict presented Bulgaria with the opportunity to modify the clauses created by the Bucharest Conference, should it act in accordance with its historical relationship with Russia.

We fully realized that the only way to make Bulgaria our ally was to give it Macedonia, as had been defined in the 1912 treaty of alliance.[28] On the other hand, if Bulgaria were to hold back her forces, we would reward her benevolent neutrality with territories up to the Vardar River. We apprised the Serbs of these conditions and requested their full cooperation to begin negotiations with Bulgaria. Pašić disagreed, explaining that the ongoing mutual hostility made any Serbo-Bulgarian joint action unfeasible. He expressed firmly that no Serb would agree to give up Macedonia to the Bulgarians. He conceded by pledging some unspecified territory to Bulgaria as an incentive for its neutrality. He even suggested that the exact parameters of those territories be left for future considerations by us. They should not, however, be extended as far as the Vardar, but only to the Bregalnitsa River. In view of this, we asked Bulgaria to maintain benevolent neutrality. We believed that Bulgaria's entry into the war would be desirable primarily if and when Turkey also joined; until then, a neutral Bulgaria was a threat not only to Turkey but to indecisive Rumania as well.

As soon as we found ourselves at war with Germany, the Bulgarian envoy Radko-Dmitriev expressed a desire to join the ranks of the Russian army. He asked for a division and was promised an entire corps. A reply to his telegram to King Ferdinand requesting approval never came, and Radko-Dmitriev left for the army. He was replaced by Counselor Patiev, who tried persistently to cajole promises advantageous to Sofia from Sazonov and myself. We made it quite clear that, should Bulgaria make a move at the appropriate time, it could perhaps receive Macedonia.

Not long afterward, Madzharov was appointed minister plenipotentiary in the place of Radko-Dmitriev. He was quite a decent fellow who had previously served in London. He repeatedly sent telegrams to his government urging them to set aside their double-dealing and support Russia openly. At this point in time, however, the Bulgarian government chose to construe the definition of benevolent neutrality to the benefit of Turkey, allowing German supplies to pass through its territory en route to Constantinople.

The war with Turkey should have induced Bulgaria to take our side, with a possibility of acquiring Thrace. Furthermore, as an adversary of Turkey,

Bulgaria could have received the rights to Macedonia as well, gaining credibility. As it happened, there was no discernible change in Sofia as far as we could tell.

It was likewise important to determine Rumania's position. The war had taken Rumania by surprise. We had only just begun to establish a friendly relationship, in spite of the fact that Rumania had not severed her ties with Austria and Germany. These ties had been growing from the time of the Congress of Berlin. Old King Carol, a Hohenzollern and a German through and through, personally preferred an open alliance with Germany and Austria. Italy declared her neutrality during a session of the Council of Ministers that the king had summoned to discuss this very question. Italy's declaration influenced Rumania to do the same. A rapport was thus established between Italy and Rumania. The aftermath was a mutual attempt to coordinate their actions during the war.

In time, public opinion in Rumania came to favor Russia and her allies. France and French culture had always been popular in Rumania. The education of the intelligentsia was based on French values. The aristocracy, powerful because of its extensive landholdings, deferred to France, influencing Rumania away from Germany. The brilliant successes of our troops in Bukovina and Galicia led to the idea of bringing the four million Transylvanian Rumanians into the Kingdom of Rumania. In contrast, there were fewer than one million Rumanians in Bessarabia. In reality, the Rumanians would have liked to have acquired both, but they never ventured to broach this subject with us openly. The fall of Lemberg provoked extreme agitation.

The king and his government were becoming alarmed that public opinion would pressure them to take some concrete action. Brătianu launched into discussions about benevolent neutrality in exchange for the Rumanian-populated lands of Austria-Hungary. Rumania would retain the option of deciding when to take over these territories.

Blondel, the French representative in Bucharest for nine years, was considered an expert on Rumania.[29] Somewhat dubious about negotiations, he exhorted taking advantage of the psychological moment and pressuring Rumania into action. By agreeing to Rumania's neutrality, we weakened the position of the proponents of immediate action. Why? Because Brătianu could then say, "Why rush when Russia has recognized our right to act when we see fit?"

Our minister in Bucharest, Poklevskii-Kozell, on the other hand, was of a completely different opinion. He favored the idea of coming to an agreement on Rumania's neutrality in order to prevent the country from changing its position. The very, very old Germanophile king was still alive at this point in time and had a significant influence on government matters, which needed to be taken into consideration.

Sazonov supported Poklevskii's point of view.

I personally felt that Rumania should define her "benevolent neutrality" more clearly. We needed assurances, for example, that Rumania would not sell food and fuel to our enemies, which they desperately needed after our capture of the oil-rich province of Galicia.

The Rumanians took offense at our mistrust. They insisted that it would look somewhat suspicious and dangerous if they were to forbid exports to our enemies. Convinced, Sazonov signed the agreement. Blondel's views turned out to be broadly correct, as Brătianu showed little concern for the ongoing pro-war agitation.

The death of the old king rekindled the hopes of the pro-war faction. News of his death reached us in St. Petersburg at the same time as news of the fall of Antwerp to the Germans.

With the king gone, the Germans had lost their most important supporter in the Balkans.

I have some personal reminiscences of King Carol. In 1908 I had traveled privately through the Balkans. In Bucharest the king granted me a two-hour audience. Just prior to this, I had occasion to visit most of the monarchs and leaders in the Balkan Peninsula. Not one of them impressed me as deeply as did this remarkable and intelligent king. Like King Ferdinand of Bulgaria, he kept full control of his country, but he used his power for the good of his country rather than in the service of personal ambitions.

There used to be two types of German landlords in Russia before the emancipation of the serfs. The first type despised the common people and treated them like vermin. The second type sought to enlighten their serfs, introducing new methods of agriculture. Carol and Ferdinand reflected these two types of German rulers in the Balkans. The former was the wise landowner and overseer of Rumania. In contrast, the latter belittled the Bulgarians, publicly referring to them as beasts of burden on more than one occasion even in the presence of foreigners.

Ferdinand envied Carol, while Carol despised Ferdinand.

First and foremost, King Carol was a reasonable ruler and landlord, who kept exemplary order on his estates. This, in turn, brought him large profits. He discussed his lands and agronomy in general with such obvious affection. Having long been plagued by absentee landlords, Rumanian agriculture could not but benefit from his example.

He showed great wisdom in his approach to the political parties of Rumania. The country was not fully developed and lacked in political experience.

Nor was there anyone intellectually or morally capable of standing up to the king. The king asserted his authority surreptitiously, promoting one party into power while dissolving another. A minister retired, not at the behest of Parliament but when the king decided it was necessary. Nevertheless, the king was held in such high esteem that there was no resentment on the part of the ministers. King Carol never forgot that he was German and a Hohenzollern. This inherent belief in the superiority of his roots convinced him that developing close ties with Germany and Austria was in the best interests of Rumania. Only once did he compromise his principles, when despite Austrian pressure, he signed the order for mobilization during the Balkan crisis. He did so with tears in his eyes, having given in to social pressures. King Carol had been ill for some time. His naturally strong constitution was weakened by pressures and afflictions. Although he passed away at the right time, Rumania was unable to replace him with a leader of comparable experience, and so the country remained at a crossroads.

Turkey opened hostilities on October 16, 1914, after which date our embassy staff left Constantinople. In October, the Austrians began their second advance into Serbia. The news from Serbia was sufficiently disturbing that I needed to go now and assume my responsibilities as minister plenipotentiary. Gulkevich, the counselor of the embassy in Constantinople, replaced me as head of the Department of Near Eastern Affairs.

From the inception of the war with Germany, when Turkey was still neutral, the thought foremost in everybody's mind was gaining control of the Straits. The conduct of the Turks seemed to suggest they were well aware of the fact that Russia would sooner or later try to resolve the question of the Straits in its favor. This was certainly reflected in my discussions with the cautious Fetkhi-Bey to which I have already alluded. When Turkey made its illegal attack in the Black Sea, the large majority of the public welcomed this, in anticipation that at last something could finally be initiated. I heard this from everyone I met: from political leaders to the ordinary man in the street. I was much surprised when I had to listen to impassioned addresses on this subject in the court of Empress Maria Fedorovna. The future of Constantinople did indeed provoke concerned dialogue, from huts to palaces.

One day in October, Witte and I attended a dinner hosted by Prince Alexander Dmitrievich Obolenskii. At the table, Witte bitterly denounced everyone who had dragged Russia into what he considered to be a useless war for the sake of Serbia, a country on whose behalf he would not sacrifice even his pet dog. He was highly critical of the grand duke's declaration to the Poles. Its provisions could never be implemented, Witte argued. Worse still, the declaration seemed to reverse overnight the concerted policy of several

Russian emperors. Naturally, Witte conveniently seemed to forget that he himself had insisted on the promulgation of the Manifesto of October 17, 1905, without any regard to how the emperors Nicholas I or Alexander III would have felt about it. However, it was impossible to argue with Witte. He never listened to what anyone had to say and silently ignored arguments he found difficult to refute.

Elaborating on the futility of the war, Witte declared, among other things: "Now, it would be an entirely different matter if we were fighting in order to acquire the Straits—I couldn't possibly argue with that. But our English friends, who are willing to fight 'to the last drop of Russian blood,' would never give us this." Witte was referring to the phrase that Baron Rozen, also at the table that evening, had used recently. I needed no persuading of the importance of the Straits Question to Russia. I had pondered it for many years. It was the main goal of my years of service and my work in the field of foreign policy.*

In practical terms, the dilemma of the Straits first came up during the Balkan Wars when we feared that Bulgaria would occupy Constantinople. We were not prepared for war then, and we realized that it would be impossible to resolve the question one-on-one with Turkey without the involvement of the other Great Powers. To consider a final resolution of the question therefore was not possible. Nevertheless, we had to work out various possibilities in the event of Bulgaria occupying Constantinople, in which case we would be forced to send an expeditionary force. On October 30, 1912, I wrote a memorandum that established nonetheless our presence in the upper Bosporus as *condition sine qua non*. This partial solution would have resolved the problem of our defenses in the Black Sea without, however, providing us with access to the open sea, which ultimately made it unsatisfactory. That is why I personally hoped at the time that Bulgaria would not enter Constantinople, thereby postponing decisions for a time more favorable to us.

My memorandum and the issue as a whole became subject to debates in the Council of Ministers. The army and navy representatives insisted that any presence on the Upper Bosporus alone would not be secure and would leave us "standing on the ledge." In order to strengthen our permanent hold of the area, we would have to acquire a territory large enough to allow us to deploy significant forces. Chief of the Navy General Staff Prince Lieven, a noble, sympathetic man who was apparently a decent sailor but unfortunately no statesman, proposed neutralizing the Straits by demolishing all of

---

* Trubetskoi actually describes "main goal" as "central dream" or *tsentral'noi mechtoi*. Tr.

their defenses. While this appeared to be a good solution in peacetime, such a provision would not have been worth the paper it was written on at times of war.

I once had an opportunity to try to persuade Lieven of the folly of his proposal. When I inquired about the enforcement mechanism the supposed international condominium for the neutralization of the Straits would employ, or how we were supposed to prevent a hostile power from taking over the Straits in case of war, he simply stated: "It is the job of diplomats such as yourself to work out appropriate guarantees and sanctions."

Sazonov was not averse to the idea of neutralizing the Straits and establishing an international condominium to guarantee the settlement. It also appealed to the tsar. At the time of the Balkan crisis, the tsar told Sazonov that he too had been enthralled by the possibility of taking over Constantinople until he had read the letter correspondence of Emperor Nicholas I on the subject. Nicholas I, whom the tsar considered to be the most nationally minded of his predecessors, had allegedly argued that control of Constantinople would be detrimental to Russia. This was the tsar's point of view; Sazonov, for his part, believed the acquisition of Constantinople would pose cultural, political, and church problems of enormous magnitude, which we would be unable to tackle successfully. He had little time for my arguments in the matter.

Just before my departure from St. Petersburg, I requested permission from Sazonov to present my arguments. I asked him not to flare up while I talked. Baron Schilling was also there. I emphasized the need of our presence throughout the entire zone along the Midia-Enos Line.[30] To my astonishment and that of Schilling, Sazonov completely agreed, although he continued to be personally skeptical of our ability to establish order in the new lands. He feared international complications, but he had to consider public opinion, which was firmly in favor of such policy.

Sazonov even went as far as persuading the tsar of how important it was to reexamine the question of Constantinople and the Straits. I was soon to receive an endorsement.

Before departing for Serbia, I had a lengthy audience with the tsar. I defined the expectations of my assignment in Serbia. I talked about our acquisitions in Galicia and Bukovina, which presented more of a burden than an advantage for us. Our chief aim in this war should be to dominate the Straits and to control the entire zone, both dry land and water, to the Midia-Enos Line. This would give us Constantinople and the islands of Imbros, Lemnos, and Tenedos, which defend the Dardanelles to the Sea of Marmara from approach.

The tsar interrupted me with a glance of approval. Encouraged, I went on to say that we needed the support of Bulgaria, without whose assistance we could not take Constantinople.

These last words of mine did not agree with the tsar.

"You have the reputation of being a Bulgarophile," he remarked.

Addendum: As he had a good memory, I imagine that the tsar was referring to the talks leading to the Bucharest Peace in 1913, when I had personally championed giving Kavala to Bulgaria. Psykha, the Greek minister who knew both me and Sazonov, had the impression that in this instance Sazonov was under my influence. At this time, the former chairman of the Greek Council of Ministers Zaimis arrived in St. Petersburg to announce King Constantine's ascendancy to the Greek throne. Presenting himself to the tsar, Zaimis complained that Sazonov was under my influence. The tsar repeated this to Sazonov who laughingly replied:

"I admit that at times I do acknowledge an influence on the part of my coworkers whom I trust and whose advice I heed."

Such a reply underlines Sazonov's nobility of character, a nature lacking all interest in petty little details.

I protested. It was easy to label me a "phobe" or a "phile" in my position. My only concern was to uphold and promote Russian state policy. The tsar, probably to soften his remark, began to discuss at what point in his opinion the Bulgarians began to draw away from us. Was it when we refused to send them the warships they required in order to take Çatalca from the rear? I observed that generally Slavic sympathies could not be relied upon, that the relationship we had with our Balkan clients reminded me of the peasant boy and the landowner, who was also his godfather. The godfather was supposed to help him to the end of his days, but he, as a godson, was not obligated in any way.

"You don't say," the tsar interrupted. "I have so many godsons!"

Coming back to the original subject of our discussions, I expressed once again my conviction that we must make an ally out of Bulgaria The only way to achieve this end was by promising it Macedonia. With this in mind, I asked for the tsar's authorization to voice this to the Serbs. The tsar wished me success but was noncommittal to my request to pursue this matter in his name with the Serbian heir to the throne.

The conversation changed to the subject of Rumania. I asked for permission to stop in Bucharest on the way to Niš in order to assess the situation.

"I would even request that you do so. It is imperative that you meet with Brătianu and government officials while you are in Bucharest. You will apprise us of the situation there."

Then he went on:

"This is only between us. Do not tell Sazonov that I do not trust Pok-levskii. He is not Russian."

I expressed my astonishment.

"Do you know him well?" he asked.

I replied that, although I knew him casually, I was surprised to learn he was not trustworthy.

"I have good reasons to think so," said the tsar.

"Poklevskii made a mistake because he was quite sure that Russia would be defeated. This formed the basis of his politics. Anyone can make a mistake, but let me tell you that whenever I make a mistake I am not ashamed of admitting it. There can be nothing worse than clinging to the error of one's ways."

In his closing remarks, the tsar wished me all kinds of success and charged me to convey his greetings to the heir to the throne and to Pašić.

I left Petrograd on November 16. The situation in Serbia was so bad at this time that I took with me only the bare necessities in case I would need to move elsewhere with the Serbian government. I arrived in Bucharest on November 20, early in the morning, and stayed with Poklevskii. I remained three days.

Bucharest left me with the impression of a noisy and joyous country fair. During the morning, various leaders of the opposition came by to see Poklevskii. I renewed my acquaintance with Filipescu, Take-Ionescu, and others.[31] They communicated the latest news: what Brătianu said to whom, what Marghiloman, the leader of the Germanophiles with whom I was acquainted from my earlier visits, did, and so on.[32] This was followed by a meeting with the old king who wanted to know which political leaders I had met. When I mentioned Marghiloman, the king remarked:

"Yes, he has some good horses."

Apparently, he had no other notable qualities. There it was. That very same gentleman, very wealthy and a big snob like many Rumanians, became the leader of the German party in Bucharest and the defender of dynastic interests.

I was left with an impression that each leader in Rumania had a tacit agreement with the others to play out a prearranged political role. The leaders of the opposition, apart from Marghiloman, called for action. Brătianu stalled. The same would have probably held true in reverse. When Brătianu was not in power, he was a warmonger. It was then that he stated that Rumania would march in February.

When I saw him at this time, Brătianu inquired whether I was aware of the date of Rumania's march. He himself preferred not to predict the actual date according to the calendar. Nonetheless, he very clearly stated his support of an alliance with us and in no uncertain terms told me that Rumania would be ready to cede a small piece of territory to Bulgaria if that would bring Bulgaria to our side. He placed great importance on determining Bulgaria's position and the concession to this end of Serbian Macedonia.

For my part, I suggested that Rumania should take the initiative in bringing together all the signatories to the Treaty of Bucharest. Rumania, Serbia, and Greece could come to some agreement regarding concessions of territory to Bulgaria. Rumania could take the lead and once again consolidate her position in the Balkans. Brătianu said that he did not trust Bulgaria at all and therefore any direct negotiations should be avoided, since they might become known to the Austrians, thereby negatively affecting Rumania's neutrality. It was imperative that our enemies remain unsuspecting of Rumania's intentions to march until the last minute.

One of the most influential members of Brătianu's cabinet was Minister of Finance Costinescu. He was in favor of Rumania making a march without delay. At the same time, he considered the possibility of ceding even more territory to Bulgaria than Brătianu did. He reiterated to me that he knew from German banking circles that Bulgaria and Germany had concluded economic and political agreements in connection to that loan.

There were obvious factors for Rumania's biding its time. In the first place, the government had little confidence in its own army. Rumania had placed orders for the military in Germany. Not trusting the Rumanians, the Germans did everything to delay these orders and to fill them out incorrectly. Brătianu feared that communications with France could be interrupted by an Austrian invasion, which Rumania could do little to stop. The national army did not lend itself to a fighting spirit. The idea of annexing Transylvania was most tempting. However, the political leaders had second thoughts. The social structure of Transylvania was much more democratic than that of Rumania. The annexation would bring into the kingdom a large class of intelligentsia whose thrust would be to participate in the political structure of the country and undermine the authority of the present leadership.

There was, then, much to be gained from maintaining neutrality. The Germans were liberal with their gold. They distributed this gold among political leaders, businesses, civil servants, newspaper editors, and generally to anyone who was open to bribes, of which there was no lack in Rumania. Rumania openly sold food and fuel to the Austrians and Germans in spite of the proclaimed benevolent neutrality. An unhealthy atmosphere of gold digging pervaded Rumania. Brătianu was quite correct in advising me not to fall for what I was told by members of the opposition and to believe that his policy was more of a reflection of the national one.

There was one more factor that influenced the leadership as controlled by Brătianu.

That was Italy. The Italian minister to Bucharest was one Baron Fasciotti. He was a typical Jew. One should not forget that during the course of this war, there was a substantial Jewish element in the Italian diplomatic corps.

They added to the somewhat nearsighted component of dry calculation of varied combinations that defined Italian diplomacy. Fasciotti was able to establish an excellent position in Bucharest. He managed to convince Rumania to follow the example of Italy and declare neutrality.

In conversation with me, Fasciotti unfolded his views frankly and openly. Rumania, just like Italy, must carefully weigh its advantages in considering when to make its move. In so doing, it must pursue its own interests only. The moment would arrive when the two sides had exhausted each other. The quality of their armies would deteriorate. In just such a moment, the entrance of the two fresh armies of Italy and Rumania would be most advantageous. Brătianu was most receptive to this view. Evidently, he believed Rumania would be able to play the same role as it did in the Balkan War.

3

SERBIA

After three days in Bucharest, I left for Serbia by the Danube River. News of the Serbian victory over Austrian forces had already reached us. From Prahova, I went by railroad to Niš, changing trains twice because there was no direct line. I arrived in Niš on November 25. The news of the war effort got better and better every day, until finally the Serbian armies entered Belgrade on December 3, 1914. Živko Pavlović, attaché to their *vojvoda* [military leader] Putnik, cabled that not a single Austrian save for prisoners of war remained on Serbian soil.[1] He was also an aide to Prince Alexander. Due to General Putnik's weak state of health, he became the de facto commander of the army.

What rejoicing there was, especially because up to this moment Serbia had been threatened by total annihilation. The Serbian people owed this turn of events to their king, the venerable King Peter. Russian artillery and uniforms also helped.

At one point the Austrian advance had completely demoralized the tattered Serbian army, which lacked ammunition, uniforms, and army boots. Somewhat belatedly, the Serbians turned to us for help. Despite our own adversity in the war effort, the Russian general staff made a heroic effort and sent 120,000 Berdan rifles, which we ourselves badly needed, to Serbia. They arrived at the last moment, turned the tide, and enabled the Serbians to repulse the first Austrian advance. Until that moment, there had been so few rifles that only the first row of soldiers were armed; the second row had to wait for the first row to fall in order to use those same rifles.

By the second Austrian advance, the Serbians lacked artillery shells and uniforms. The artillery shells came from our booty from Galicia. We were able to send 200,000 overcoats as well.

At the time, I was still in St. Petersburg in charge of the Department of the Near East. I stopped by the office of General Belaiev. He insisted that enormous efforts were being made to obtain enough overcoats for our army and that he had no idea how to alleviate the desperate situation. As I was leaving I met up with Prince G. E. L'vov, chairman of the Union of Zemstvos (*Zemgor*) and asked him for a few minutes of his time.[2] We walked together across Palace Square to the Ministry of Foreign Affairs. I explained the situation and asked whether he could help obtain 200,000 warm overcoats for the Serbian army. Without more ado, he agreed. I telephoned Serbian Minister Plenipotentiary Spolaiković to get over to the ministry right away. He beamed at such news, thanking Prince L'vov very warmly, and left to send off a telegram to Pašić for official confirmation of acceptance. L'vov remained in my office and telegraphed an immediate order for 50,000 half-length fur coats. I reminded him that we needed confirmation from Pašić, to which he replied, "I don't need it. Do you really think that Pašić would refuse? Let the civil servant telegraph and wait. We'll get the ball rolling. And if Pašić does refuse, I'll find some use for the coats here."

Indeed we received an answer from Pašić right away thanking us and requesting that we not delay.

Communication with Serbia was by way of the Danube River. We established a special flotilla under the command of Adjutant Veselkin. The first transport with the artillery shells arrived in the second half of November 1914, right at the time when the second Austrian advance was at its height. Until this moment, the Serbs were forced to relinquish well-fortified positions without a fight because they had nothing with which to defend them.

Consequently, the Serbian High Command had to move from Valiev to Kruševac, where the main arsenal was located. In some areas, the Austrians and especially the Hungarians treated people with cruelty and violence. A catastrophe was inevitable.

The elderly king, who had retired to Topola transferring the reins of power to his son and heir, Prince Alexander, left his self-imposed exile.[3] In Topola, the king was building a magnificent cathedral complete with a vault for his ancestors. He himself lived in a small modest home belonging to the village priest. He suffered greatly from gout and rheumatism, which he had developed while fighting in French ranks against the Germans back in 1870.

Taking in the overall confusion and becoming aware of the potential devastation of Serbia, the king decided to join his army, against the advice of his ministers. It was after the fact that the king himself told me the following with touching modesty.

"People say all sorts of things about me," he warned. "Don't believe everything you hear. I didn't do anything special. You know that I am old and not much good for anything. It is no surprise that I preferred to die for my country rather than watch its shame. I went to the trenches and told the soldiers just that. I told them that whoever wants to go home should. It's all right. I shall stay there and die for Serbia. Ah! If only you could have seen our soldiers! What extraordinary people. They cried, kissing my coat. All of them remained and fought like lions. The Serbs are capable of remarkable feats of courage in the presence of an audience."

What the king had said was indeed true. According to eyewitnesses, his arrival utterly transformed the army. The Bulgarian military attaché in Niš referred to this incident as "a case of war pathology." Happily, the Russian artillery shells contributed to the transformation of the army by getting there on time. Raging anger at enemy atrocities gave further incentive.

According to the same military attaché, the Austrian High Command, lacking in genius, was slow to react. Thus, the Austrians suffered resounding defeat, and a potential devastation of Serbia was averted.

About his entry into Belgrade, again the king described to me what happened.

There was still some fighting in the streets as the king, ignoring once again the warnings of those trying to stop him, entered the city. People thronged around him touching him, shoving small icons and crosses into his pockets. Proceeding slowly, the king stopped at the first church. It was locked. He then proceeded to the cathedral, followed by the throngs. It too was locked. However, there was a key visible in the alcove above the interior door. Someone climbed through the window into the cathedral and opened the door. The king entered with the crowd close behind.

"There was no priest. We all got on our knees and prayed as we never prayed before. Everyone cried."

This involvement on the part of the king—his simple, spontaneous words coming from the heart, words that reignited the lost faith of his soldiers, the entry into Belgrade freed from enemy occupation, and the act of prayer with the people in church—all this is but a fragment of a heroic epic that transcends the present day. This fleeting bright ray of light brought a momentary respite to the soul of the Serbian people, a people as yet unaware of the great suffering they would have to endure.

Great excitement pervaded Serbia and Niš in particular. Seventy thousand prisoners had been taken, along with weapons and all kinds of other booty. Every day, prisoners of war marched through Niš. Many of them were

3. Niš, circa 1914. King Peter I Karađorđević. King from 1903–1921.

Slavs and sang Slavic songs as they walked. Civilians in the street gave them bread and shared cigarettes.

The residence of the Russian mission was an old colorful Turkish konak.[4] It had once been a residence of the Turkish pasha and was taken over by King Milan.[5] It belonged to Queen Natalia after his death, and she turned it over to the city of Niš. There were plans to move the Russian School for Girls from Cetinje to this building after the war.

The konak, which housed the entire Russian mission along with the chancery, was the best residence in the city. The rooms were spacious, with high Turkish ceilings and exquisite woodwork. The entrance led into an enormous hallway, separating the men's chambers from the women's quarters, or harem.

My foreign colleagues had to contend with smaller apartments in the city center. The birthplace of Constantine the Great, Niš was a picturesque city located along the Nišava River and surrounded by mountains pointing in the direction of Bulgaria. It was the second largest city in Serbia, and its citizens referred to it as Proud Niš. In reality, it was a miserable dirty little town whose streets were often covered with enormous puddles. We referred to one of them, which we had to negotiate en route to the Russian hospital, as the Dardanelles. One time when I was passing through the Dardanelles, my horses, which were entirely blind since one could not obtain healthy horses in Niš during the war, became frightened and trotted violently, covering me in mud. The situation was critical, as I could not get off the hansom without finding myself knee-deep in the dirty, stinking Dardanelles. I started to call for help. Luckily, a soldier was lazily observing my travails in the puddle. Although he had not the slightest intention of forcing the Dardanelles, the silver coin I showed him proved sufficient to convince him otherwise. He came to the hansom and offered me a piggyback ride to the pavement, from where I proceeded to make my way home through the entire city covered in mud. This is what the proud city of Niš was like.

Luckily for me, the first secretary of the Russian mission, V. N. Strandt-mann, had been appointed to Serbia at the start of the Balkan crisis. He was a young, intelligent, and tactful diplomat who, having a solid knowledge of Serbian politicians and affairs of state, had formed a close relationship with the Serbs.

The other staff members included Second Secretary Zarin, Vice-Consul Emel'ianov, and Secretary to the Consulate Iakushev. The dragoman of the mission, Mamulov, came from the Caucasus. Mamulov had been an officer in the cavalry and stationed in Serbia for twenty years. He spoke Serbian like a native and knew absolutely everyone. His thorough knowledge of horses was to be very useful during our subsequent retreat. We all lived like one big family.

The liberation of Belgrade brought the campaign of 1914 to an end. The consensus among military representatives was that the Serbs did not capital-ize on their victory over the Austrians. They should have pursued the enemy to the end, beyond the Danube River. The Serbs maintained that their cav-alry was not strong enough for this. Besides, their forces were exhausted and badly needed a respite.

On December 4, I left for Kragujevac, accompanied by Pašić and two secretaries from the mission, to present my credentials to Prince Alexander. Veselkin and his officers, who had come to Niš, also joined us. We traveled along the picturesque Morava River valley.

Traveling in the same coach with Pašić gave me the opportunity to pur-sue my mission, which was to initiate tentative discussions regarding the need for Serbia to relinquish Macedonia to Bulgaria within the framework of the Agreement of 1912. This was a preliminary talk. I told him that as a representative of Russia it was my duty to be completely frank, whether that suited the moment or not. In view of this, I considered it imperative to forewarn him of our conviction that this was the only way to bring Bulgaria to our side. Obviously, such a concession depended entirely on Bulgaria's becoming our ally against Turkey. Such a sacrifice on the part of Serbia would be rewarded accordingly, and Serbia could count on acquiring territories elsewhere. Just as it was in the interest of Russia to strengthen Serbia by bringing about the unification of Austrian Serbs with Greater Serbia, so it was in the interest of Serbia to have the total support of Russia in this matter. Obviously our other allies, France and England, would not be as keen in this matter. They might even question whether the dissolution of Austria and the concomitant strengthening of Serbia along the Adriatic were advisable developments.

Pašić replied that there should be no doubts in my mind regarding the enormous obligation of Serbia to Russia. If Serbia were indeed to agree to such a sacrifice, it would be only because of us and not because of our allies. He then added that not a single responsible person in Serbia would agree with the provisions of the Agreement of 1912. Moreover, he regretted that we placed such hopes on Bulgaria. In his opinion, this was not a very good approach. It would be easier to influence Bulgaria with threats of what it stood to lose. Bulgaria was not worth this great sacrifice, and it would probably refuse to join the war in any event. He was to put forth these arguments many times in the future.

We arrived in Kragujevac that same evening and spent the night on the train. I had an audience with Prince Alexander the next day, on December 5. A state carriage arrived at the station for the grand marshal and me. The secretaries followed in another carriage. We were escorted by the Hussars, the king's guard of honor. Throngs of people lined the streets of this little town. They warmly greeted the Russian minister, removing their hats, waving handkerchiefs, and shouting "long live."

The prince lived in a small stone house. As we drove up, ranks of soldiers saluted and music played "God Save the Tsar," the Russian national anthem. This one-story house had but three or four rooms. In order to be able to receive me, the prince had his bed removed and the bedroom converted into a reception room.

As was the custom, I had acquainted Pašić with the text of my speech so that he could prepare an appropriate answer. Usually, the exchange of speeches during the ceremony of the presentation of credentials really had no substance, just greetings and compliments.

This time, however, I felt it necessary to depart from strict protocol. Apart from the very warm address to the Serbian people and assurances that Russia would not abandon them, at the end of the speech I added that Russia's primary obligation was to bring peace to the Balkans no matter how great the sacrifice. Russia expected assistance from Serbia in this endeavor.

4. Kragujevac, 1914. Trubetskoi on his way to present credentials to Crown Prince Alexander with High Marshal of the Court and Chief of Protocol Ostojič.

5. Kragujevac Station, 1914. From left to right are Russian War Agent Artamonov; Filaliti, Rumanian Ambassador to Serbia; Second Secretary Zarin; Trubetskoi; High Marshal of the Court and Chief of Protocol Ostojič.

The return speech by the heir to the throne was an indirect response to mine. There was confirmation of Serbia's empathy toward Russia and the willingness of Serbia to support Russia in every way, but it was nonetheless hoped that the vital interests of Serbia would be taken into consideration. The two speeches were made public, and the Russian and Bulgarian press subjected them to lively debates.

After luncheon with the prince, we hastened back to Niš because the next day was the tsar's saint's day (December 6/19). There was to be a solemn liturgy at the cathedral followed by lunch and a reception at the mission. Thanks to the efforts of Mrs. Strandtmann, the reception was well organized. An orchestra played military music in the large room by the entrance hall.

Almost all the rooms were turned into dining rooms. We had invited 120 guests. More came, however, because the Serbs, generally deprived of festivities, did not want to miss this one. We brought trout from Lake Okhrid.

There is, by the way, a story connected with that. Prince George had a noted professor of mathematics, Petrović, in his entourage doing military duty. This luminary was also an avid fisherman. Two days after the event, he met French Minister Plenipotentiary Bopp in the street.

"Did you eat trout at the Russian mission?"

"Yes."

"Well, it was I who caught them," the mathematician said proudly.

It turned out that the chef who needed fish turned to Prince George for help. He requested the prince to send the professor on a mission to Lake Okhrid, and that is how fish came to be served for lunch, a rare treat in Niš. The English minister told me that this was the first time he had eaten fish since the start of the war. Life in patriarchal Serbia was quite simple.

Bulgarian Minister Plenipotentiary Chaprashikov, who was leaving for Sofia that same day, had been invited as well. In my very first days in Niš, he came to see me and asked outright what Bulgaria could expect. Without any hesitation I replied the following:

"We are very well aware of Bulgaria's concerns. You would like to revise the Treaty of Bucharest and acquire the part of Macedonia designated in the Agreement of 1912. Let me tell you exactly on what you can and cannot count. You can receive Macedonia. As for the lands that went to Rumania and Greece, we can only promise our firm commitment to press upon these governments the exigency of ceding to you these lands. These territorial revisions would apply only at the end of the war and on condition that you set aside your hypocritical policy that the Russians regard with indignation, and openly, honestly, support us when the time comes to do so. You will also gain Thrace as far as the Midia-Enos Line. You will gain your rights to Macedonia when you advance against the Turks in Thrace. You are personally close to the king. If you succeed in swaying him then you shall have served not only your country, but your king himself. He will be able to rely on Russian backing of his dynasty, thus strengthening it."

Chaprashikov expressed total satisfaction at my words. He also posed the question whether, if Bulgaria were reconciled to Serbia, we would agree to Bulgaria having its own way with Greece. I replied that we would not tolerate any kind of aggression in the Balkans.

He departed for Sofia with expressions of hopes for success. My conversation with him, which I subsequently relayed to Petrograd by telegram, was approved.

Chaprashikov returned at the beginning of January. He had not had a chance to see the king, and the ministers had been too busy with the budget. He felt certain, however, that the issues we had discussed previously would be taken into serious consideration once the holidays were over and the budget tabled. I listened silently to his somewhat awkward explanation and said:

"If the budget takes priority over Bulgarian interests in Macedonia, that's your business. I for one will never bring this subject up again. It will be for you to do so in the future."

Chaprashikov tried to talk to me about these issues on more than one occasion. My replies were rather lackluster.

From the beginning of my stay in Niš, I cabled and wrote regularly to Petrograd stressing the urgency of compensating Serbia for the very real sacrifice we required of it—Macedonia as per the Treaty with Bulgaria on February 29, 1912. Compensation was a necessity, and we needed to define certain new borders and territories. Professor Cviić was Serbia's designated and official cartographer, an expert in carving up territories. His new boundaries included the entire Adriatic coast to Trieste and a large part of the Banat district.[6] Far be it for us to contravene against his map. A northward expansion of Serbian territory at the cost of Austria was surely in our interests. At the same time, we had to consider the interests of Italy in the Adriatic, since involving Italy in the war was imperative for our allies. As far as I can recall, I sent Cviić's map to the ministry on January 9, 1915. That same month I persuaded my French and English colleagues to send telegrams to their respective governments, apprising them that a solution for the compensation to Serbia was in place.

We believed it essential to adhere to the principle of reciprocity. To prevail upon Serbia to give up Macedonia was impossible before the end of the war. Serbia should be held to its promise to surrender Macedonia only in an equal exchange and only if Bulgaria were to come to our support.

The French and English ministers were in full accord and upheld the three basic principles for the surrender of Macedonia by Serbia:

1. To define exactly Serbia's compensation.
2. Macedonia to be surrendered only after the war, upon receipt of the promised territories.
3. The immediate entry by Bulgaria into the war.

The Ministry of Foreign Affairs supported my resolutions. England, however, wavered. Grey had little desire to grasp the importance of clearly defining Serbia's compensation; nor did he want to commit himself. Discussions in the respective cabinets were slow moving, undefined, and vague, causing a rather dangerous impression in the Balkan capitals: the Entente powers were weak and incapable of agreement among themselves.

It was the same in Sofia, in Athens, and in Bucharest. In addition to the uncertainty of the conditions to be presented to the various Balkan governments, there was little agreement on how negotiations were to be conducted. Time and time again, my colleagues in Niš and I pressed our governments at least to secure a commitment either from Bulgaria or from Serbia. Prevailing upon one side, we could negotiate then with the other. Instead, declarations were being made simultaneously in Niš and Sofia and immediately became public knowledge. At the same time, there was little follow-up. The powers did not bring any of these initiatives to their logical conclusion.

These details, many of which were to be overshadowed by larger events, have gone down into the annals of history. My purpose here is to write about my personal impressions of this time in Serbia, of events I witnessed, and of the people around me during these historical moments.

Three main political parties formed a coalition cabinet in Serbia at the inception of the war. They were the Old Radicals, the Young Radicals, and the Progressives. These three parties did have some historical foundations. Differences were minimal. There was no social conflict, nor was there a consciousness of class in Serbia. Mostly agrarian and lacking in a strong urban culture, all the Serbs were democrats. However, the three parties differed in their views on foreign policy. The Congress of Berlin placed Serbia at a disadvantage vis-à-vis Bulgaria. Serbia found itself hemmed in by Austrian territories with no outlet to the sea. Russia, ignoring Serbian interests, had clearly favored Bulgaria and also allowed the occupation of Bosnia and Herzegovina by Austria. Turning away from Russia, King Milan, supported by the Progressives and Liberals, concluded a military convention with Austria.

This policy was never really popular in Serbia. The close proximity of military headquarters, the threat to Belgrade of a possible bombardment by Austrian cannon, and finally, empathy for the Serbs beyond the border, all contributed to enmity and mistrust. Rapprochement with Austria, however seemingly logical, was certainly unacceptable to the psyche. The ordinary Serb had every reason to be bitter over Russian diplomacy, yet he continued to believe in Russia. The mistakes on the part of our government were attributed to German influence, and Russia remained popular. This became evident at the time of the war between Serbia and Bulgaria in 1885. When Serbian forces were defeated at Slivnitsa, Austria stopped the further advance of the Bulgarian army. The Austrian minister in Belgrade at the time wrote in his memoirs that, when the news broke, people began singing "God Save the Tsar" on the streets.

The Old Radicals Party reflected this popular view. The party leaders, with Pašić at the helm, were influenced in their youth by radical Russian literature. Pašić was a student of the revolutionaries Lavrov and Bakunin. The years of this youthful enthusiasm went by, but the pull toward Russia remained. Milan regarded the Old Radicals Party with hostility and persecuted them ferociously. He instigated procedures against them, accusing them of treason. Pašić was imprisoned. He managed to extricate himself, but the party fell apart, and the Young Radical Party was formed.

The Austrophile tendency could not last long in the country. Already King Alexander turned toward Russia, as did the Progressives. With the king's permission, the Progressive leader, Novaković, revealed to the Russian minister the details of the military convention between Austria and Serbia. The advent of the new Karađorđević dynasty completed the Russophile shift. Pašić became its most ardent advocate.

From the time of the new dynasty, Pašić led the country almost without interruption. Even at such times when he thought it better to distance himself from leadership, he still kept control. At seventy years of age, Pašić was a strong and energetic patriarch with a long white beard. His youthful blue eyes were alert and cunning. He led a moderate lifestyle, did not smoke, did not drink wine, was an early riser, and was in bed by ten o'clock in the evening. The strongest quality in his character was his self-control and equilibrium. I would see him during the worst of times for Serbia. He always remained calm and collected. It was only when I watched him pace that I could sense his mood.

In Niš, Pašić lived on the same street as the Russian mission, in a small one-story stone house. His wife was an uncomplicated person, somewhat anxious, yet doting. They had two grown-up daughters and a son.

Pašić went to work at the ministry first thing in the morning. There he would spend the entire day, taking an occasional short break. He determined all affairs of state, large or small. He was able to do so because of his official position and his enormous personal authority. There was only one other civil servant his age, and that was Minister of Finance Lazar Paču. He was intelligent, a brilliant accountant, and a follower of Pašić from childhood. Pašić valued his opinion. Paču died in the autumn of 1915 during the Serbian retreat.

The rest of the civil servants were considerably younger than Pašić, and he, of course, would treat them as youngsters, addressing them with the familiar "thou" and calling them by their nicknames. This was perfectly in accordance with Serbian patriarchal tradition. Pašić himself occupied the opposite corner of the table across the room. All the ministers worked in one large room. The impression was that of a professor and his students, especially during those moments when they would come up to Pašić requesting his permission to go home.

Overall, Serbian governance was somewhat disorganized because of the constitutionally weakened monarchy. The nature of the Serbian constitution was such that the king was bound hand and foot. When the Karađorđević dynasty was established, the Radicals insisted on limiting the king's power to forestall initiatives similar to those of King Milan, which is why the authority of the monarchy was quite feeble. The power of the executive was also curtailed, thereby limiting individual responsibility. A basic mistrust of authority resulted in slow-paced decision-making.

Every small problem was relegated to a special commission, which was assembled with difficulty. I was fascinated by the discovery of how their system of government contrasted with our own, where there was too much room left for individual initiative. In short, there was as much disorderly confusion in little Serbia as there was in Russia. One's health could easily be undermined if one was attempting to obtain an immediate decision. I learned quickly to go directly to Pašić, whether it was to discuss Macedonia or washboards for the hospitals. He would write a note to the right person, without going through a corresponding commission. The washboards would eventually arrive.

Pašić governed Serbia like a village elder looking after a large underdeveloped village. He knew absolutely everybody of consequence. He eliminated rivalry either by a distant appointment to some post or by awakening an interest in some distant enterprise. He reminded me of a village elder especially in his relationship with the big landowner Russia. The landowner

6. Niš, 1914. Nikola Pašić, Grand Marshal.

might get angry and shout at him, but Pašić would bide his time and eventually secure money for his village.

The commanding nature of Pašić did not leave room for the advancement of other political leaders. He represented Serbia to such an extent that he would effectively threaten the allies with resignation over some policy or other, and the allies would give in rather than lose Pašić.

In all fairness, there were some capable people in the Serbian cabinet. Besides the elderly and somewhat infirm Paču, who was the closest to Pašić, there was Drašković, the remarkable minister of transportation and leader of the Young Radicals Party. Still young and sincere, he was passionately patriotic. One could rely on his efficiency and, above all, on his word. Such a person was a rarity in a country permeated by Slavic negligence.

I would like to mention Minister of the Interior Ljubo Iovanović. A political immigrant, he was known for his gift of oratory. He was honest, open, and intelligent. In Serbia everyone has a nickname by which he is better known. Ljubo Iovanović was "Patak" (Drake) because he tended to waddle. Davidović, the minister of education, was dubbed "Ant." The Minister of Trade and Agriculture Voja Marinković was given the nickname the "European." He stemmed from the Progressives, that same party which for many years was oriented toward Austria, something that did not dampen his chauvinism. Serbian culture was influenced by its close proximity to Austria and by Russian literature. Russia was not much of a trading partner, being far away, whereas Serbia found it exceedingly difficult to become economically independent of Austria.

Serbs journeyed to Budapest and Vienna, the closest European centers, to trade their goods or attend institutions of learning. Despite an inherent animosity toward the Krauts as a whole, the Serbs absorbed some of their lifestyles and attitudes, to the point of scorning Russia as a "barbarian country." Marinković, initially sympathetic to Austria, adjusted to the present situation by becoming a Russophile.

Ioco Iovanović was the Serbian representative in Vienna when the war started. Pašić appointed him as his aide in the Department of Foreign Affairs. He still bore the nickname "Dandy" from his school days. Actually he was an intelligent gentleman, educated, modest, and conservative. It was with him that I dealt for the most part, and working with him was indeed a pleasure.

Although I was the Russian minister and given consideration in all business transactions, I must say that I encountered a major obstacle in the national character of the Serbs, found not necessarily in their lack of organization.

The Serbs tend to counteract a direct question with another question followed by a roundabout statement finishing up with a tentative answer. "Why did you ask this?" They could not be relied upon to carry out promises, especially if there was a deadline. Answers to any inquiry on my part were completely contradictory. If information had to be ascertained in two different institutions, you could bet on there being a discrepancy. Their entire history, made up of incessant wars, taught them to be cunning and guarded, especially in their dealings with the Turks, the Krauts, and the Bulgarians. It took its toll on my health.

The Serbian personality is dreamy and imaginative. The absence of detail in their answers reflects the same in their way of thinking. The Serb will not see something truly for what it is, preferring to regard it as better or worse instead. Their mood swings during the war played a significant role as well. This was ever so apparent during the second Austrian advance, when the mood fluctuated between despair and victorious enthusiasm. This very characteristic, however, defined the extraordinary vitality of this tiny nation.

The extreme chauvinism of the Serbs often led to comical exaggeration. Many Serbs genuinely believe they are the first nation in the world, with the best army in Europe. The same goes for their literature and scientific achievements. For instance, there was a lecture on Serbian influences on

European literature. There were no more than a couple of Serbian scientists of international repute—Novaković, Professor Cviić, and Petrović (the same Petrović who went fishing on December 6). These men have the reputation of geniuses in Serbia. On one occasion, Prince George ardently endeavored to persuade me that Petrović was the most talented mathematician in the world; compared to him, the famous French mathematician Poincaré was a nonentity.

The best Serbian academic was actually Novaković, who died in Niš in the spring of 1915. He was a political activist and the leader of the Progressive Party. He had served as prime minister and minister plenipotentiary in Petrograd and Constantinople. He specialized in history and philology. He came from a poor family and died a poor man. It is worth pointing out that politics in Serbia is not seen as a source of personal enrichment, which is quite common in Bulgaria. Novaković lived in a small room in Niš, which simultaneously served as his bedroom, dining room, and study. There he wrote a series of articles developing his ideas about a South Slav federation. He led a simple life, remaining intellectually alert until the very end. He was tall and slim. Although he stooped a little, he went for a daily walk along the waterfront. Even his political adversaries respected him. In political circles, his name was second only to that of Pašić. He was less cunning and generally less savvy than Pašić. He was more of an academic than a politician, but his main incentive in life was the advancement of Serbia. An ardent patriot, he knew of nothing else in politics or in academia.

Novaković's views on foreign policy were opportunistic. He favored Austria after the Congress of Berlin, until he realized this was not beneficial to Serbia. Thereupon, he drew closer to Russia and, as I mentioned earlier, read the text of the military convention with Austria to the Russian representative Baron Rozen. Novaković was neither an Austrophile nor a Russophile—he was a Serbian patriot. Toward the end of his life, he bought a small vineyard on the outskirts of Belgrade by the Danube. He built himself a small hut, from which he used to gaze longingly in the direction of Bačka and Banat and dream of their future unification with Serbia. He did not live to see his dream come true. Everyone of consequence attended Novaković's funeral in Niš; it was decided that his remains would be transferred to Belgrade at the end of the war. Novaković was an outstanding representative of Serbia's intellectual culture. The Serbs were proud of him, citing him as an example of their ability to rise to the highest level of European culture.

The bishop of Niš, Dosifej, was another outstanding representative of high spiritual culture. It is with the deepest emotion that I write about Bishop Dosifej. Not a tall man, he would have gone unnoticed were it not for his expressive, large, dark eyes. They exuded a tranquil radiance, extraordinary kindness, and deep spirituality. He lived in a small stone house, the roof of which was covered with clay tile. His father often worked in the tiny front yard, which was crowded with people seeking spiritual advice. Bishop Dosifej was thirty-five years of age. His family most likely came from the countryside. He received his initial education in Belgrade and at eighteen took monastic vows. He was sent to study at the seminary in Kiev. Further studies were at the University of Leipzig in philosophy and ecclesiastic history. He spent some time in Geneva, where he met one of our church officials, Sergei Orlov, with whom he became very close. He also became acquainted with the rector of our church in Berlin, Archpriest A. P. Ma'ltsevyi, a remarkable person who died at the beginning of the war. Divine Providence decreed he should maintain close relations with these two outstanding representatives of our church.

Bishop Dosifej was an ardent Russophile. He considered himself both Serbian and Russian. Unlike the majority of his Russian-educated compatriots who often formed a negative view of Russia, he endorsed the best aspects of our religious thought and faith. He did not favor Russia purely as a means of achieving Serbian national aspirations—he admired the beauty of the Russian mind and its spirituality. He dreamed of uniting his country with the treasures of Russian culture. I considered him the best example of the proper attitude of the Balkan peoples toward Russia, an attitude both sides should have.

We soon formed a close bond, and I visited him every day. Although we avoided all political discussion, I found myself confiding in him, always to a warm reception. On occasion he was overcome with childlike joy, his ringing laughter an expression of his purity of heart. He was a mainstay, not only for me but also for my wife. Bishop Dosifej and I established a number of institutions. I encouraged him to discuss religious matters with my eldest son, Constantine.

Dosifej led a busy life of social work. He received a constant stream of poor people whose lot he strove to improve.

Civil society was remarkably underdeveloped in Serbia. There was nothing comparable to our zemstvo, with its spirit of public service and civic-mindedness. There were very few Serbian Sisters of Mercy, who on top of everything else refused to see contagious patients or take night shifts in hospitals. Even before we opened our institutions, plenty of Russian medical doctors and nurses had come to work in Serbia. They did this not for money—which was not very much, anyway—but because they genuinely sympathized with Serbia and wished to help. These noble men and women risked their lives, and many died. Few Serbs appreciated their efforts fully; among the few, naturally, was Father Dosifej, who always recognized good deeds and turned away from all evil in life. He never tired of pointing out to ordinary Serbians everything that Russia was doing for them. The Russians treated him as one of their own, and even the less religious among them went to see him. Everyone came to him.

Father Dosifej never had any ulterior motives. In contrast to most of his compatriots, he kept away from politics. Hence, most political activists believed him to be a good but somewhat naïve man. I once told the crown prince that coming to Serbia had been worth my while because, if nothing else, I had had a chance to meet Father Dosifej. The crown prince burst out laughing at what he thought was a joke; he was rather bewildered when he realized I was serious and inquired whether I really thought so—although he admitted to knowing little about the bishop.

Metropolitan Dmitrij of Serbia, a handsome old man, lived with Father Dosifej. The metropolitan was the head of a relief committee for devastated Serbian lands. On Father Dosifej's insistence, I often joined the metropolitan on his trips.

During one excursion in the countryside, the metropolitan told me that Serbia owed its roads to the Turks. Moreover, the cathedral in Niš was built thanks to the efforts of the famous Turkish Pasha Mitrakhad, who coerced the inhabitants of Niš to donate money for the construction. In fact, I met an old Serbian in Niš whom this same Pasha had used as an errand boy. He told me that the Pasha would stroll around the city knocking on doors with his walking stick, demanding money for the cathedral. Most Serbs remember him fondly. It is surprising how little animosity toward the Turks exists in Serbia, in spite of the century-long Turkish rule.

Atrocities are quickly forgotten, perhaps because in the Balkans they are not the sole preserve of the Turks. Besides, Turkish rule was not particularly harsh. They did not interfere with religious life and generally confined themselves to collecting tribute. The Turks did not create anything new and left nothing of their culture. They set up a military camp in Europe and subsequently vanished without a trace. The Turks who did not emigrate became model subjects.

Niš was a large city of eighty thousand under the Turks. After the Serbs gained control, its population declined to a little over twenty-three thousand in peacetime. Few Turks remained; they were most notable around the religious holiday of Ramadan, when the mosques were lit and the religious gathered for prayer. I have already described the Serbs I was in contact with. Apart from my interactions with them, there was little social life in Niš, not only because it was a small town but because life was basically simple. Large Serbian families dwelled in two or three rooms. It was common to see the wife of a minister of state, shopping in the marketplace for food, hurrying home with a piglet under her arm. This was especially so around Christmas, when the entire town resounded with the squealing of piglets, pork being the traditional holiday dish. From the square by our house came a litany of different sounds. Peasant women in their beautiful costumes, with flowers attached to their head scarfs, rode on carts pulled by oxen. There were soldiers, civil servants, officers, and women of every social position. Only foreigners found it odd to see, for example, a venerable colonel with a piglet in each hand.

I associated mostly with my colleagues in diplomacy. The French minister was Bopp. I knew him from Constantinople when he was a secretary at the embassy. He had spent most of his diplomatic career in the Near East, primarily in Constantinople. He had also served as consul general in Jerusalem. Bopp was educated, well read, intelligent, and cautious. A fervent Catholic, he delved into the politics of religion. I was astonished to find out he had once read Porfirii Uspenskii's vita in the original Russian. He adored the Serbs and detested the Bulgarians. Consequently, he tried in every way to convince the French government not to insist on the handing over of Macedonia. He missed his family terribly and would fall into bouts of melancholic despondency.

Bopp exerted a strong influence on the British representative, Des Gras, who usually passed the mornings with him. Des Gras, a confirmed bachelor in his senior years, was a most pleasant gentleman, and eventually we became quite close. His health was weak. He was considerate of others, kind, and to some extent naïve. He was unable to sort out the general situation and relied on Bopp for guidance. Both timid men, they preferred to avoid confrontation with their respective governments. It was not easy for me to persuade them to come up with joint initiatives when I considered it necessary.

The Italian minister, Baron Schvitti, was sixty years old. While Italy remained neutral, he kept to himself and seemingly avoided the company of the other representatives, in light of the awkward situation. Subsequently, we became close. An intelligent, delicate man, he had a lovely sense of humor. The Belgian, Rumanian, Greek, Montenegrin, and Bulgarian ministers also resided in Niš. The Belgian representative, a dean of the diplomatic corps, lived in two tiny rooms with his wife, teenage daughter, and governess. Prior to coming to Serbia, the Montenegrin minister, Lazar Miušković, had served as prime minister in his homeland. He was married to the half-Russian, half-Albanian daughter of Russian Consul Krylov and had a large family. I

7. Niš, 1914. Seller of kvass at the marketplace.

have already mentioned the Bulgarian minister, Chaprashikov. He came to visit me often and tried to establish a close working relationship with me in order to secure his position. He tried to appear polite and amiable, but his lack of tact made him very unpopular with everyone. It appeared to me he genuinely desired to restore friendly relations between Russia and Bulgaria, but he went about it the wrong way. Serbian and Bulgarian newspapers were full of mutual accusations, often quite scandalous. Chaprashikov was constantly complaining to me about some newspaper. I attempted to improve the situation through Pašić but soon discovered the personal involvement of the Bulgarian representative only made matters worse. He had the rare ability of making even the restrained Pašić lose his temper.

The Serbian representative in Sofia, Čolak-Antić, was his complete opposite. Like Chaprashikov, he began his career as a court attendant but, unlike Chaprashikov, he was a well-behaved and pleasant person. Even though they detested the Serbs, the Bulgarians could not help but respect him. At the very least, they never voiced any displeasure. In contrast, not a single Serb could remain dispassionate when hearing Chaprashikov's name.

Initially, my daily routine in Niš was interspersed with the comings and goings of various people. From a simple crossroad, Niš grew into an important railroad center connecting civilians stranded in Greece to Europe and Russia through Bulgaria and Rumania. The Serbs welcomed all Russians passing through their territory, although poor rail connections between Salonika, Niš, and Sofia left hundreds of people stranded in Niš. There were but two, most dingy, hotels in Niš: the "Europe" and the "Russian Tsar." Every inch was occupied, and inevitably forlorn and irate travelers would find their way to the mission.

We did what we could. At such time, when we could not find any other accommodation or billeting, we would have to put up complete strangers at the mission. This presented some difficulty because I had brought only the essentials with me. All of us had to give up a pillow or a blanket. It took two months of incessant nagging on my part for the train schedules to be finally coordinated.

Not long after the successful expulsion of the second Austrian attack, the tsar wished to confer medals of honor upon the Serbian king and his army. At the end of December, we had a visit from General Tatishchev, the same person whom I mentioned earlier as having been sent by the tsar as liaison to the court of Kaiser Wilhelm. He arrived in Niš to present King Peter with the Order of St. Andrew with Swords on behalf of the tsar. This was a distinction previously given only to Alexander I of Russia. Prince George and Prince Alexander—as well as four Serbian generals—were to receive the Medal of St. George. There were also other medals of honor for Serbian soldiers. General Tatishchev stayed with me at the mission.

The king traveled to Niš accompanied by the heir to the throne, Alexander, to greet Tatishchev. He received the general in a private audience. When Tatishchev handed him the medal of St. Andrew, the king solemnly brought it to his lips. A small luncheon followed, attended by the king and his two sons, me, and Tatishchev. All this excitement exacted a toll of the king, who was forced to retire after lunch as he was feeling faint. He was unable later to attend the official ceremonial dinner. He was, after all, seventy years of age. At times he looked much younger, at times significantly older. When he discussed a subject close to his heart, his eyes sparkled with youthful vigor. As soon as he had finished, however, his eyes lost their sparkle, and he turned into a tired old man. He was charming in his simplicity and warmth. One sensed the old soldier. Those close to him, however, were occasionally subjected to his quick temper and bouts of willfulness. His oldest son, George, unfortunately inherited these qualities.

Prince George was a handsome young man with fine, somewhat exotic features; he resembled a highlander from the Caucasus. He was very courageous and was wounded twice in battle. He had been convalescing in Niš and was now beginning to become rather restless.

However, the military authorities were unwilling to give him command even of a single battalion for fear that he and the entire battalion would perish on the battlefield. He lacked all self-control, beating up his servant and adjutants, who were continually moved about for this very reason. He was quite popular with the youth, who admired his fearlessness.

He once kicked his butler so hard in the stomach that the man died from internal bleeding. In 1908, overwhelmed by remorse, he gave up his claim to the throne in favor of Alexander, a decision he subsequently regretted and hoped to undo.

He would stop by the mission for a visit or a chat and remain until late hours chiefly out of boredom. I would have to leave him on a pretext. Heaven forbid if he had his penknife along.

He would then make scratches and carvings on the tabletop or cut up some serviette or tablecloth. He used this same penknife to put out his cigarette and listlessly put his feet up on a chair. Strangely enough, he could also be shy. He was, all in all, an unbalanced person. He could not stand his younger brother, Alexander. On New Year's Day, when they both came by, I sat on the edge of my chair in trepidation that he might make a scene, as he teased and goaded his brother. Prince Alexander kept his composure, trying in every way to soften the situation, while Prince George went on about the weak Montenegrin blood flowing in his brother's veins.

Prince Alexander was the complete opposite of his brother. Although he was not as dashing and wore glasses, he was always composed, even reserved. He clashed with Pašić, who inevitably got the better of him. The old king—seeing in George a reflection of himself, to some extent—favored this son in spite of everything. Prince Alexander attended the imperial Page Corps in St. Petersburg before returning to Serbia. The political situation in his home country meant that he was unable to complete his education.

During the Balkan War, Prince Alexander already commanded the First Army. After this war, when King Peter retired to Topola, Alexander became prince regent.

Circumstances completed Alexander's training as a statesman, although he still suffered at times from an incomplete formal education. To compensate for this, he continuously strove to improve, develop his qualities, and gain much-needed experience. (Timid yet ambitious, he tried to distance himself from the authoritative Pašić and act on his own, although he was not always sure how best to do so.)

Prince Alexander regarded me at first with a justifiable suspicion, because of my alleged Bulgarian sympathies. It was not easy for me to replace the popular Hartwig, whom the Serbs had regarded as one of their own. I was aware of Alexander's open animosity toward Bulgaria but chose not to comment, knowing that in the end Pašić would make the decision. But I digress.

Along with Tatishchev, there was another general, Prince Iusupov, passing through Niš on his way to France, England, and to the Belgian king, to confer medals of honor upon the Allied armies. Iusupov stayed in Niš for a day, and the prince invited him to the formal reception organized for Tatishchev. He spent the time until his departure at the mission with me. Tatishchev told me he was supposed to travel on to Montenegro and confer the Order of St. George IV class on Crown Prince Danilo. I had recently heard from Pašić that the admiral in charge of the small French squadron in the Adriatic had accused Prince Danilo of colluding with the Austrians; the French were even thinking of withdrawing the troops they had transferred from Scutari to Montenegro at the beginning of the war. Given these circumstances, awarding Prince Danilo a medal of honor would have been awkward. I immediately telegraphed Petrograd with a request to cancel Tatishchev's trip to Montenegro, ostensibly on account of the intractable Montenegrin mountain passes covered in snow. The Foreign Ministry took my advice, and Tatishchev stayed longer in Niš than was originally planned. We all enjoyed his company.

France and England, following our initiative, also sent representatives to Niš to confer appropriate medals. We had visits from General Paget and

General Pau.[7] Both were on their way back from Russia via Niš. I especially enjoyed meeting the charming and amiable General Pau. He was just such a perfect representative of the French army, loyal and patriotic. He had lost an arm during the Franco-Prussian War of 1870. For meals he used a special knife, the tip of which had prongs that served as a fork.

The English general Paget was close to his king. On his way back from Russia, he made a stop in Sofia and was received by King Ferdinand. While in Niš, he related to Prince Alexander the substance of this meeting, which the prince then passed on to me in confidence. Paget was trying to convince King Ferdinand to join with the Triple Entente and attack the Turks. He had cautioned Ferdinand against attacking Serbia.

"Well, what would you do in such a case?" Ferdinand asked.

"We could always find a way of bringing two hundred thousand men from Egypt to Dedeagach," the general answered.[8]

In answer to the proposal of a war with Turkey, Ferdinand replied that the hindrance lay with Russia's pretensions to Constantinople.

"In that case, you should enter Constantinople yourselves and stay there. England would much prefer a Bulgarian presence in Constantinople to a Russian one." Ferdinand's reply was a theatrical gesture.

Undoubtedly, Paget was unaware of questions of international relations and was overall a bad diplomat. He should have known better than to discuss this issue with Prince Alexander, who opposed any Bulgarian takeover of Constantinople. Paget was a person of consequence both in the army and in the English court. His dialogue with Prince Alexander may not reflect the opinion of responsible English circles, but it does certainly underline the long-standing prejudice toward us on the part of the English, a prejudice that only a prolonged conflict with Germany could erase.

From time to time, Austro-Hungarian politicians would come to Niš. The most notable was Supilo, a Croatian statesman.[9] Serbian dreams of uniting all South Slavs—and of unification with Croatia—were somewhat vague and did not explain how to achieve this end. Novaković dreamed about a federative Yugoslavia; that is, a large Slavic state wherein various regions would enjoy substantial autonomy. This view did not enjoy widespread support. The majority of Serbs imagined unification as Serbian annexation of certain Slavic territories.

The Serbs were chauvinistic. They firmly believed in the superiority of their culture. Optimistic by nature, they preferred to avoid complications, while failing to see the very basic differences between themselves and the Croats. The Serbs were Orthodox and the Croats Catholic. Serb society was classless and overwhelmingly rural. The Croats had a longtime aristocracy and a culture heavily influenced by German values and mores. It was a gap similar to that of a peasant and an urbanite.

Serbia, on the other hand, had the advantage of being a sovereign state with a first-class army. Hence, unification would be paid for with Serbian blood. In a potential federation, Serbia certainly would demonstrate strong leadership in resolving the many potential international problems the new state would face.

At the same time, one could not speak of mere annexations. By themselves, Serbia's forces were insufficient to conquer several Austro-Hungarian provinces. The question could only come up after a victorious war undertaken by Russia and its allies against the Central powers. Any union, however, would depend on the Croats. As part of the Austro-Hungarian Empire, they detested the Krauts and, from the start, were drawn to Serbia. Once faced with the prospects of immediate unification with Serbia, however, that could very well change. Despite their common background, the social differences were too great. Just recently, in Agram [Zagreb], Serbs were barred from cafés frequented by Croats and vice versa. Even so, the idea of a Serbo-Croat political alliance gained ground, winning a majority in the last elections to the provincial diet. At the same time, there were the Frankovci, a political party made up of Serbophobic Croats. All these factors had to be considered. How to respect the Croats while convincing them that it would be to their advantage to form a federation with Serbia was the essence of the matter.

There was another hurdle to overcome in the successful resolution of the South Slav Question: Italy, which in no way sympathized with the idea of a strong Serbia. In its pursuit to control the Adriatic, Italy claimed the Adriatic coastline inhabited mainly by Slavs. The antagonism between the South Slavs and Italy was quite evident. It was in Italy's interest that Croatia become an independent nation, separate from Serbia. Italy relied heavily on the support of the Croatian aristocracy. The more Italy pursued this policy, the more the ordinary people stopped trusting Italy and began looking toward Serbia.

At one point, when hostilities between Serbia and Austria temporarily ceased and Italy was considering joining the Entente, their mutual animosity seemed to abate somewhat, since both regarded Italy as a common foe. Austria was hoping to capitalize on this mood in order to garner support among its Slavs for an upcoming attack on Italy. I often heard political leaders in Niš expressing the most dangerous sentiment that Austria should thoroughly beat the Italians.

A solution of the South Slav Question in favor of Serbia was definitely advantageous to us. We would naturally welcome the maximum strengthening of Serbia, as we would continue to have common enemies after the war. There-fore, we could not desire the creation of an independent Kingdom of Croatia, which would result in artificial tensions between the Serbs and the Croats, but neither could we afford to totally support Serbia's narrow perspective. The entry of Italy into the alliance was so essential for us that we had to consider its interests, even if this meant curtailing ethnographic principles. It was at this point that Supilo arrived in Niš.

Supilo was an intelligent, educated gentleman imbued with Italian culture. He worshiped the Italian Risorgimento and spoke the language like an Italian.[10]

Nonetheless, he bore the mark of an Austro-Hungarian political activ-ist—he was a politician through and through, enthusiastic, sly, and ambi-tious. He stopped at nothing in the pursuit of his ideas, resorting to flattery, intrigue, and misinformation. His arrival caused a resurgence of the South Slav Question. He frequently visited Pašić, the crown prince, and other leading Serbian politicians and told me that what he heard had been most satisfactory.

I hoped that Supilo's visits would have a positive impact on the Serbs. An actual perspective of a South Slav union could possibly bring about a change of mind regarding Macedonia. A bird in the hand is worth two in the bush. Supilo told me that the Croats could not condone the intractability of the Serbs, which diminished their attention and strength from the real job in hand. He maintained that Croatia had a long-standing good relationship with Bulgaria and that Bulgarian youth came to Agram to complete their studies. Whether Supilo said the same to Pašić I shall never know. I doubt that he would seriously try to meddle in internal Serbian affairs. To me he talked much about the warm sentiments he felt toward Russia, on whom he was placing all hopes for the realization of his personal dreams for his nation. Let Russia christen the future nation with whatever name, Yugoslavia or Serbo-Croatia. He was not averse to even keeping the name of Serbia.

Supilo had arrived from Italy, where a South Slavic committee had been established, with him as chairman. He discussed with me his conversations with Italian leaders. He developed the thought that, given the present situa-tion as well as Italy's past, recognition of national rights for the South Slavs would be in order. Developing a solid relationship meant that Italy would be in a position to assert not only its influence along the Adriatic but its trading rights as well. Otherwise, by seeking to annex territories in the area, Italy could find itself involved in some future conflict, a result of increasing feelings of hostility. His eyes filled with hatred as he spoke about Italy, laps-ing unconsciously into the language closest to him, Italian. From Niš Supilo went on to St. Petersburg. A delegate from Bosnia went with him to attest to the fact that agreement between the leaders of the different Slavic territories was indeed in earnest.

Apart from Slavic political activists coming to Niš, I should mention the Bexton brothers, the older of whom chaired a very influential Balkan committee in London. They came from Bucharest, where a Turk had tried to shoot them, wounding one of the brothers in the process. The Bextons were ardent Bulgarophiles who believed, as strongly as any Bulgarian did, that Macedonia should belong to Bulgaria. Understandably, their arguments found little support in Serbia. They paid me a visit and subsequently wrote me a letter from Macedonia, reiterating their beliefs. Seton-Watson was another Englishman I came to meet. He had a keen interest in the South Slav Question and wrote much on the topic. Along with the *Times* editor Wickham-Steed, who had studied the nationality question during his long stay in Vienna, Seton-Watson acquainted the English public with the desirability of South Slav unity, much to the benefit of Serbia.

THE EPIDEMIC AND THE RUSSIAN RED CROSS

I have already referred to the outbreak of the epidemic in passing. Medicine and sanitation in Serbia were badly organized. There was no school of medicine at the University of Belgrade. A handful of Serbian doctors received their medical education either in Russia or in Austria. There was no organization of nurses, and few Serbian women dedicated their time to look after the wounded. Nonetheless, in spite of this shortage, the care for wounded soldiers was somewhat organized.

I arrived in Serbia at the end of November, during a period of fierce fighting. On the way to Niš I was met in Zaičara by Sychev, the senior doctor from a medical brigade funded by the Society for Slavic Charity. Along with a handful of nurses, he toiled unceasingly not only in his own hospital but in the nearest Serbian hospital where there was but one doctor who had no help for several hundred wounded. That doctor, Sychev remarked, was about to lose his mind.

For those stricken with infectious disease, however, the situation was dire. During their second invasion, Austrian forces devastated the entire northwestern part of Serbia and carried out a number of atrocities. Whatever roadways remained were swamped with refugees, most of whom made their way to Niš, seeking government aid. In peacetime, Niš had a population of 23,000 inhabitants. During the war, it expanded to 147,000 people. Obviously, there was not enough space in the town to accommodate the flood of refugees. The cafés were filled with people drinking coffee or beer by day; at night, people slept on tables, on benches, on the floor. Families who were more impoverished simply camped on the streets. All of these people were starving. In the town, where refugees and prisoners of war were based, every last hospital or hastily converted building was overflowing with wounded. In the circumstances, it was only a matter of time before epidemics became rampant.

I sent reports to Petrograd and wrote to my wife in Moscow. She was intending to join me soon in Niš with our eldest son, aged twelve. She published my appeal for aid to Serbia in the newspapers as well as a letter of her own advising of her impending visit to Serbia and that she would be accepting donations.

The results of this appeal were stupendous. The Moscow Duma, which previously had raised fifty thousand rubles for Serbia, once again gave my wife an equal amount. Donations and letters from every part of Russia arrived daily. There was one touching letter with twenty kopecks from a prisoner doing hard labor. On a train somewhere in the Caucasus, wounded soldiers making their way from the front collected three rubles and fifty kopecks.

There was one widow who, with tears in her eyes, brought my wife her late husband's gold cross and wedding band. There were donations of clothes, crackers, and all sorts of other things. Physicians, nurses, and students signed up every day.

PRINCESS TRUBETSKAIA REGARDING THE DISTRESS IN SERBIA

A telegram from the wife of the Russian ambassador in Belgrade. Niš. 14–02 (1914). 4:10 p.m.

I am grateful to the *Birzhevye Vedomosti* for offering me the opportunity of writing about the needs of the Serbian nation.

From the very beginning of its heroic struggle, the Serbian people have uncomplainingly endured deprivation, suffering, illness. Every month, there is unavoidable pressure resulting from constant, increasing casualties. Those areas passed by Austrian soldiers at the beginning of the campaign are completely devastated. Old men, women, and children who lost their parents made their way to unaffected towns. Due to the large concentration of refugees in smaller centers, there is a significant increase in the price of essential goods.

There is urgent need for generous brotherly aid, for the organization of centers for food distribution, for all forms of medical assistance.

The committee of the Russian mission is attempting to increase assistance in this direction. This work is bringing relief to those in need and is strengthening the brotherly ties between Russia and Serbia.

Committee Chairperson, Princess Trubetskaia.

[On January 27, 1915, Alexander Scriabin played a fine recital in Moscow organized by my grandmother the princess Trubetskaia, in order to raise money for the Serbs. The tickets cost from eight rubles ten kopecks down to fifty-five kopecks, the highest any pianist at the time drew. Half the proceeds went to the Serbian Red Cross. This was Scriabin's final public appearance in Moscow.][1]

Thanks to the incoming charitable donations and widespread public sympathy, my wife was able to put together a hospital team of around thirty-five people, including four medical doctors and several nurses. The team also acquired valuable equipment such as an X-ray generator. At the end of December, my wife informed me of her difficulties in finding a suitable building for the hospital. Although there was a spacious edifice in the center of town earmarked for a high school, it had neither a roof and floors nor windows and doors. At the same time, it was large enough to set up a model hospital, and Pašić promised to have it ready as soon as possible. However, these things take time, especially in Serbia, due to the shortage of construction workers. He deployed prisoners of war, but about half of the 150 men fell seriously ill after two or three weeks. The rest were too malnourished to be of much use.

I tried to delay the hospital team's arrival, which was no easy task, as they were eager to get to work. Furthermore, their medical supplies had to be transported by train, and one could not easily change the timetables. The team set off from Moscow on a special train, which traveled via Rumania and Bulgaria and arrived in Niš on January 25. A large flag of the Red Cross waved from the top of the locomotive. My wife and son departed the train, along with the rest of the medical team, to a warm welcome. The team was comprised almost exclusively of high-spirited young people, who were eager to get going; they quickly grew to resemble a large family. However, they could not start working as quickly as they had wished, as the designated building had not been completed. They set up shop temporarily in one of the Serbian hospitals, before moving into the unfinished building.

The new Russian hospital in Niš was quickly filled with wounded soldiers transferred from other medical hospitals and field hospitals, who required more complicated surgery and medical attention. S. I. Sirotkin, a wonderful surgeon, became the head of the medical team. His closest associates were Dr. V. V. Semiannikova and Džuverović, who was originally from Serbia. The former, a reasonable, well-balanced young woman, quickly became the heart and soul of the team. She was quick to settle all misunderstandings and did her best to keep up the spirits of all those who struggled to come

8. Niš, 1915. Crown Prince Alexander with the Russian medical brigade. Trubetskoi is on the far right. In the middle is Dr. Malinovich.

to terms with the malady they were suffering from. There was also Dr. N. V. Martsinkevich, who specialized in the treatment of contagious diseases. Most of the nurses were the epitome of kindness. Some, most notably Marianna Goriainova and Sofia Gorbova, came from respected Moscow families; the rest were university students. My wife's first task was setting up a separate hospital for patients suffering from contagious diseases. This was of the utmost necessity, because the epidemic had reached enormous proportions by the time the medical team arrived in Serbia.

Eventually, I met a wonderful doctor by the name of Sofoterov. At the outbreak of war he chanced to be working in the Russian hospital in Salonika. The Ministry of Foreign Affairs had transferred him to Serbia where he became the head of a Serbian hospital. This hospital eventually became known as the "Russian Pavilion" because Russian nurses were already working there and because it had been subsidized by the Russian Duma at the very beginning of the war effort. Sofoterov had previously already worked in Serbia, where he acquired a sound reputation as a surgeon.

He described to me the previously hopeless situation in Serbia. At the time of military action along the rivers Sava and Danube, there were two contributing factors to the spread of infectious diseases. First, the Austrian occupation of northern Serbian territories created a deluge of refugees, who tried to reach the interior of the country primarily by the railway line Belgrade-Kruševac-Niš-Skopje. Along with them traveled tens of thousands of prisoners of war, who often came into contact with the local population. A tired, starving, wounded population cramped into small quarters provides ideal breeding ground for typhoid fever and similar diseases. Soldiers, deserters, and prisoners of war in the trenches and elsewhere did not have the necessary facilities to wash themselves or their clothes. For months on end, they had to lead an utterly wretched existence in inhumane conditions. While soldiers received reasonably decent food rations, deserters and prisoners of war roamed the countryside starving. This large mass of refugees and prisoners of war streaming into the home front was subject to no controls. The situation regarding wounded soldiers was little better; trains arriving in Niš from the front were filled with wounded soldiers who had caught typhoid fever en route. There was no separation between wounded soldiers and soldiers infected with typhoid fever and other diseases; the dire circumstances made this unfeasible in any event. Upon arrival in Niš, the sick were transferred to the hospitals on bull-drawn open carriages, where one could often observe people in death throes and even corpses. Bystanders could often be seen smoking in close proximity to the carriages and encouraging the sick. The limited capacity of the hospitals meant that oftentimes three or four patients had to share two beds. To make matters even worse, patients being transported out of Niš occasionally ran away from the carts in delirium, and the accompanying old men could not catch them. There were no lodgings to be found in Niš around this time. Schools, restaurants, and cafés went about their business by day and accommodated the wounded by night. Newly arrived patients were assigned a chair in a restaurant, where they had to spend their day and sleep at night. The majority of refugees had to make do with makeshift hovels set up in the city streets and squares. The healthy and the sick were in constant contact, starting with the insect-filled carts and ending with the open markets. Uncontrolled contact thus contributed to the further spread of the epidemics. Those released from hospitals were given the same clothing, clothing that had not been disinfected and was riddled with body lice. Upon their return to the villages, they transferred the diseases.

There were few means to contain the epidemics, as the hospitals did not even have disinfectants. The nurses tried to wash incoming patients, but this did little to remove lice and other insects from clothes and bodies. The amounts of insects were truly astonishing. I will never forget one unfortunate patient, whose entire body was covered with insects, as if by a thin blanket. I shiver to this day when I think of the nightmare that reigned in the hospitals.

In Niš alone, around thirty-five thousand people died in four months, according to my calculations. They died not only from typhoid fever, but from typhus, smallpox, and diphtheria. Typically a stable, calculated to house from twelve to fifteen hundred horses, maintained from five to six thousand prisoners of war who, if they were still unaffected by an epidemic disease, died of weakness or dysentery. They were fed once a day, and the dead were carried out once a week.

The stench was overwhelming. Yellow-faced men lay in a formless mass or stood on the floor like wax figures; some tore the rags from their bodies amid the throes of delirium; some slept peacefully, their heads on the corpses of their dead comrades. There was no one to distribute the food, so everyone looked after himself. Corpses were left by the door. In addition to Dr. Sofoterov's description, I would also like to highlight the complete absence of facilities—one unfortunate man who fell through the rotten floor literally drowned in feces.

The principal reason for such circumstances was the inability and lack of resources in Serbia to cope with the epidemics. Naturally, prisoners of war received the least attention. At the same time, they were quite free to roam about town and often took bread from the sick and the dying.

The refugees were not much better off. There was a two-story building by the cathedral that had once been a school. Gypsies occupied the upper floor, and Serbs the ground floor.

What was strange was that, inevitably, all the Serbian refugees died from the crowded quarters, whereas the Gypsies survived unscathed. Unfortunately, there was no one to study this interesting case of immunity from infectious diseases.

In spite of our efforts to attract medical doctors, there were only about 540 of them in Serbia at the beginning of the war. Many of those were Russians from Russia or Russian Jewish émigrés from Switzerland. In a mere four months, 160 died and another 130 fell ill. One hospital for infectious diseases on the outskirts of Niš accommodated all those suffering with typhoid fever. It was so crowded that the sick were placed not only on cots, but under them.

There was hardly any care due to lack of personnel. Those who were sent to this hospital knew they would never be back. The place was nicknamed Chele-Kule. In Turkish that means Hill of Skulls. In bygone days, the Turks quelled a Serbian uprising. To commemorate this event and to instill fear in future generations, they piled up the bodies of dead Serbs in a pyramid shape. Eventually, a chapel was built on this hill.

Being taken to Chele-Kule meant certain death. Everyone knew this, and heartbreaking scenes frequently occurred when a patient was about to depart. A French medical doctor once told me the following story. A doctor working in Chele-Kule suddenly vanished without a trace. A thorough search found him lying on the hospital floor in agony amid the patients. A simple visit to a patient was fraught with danger and took place only rarely.

In the prevailing circumstances, the infection spread daily. Carts carrying troops became a common sight. There were insufficient materials to make individual coffins or gravestones, and several corpses were often hastily shoved in a box, arms and legs sticking out grotesquely. On my daily walks along the Nešava waterfront, I constantly encountered delirious, shivering people. My wife once happened to overhear a conversation between two friends in the street, which began with the words: "Hi there! Seems you are suffering from typhus, are you not?" This appeared to be a perfectly normal greeting even though it was common knowledge most cases of typhus were fatal.

Among the medical personnel, there was a female epidemiologist, Dr. Martsinkevich, who, in a highly fortuitous manner, managed to discover a building suitable for a hospital for infectious diseases. During one of her visits to the Military Sanitation Authority, which had previously provided little useful information, she happened to come across a newly arrived army officer. Upon discovering the purpose of her visit, the officer remarked: "Why don't you move into the barracks by the railway station, which were built two years ago in the expectation of a cholera epidemic?" Our medical personnel immediately went about looking. The barracks stood locked and unused. Inside, they found piles of fresh underwear, which was badly needed in Serbian hospitals. Given that Niš is only a little town and that there were two hospitals by the railway station, it took a remarkable feat of Serbian negligence to forget about the barracks and the stockpile of underwear.

In no time at all, a hospital for infectious diseases was set up under the direction of our competent Dr. Martsinkevich and with the help of five volunteer nurses. In particular, Bishop Dosifej's assistance in this endeavor was invaluable. They worked tirelessly, thirty-six hours at a time, even though two nurses and Dr. Martsinkevich herself fell ill with fever. The hospital acquired quite a reputation, and everyone who became sick hoped to be taken in, since death cases were rare. Dr. Martsinkevich soon recovered and opened an ambulatory clinic where she saw one hundred patients a day, every day.

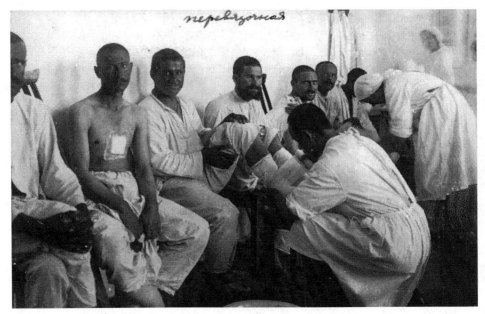

9. Niš, 1915. An ambulatory clinic.

The clinic was so successful, since it was the first of its kind in Serbia, that we opened more medical and surgical clinics in our hospitals. Free clinics were a novelty in Serbia, where civic institutions are virtually nonexistent. It was decided from the start that aid was to be a joint Russo-Serbian effort that drew on local civic groups. The committee spearheading the effort included Mrs. Pašić and Bishop Dosifej. The Serbian medical team was involved in consultations. Eventually, it became obvious that hospitals alone were not enough to control the epidemics.

Sanitary conditions in Niš needed to improve. The energetic Dr. Sofoterov, who as previously noted was more than familiar with the situation, drew up a plan that was accepted by the government and financed by us.

We also decided to organize soup kitchens, where impoverished people could get a hot meal at least once a day. The municipal administration in Niš compiled a list of those who were most in need, and they received meal tickets. Thus, in four city districts 283,000 dinners were distributed.

A location next to the railway station dispensed hot tea to anyone who wanted it. These measures definitely contributed to eliminating the epidemics, since many refugees had not had a hot meal in months.

The destruction of Serbian villages and cities by the enemy displaced many hundreds of children who lost their homes and families. At the initiative of

10. Niš, 1915. A soup kitchen.

11. Niš, 1915. A tea room.

Bishop Dosifej, the committee organized an orphanage by the St. Nicholas Church on the outskirts of town. Obviously, my wife gave all her energies to this project. At first only 40 children received permanent placement in a small, recently renovated house. After some additional renovations, the orphanage was able to accommodate 150 children.

Initially, a Serbian schoolteacher and her two daughters undertook the education of the orphans. At the insistence of Bishop Dosifej, a Russian teacher was brought in. She was a nurse by profession and had no prior pedagogical expertise but agreed to try her hand at teaching. She had so much warmth of character that the children came to adore her. Under her guidance, the pupils quickly picked up Russian. The orphanage became our favorite child. My wife used to visit daily for the duration of her stay. Once she left, Father Dosifej and I made frequent visits. We often encountered the following scene: a Czech prisoner-of-war officer who was also an amateur violin player was teaching the Serbian children to sing the Russian national anthem.

12. Niš, 1915. The orphanage.

It is worth saying a few words about these Czech prisoners of war. The Serbs had captured approximately seven hundred Austro-Hungarian officers, who resided in a splendid building located in the Niš city park. They tended to divide along mutually antagonistic national lines, constantly argued, and even used separate kitchens. There were forty or so Czechs. One of them, a conductor from Prague, set up a wonderful choir and even a small orchestra. Their chief overseer was a Serbian artillery major called Šapinac who had been seriously injured in a factory explosion. An amiable person who liked to get things done, he made sure the prisoners of war for whom he was responsible were living comfortably and did not want for anything. I visited them once and could only hope our own captured officers lived as well as they did. Thanks to Šapinac, we were able to often have the Czechs over to our hospital, where they performed splendid concerts for the wounded.

A children's sanatorium for tuberculosis was organized on the outskirts of the city in the beautiful monastery of St. Petka. At the behest of Bishop Dosifej, the monks gave up their cells and residences.

The epidemics subsided at the beginning of spring. Around this time, a group of six doctors and thirty nurses arrived from Moscow and set up a new hospital. Thanks to the warm southern sun and the concerted efforts of the Russian institutions in Niš, the number of sick people decreased significantly. Our committee focused on Niš and environs,

13. Niš, 1915. Cemetery for Austrian soldiers, victims of typhus.

as we did not want to spread our resources too thin. In the meantime, England, France, and America sent help to other parts of Serbia, which was divided into sectors.

The contributions from the Petrograd city committee were so generous that we were able to organize similar soup kitchens in Belgrade, where more than 130,000 meals were distributed. We were able to send a trainload of things and money to our consuls in Skopje and Bitola and to contribute money to Serbian organizations. We conveyed two hospitals to Montenegro, one of which went to the front line. A second field hospital was dispatched to the Dečani Monastery. It was decommissioned once the epidemics subsided, leaving behind three medical personnel who continued to work there until the Austrians arrived.

These monumental endeavors were only possible thanks to extraordinarily generous support from the Russian Red Cross and various Russian organizations, cities, and zemstvos. We were also fortunate to find suitable people to carry out the necessary tasks. I have already referred to many of them. It is also worth mentioning Lieutenant Colonel Novikov who was in charge of the committee's administrative affairs. As an officer in the Direction of Military Communications, Novikov had served as commandant of the Voronezh railway station prior to his arrival in Serbia. His main assignment in Serbia was to oversee the transportation of the military orders we had placed in western Europe via Salonika-Niš-Danube and then on to Veselkin's ships to Russia. Once the route had been set up, this required little additional effort, and Novikov willingly devoted all his spare time to the Russian relief effort in Serbia. Up to this point, our accounting and inventory had been poorly run. Novikov was able to set things in order by working with the appropriate people. After some initial complaints, everyone came to appreciate his strictness. Novikov quickly became one of the Moscow hospital's own. His assistance proved invaluable to us.

N. O. Ezerskii also arrived in Serbia to assist the person in charge of our committee. A member of the first Duma who had once dabbled in social activism, he was a noble and actually quite reasonable person. He was impractical and rather loquacious, which put him at a disadvantage at first. However, one quickly grew to appreciate his valuable skills and to sympathize with his ardent and pure desire to help others. Since everything was running smoothly in Niš, Ezerskii traveled to Montenegro, where he helped set up the two aforementioned hospitals and supervise the use of funds to obtain food for the local populations.

I will dwell a little longer on the Russian aid to Serbia, as this aspect of my stay in Niš is especially dear to me. All through our stay, we enjoyed the full support of the Russian Red Cross, cities, zemstvos, and civic organizations. As I have already mentioned, my wife was heavily involved in all relief efforts. The wave of public sympathy with heroic Serbia inspired plenty of Russian doctors, nurses, and medical students to offer their services. These amiable young people were fully devoted to the relief effort. Thanks to their common work with our inspired energetic youth, the Serbs learned to value the Russians and grew closer to them.

I also need to mention the church we set up at the Moscow hospital and the spiritual satisfaction it gave us. We used the field church that the representative of the Slavic Society, N. N. Ladyzhenskii, had brought at the beginning of the war. My wife added what was lacking. The church was duly consecrated during Lent, and we held a service.

Our church services took place in a spirit of utmost religiosity. We had a church choir, and the deacon of the main cathedral, a wonderfully kind person who considered himself as much Russian as Serbian, was a frequent guest. Greeting the holiday in our church was a most pleasant experience.

Father Epiphanius, a monk from Mount Athos, was our resident priest. He had brought along with him several other monks, one of whom, by the name of Father Dorofej, worked tirelessly in the Serbian hospital, where he caught typhus. He was transferred to our hospital where, thank God, he made a full recovery and stayed with us. He was an extraordinarily humble man, who willingly took on the most punishing menial labor. Everyone liked him.

This boundless idealism was not the sole preserve of the monk. With regard to this, I need to mention a person whose brief tragic visit has left an indelible memory. A Russian physician by the name of Baraboshkin arrived in Niš from Switzerland at the high point of the epidemic. He had previously been involved in some political movement in Russia. Baraboshkin had apparently not committed a great crime, but his involvement had been sufficient to force the young promising doctor to leave the country of his birth and settle permanently in Switzerland. He got married and started a respectable family, but times were hard. He had little money, and it was not easy to make a living in a foreign land; perhaps he also suffered from homesickness. Such was the life of this typical member of the Russian intelligentsia, who was an idealist with a pure soul.

When the Serbs began to hire medical doctors at the beginning of the war, Baraboshkin felt it his duty to answer the call, even though the work was very hard and the Serbs paid his salary in the local currency (dinar) instead of Swiss francs, as the original contract had stated. He did not complain even when he was posted to the miserable hamlet of Aleksinac, where he was the only doctor in a hospital with six hundred wounded patients suffering from typhus.

Baraboshkin visited the Moscow hospital en route to Aleksinac and expressed his desire to join one of the Russian medical institutions in Niš. He immediately made a most favorable impression on everyone there. His tall, slender stature was that of the typically idealistic Russian intelligentsia. However, we had no openings at the time, and I was reluctant to engage a person the Serbs had already hired and were clearly in need of—although I hoped to be able to do so once a suitable substitute had been found in Aleksinac.

Baraboshkin went to Aleksinac. It proved possible to recall him in little over a month, and he arrived beaming at the opportunity to work in one of the Russian institutions. However, he immediately diagnosed himself with typhus and had to be hospitalized. His body was weak, and the most diligent efforts of our doctors were in vain. We had all grown to like Baraboshkin during our brief acquaintance with him; in fact, he died surrounded by fellow Russian idealists. Perhaps this made his lonely death less painful. After his death, I was given a letter Baraboshkin's wife had sent to him. This letter disclosed fully the tragic destruction of a perfect family Baraboshkin's death had engendered. It was filled with gentle love, pride at Baraboshkin's new position in the Russian hospital, and hopes for the future.

May this pure, good Russian man rest in peace.

In a detailed report to the Moscow Medical Mission, Dr. Malinovich wrote:

> There were so many supplies at the "Russian Pavilion" organized by Princess Trubetskaia that we did not have to limit our resources to helping only the wounded. Drawing upon my knowledge of the Russo-Japanese War, of the Balkan Wars and the current war, I calculate that 35 percent of wounded are serious casualties. By serious casualties I mean those soldiers maimed by exploding artillery. There is nothing to which I can compare these wounded. We surgeons turned out to be totally unprepared and had to learn to work in the field under fire. All operations are done without anesthetic. Serbian soldiers go into surgery bravely and calmly and have a great ability to endure suffering. I average 8 operations a day. The months of December and January were the heaviest in casualties and I performed 12 to 16 operations a day. The most operations in one day were on December 15, 1915, when I performed 24.

For 20 days I lay ill with rheumatism and dermatitis from using disinfectants. It is only thanks to the energies of Princess Trubetskaia that Niš became the first city to host the Medical Team from Moscow. By organizing hospitals for infectious diseases and free meals the overwhelming epidemic was contained. Our teams of medical personnel visited 125 villages surrounding Niš in an 80-kilometer radius. It is difficult for me to describe the images of children dying from dysentery or diphtheria because their parents lay dying from typhoid fever incapable of giving them care. All this because of the lack of medical help.

THE DARDANELLES

The expedition to the Dardanelles by the English and the French began in February 1915. It was only later on that I learned of the origins of this ill-fated expedition from my good friend Prince Kudashev, who headed the field diplomatic chancery of Commander in Chief Grand Duke Nikolai Nikolaevich.[1]

Back in November/December of 1914, our situation in the Caucasus was precarious. We had very few forces at the time. At one point we even considered evacuating Tiflis because of Turkish aggression. The grand duke requested the English and French military representatives to his staff to convey to their governments by telegram the need for some kind of diversion against the Turks. It really did not matter where—in Smyrna or in the Straits. In the meantime, our situation in the Caucasus had improved considerably, and by Christmas we celebrated a brilliant victory at Sarikamish, where the Turks were soundly defeated.

In the meantime, the grand duke forgot his idea of a diversion, broached to the Allies some months back. The English, however, latched on to this idea. Perhaps it was our victory over Turkey's superior forces that emboldened them to take action in the Straits. Whatever it was, they persuaded the reluctant French to send battleships. It seems the French only acquiesced in the matter out of desire not to alienate their allies.

In a matter of days, the first actions of the Allied fleet in the Balkans left an impression of quick and brilliant success. At the beginning of March our officer Smirnov passed through Niš en route to Salonika, where he was supposed to join the fleet in order to liaise with our Black Sea Fleet. He soon traveled back and assured us the taking of the Straits was only a matter of time.

We ourselves had a single warship, the *Askol'd*, which made her mark.

Also at this time, Sazonov informed me by telegram that, since Constantinople would fall shortly, he was appointing me high commissioner on behalf of Russia. France and England were appointing their own commissioners.

I kept a close watch on all the events in the Dardanelles with some misgivings. I doubted in the success of this venture from the start. How could I even assume that this success was a fait accompli? Influenced by the prevailing general optimism and belief in Allied success, my skepticism was short-lived. Furthermore, Sazonov subsequently wrote that the Allies had agreed to Russian control of Constantinople and the Straits, under certain conditions. I acknowledged the honor of such an appointment in a letter to Sazonov. I assured him of my total dedication.

A week later a package came by mail with notes, letters, exchanges, and instructions to leave via Salonika at the appropriate time. My staff had also been selected.

This brilliant diplomatic success was not without its price, and my uplifted mood was soon to be quashed by the conditions our allies put forth. The State Duma played a role in this. Its unanimous declaration of Russia's utmost need to annex the Straits strengthened the position of Russian diplomacy. Our allies realized that it would be impossible for us to renounce the Straits without risking the disillusionment of Russian public opinion with the war. The English naturally resented this but decided to accede, keep calm, and carry on in typical fashion. Unfortunately, the French delayed making a statement for some considerable time, agreeing only if certain conditions were met.

Russia was to receive Constantinople only at the end of the war and then only after each ally had achieved its claims. The French were keen on defending their economic financial and cultural interests in the city. To this end, they came up with the idea of three commissioners, each of whom would take control of an area with the army of its country. We were to occupy the Upper Bosporus and the Phanar (the see of the ecumenical patriarch).[2] If I remember correctly the French were to occupy Pera; and the English, Stambul and the Prince Islands.[3]

These conditions were to make my future position extremely difficult. Governing Constantinople with French and English colleagues on equal terms, I risked always being in a minority, since the short-term interests of the two Western powers differed dramatically from those of Russia, which could only view the situation as a temporary arrangement pending its permanent acquisition of the Straits. I was of the opinion that our allies had every right to safeguard their interests in Constantinople. However, it had to be made clear that the Russian commissioner held supreme power in the city, with the authority of his English and French counterparts limited to the protection of their respective government's interests. I immediately telegraphed Petrograd to this end and stressed that it was absolutely necessary for me to travel to the capital to confer with the government and form my own staff of counselors. Apart from international complications, I worried about interdepartmental tensions and the relationship between the military and civil administrations in Constantinople. I had decided to accept the position only if I were the sole representative of Russian state power. I would insist on being able to send packing any civil servant or head of department pursuing his own policy. Otherwise, I would take the first ship back to Russia myself.

Permission to travel to Petrograd was my *condition sine qua non* for accepting the position. I was told that I would be unable to make such a trip, in light of the imminent capture of Constantinople, to which I replied that I should no longer be considered a potential candidate. I received no reply and considered the matter settled. However, passing through Niš en route to his posting, the new Russian ambassador in Rome, Giers, informed me that the government still hoped I would accept the position. I reiterated my desire to travel to Petrograd and discuss it in person.

In May, leaving the Russian mission in Strandtmann's capable hands, I left for Petrograd, where I found out that we had already accepted the three-power condominium of Constantinople. Bearing in mind this impossible power-sharing situation, we needed to find ways to safeguard our interests in the best possible way. To this end, A. M. Petriav (nominally consul general in Albania working in the Foreign Ministry) and I worked out the following agenda: The three commissioners together will remain sovereign until such time when a peace treaty will be signed. The executive will consist of a subordinate council of department heads who will administer departments of internal affairs, justice, finance, trade, education, and confessions. The consensus was to cede finance and trade to the English and French, leaving internal affairs and justice for ourselves.

This project failed to materialize, owing to the changed circumstances. However, we had little to regret. Had we received Constantinople from our allies in this manner, our hands would have been tied by numerous concessions. Naturally, I could not know this at the time, which is why the matter was of great concern to me.

I had already sent a telegram from Niš about the need to define our relationship with the ecumenical patriarch. While in Petrograd, I wrote another note concerning our future administration of Constantinople. The gist of these two notes is as follows. In light of the numerous qualifications and conditions our allies put forth regarding the situation of Constantinople until the end of the war, it was in our best interest to maintain the status quo and reject the introduction of any provisions that might limit us in the future. This situation would also benefit our long-term interests, first and foremost regarding the naval question. It was absolutely necessary for us to control the zone of the Straits, where we would introduce a military-naval administration. As far as the hinterland was concerned, I considered it best to set up a protectorate but allow the natives substantial local autonomy, especially bearing in mind the multiethnic composition of the population and the presence of international interests. Constantinople might become a free port under Russian administration, thereby retaining its huge role as a gateway between Europe and Asia. I thought we should avoid forced Russification but also ensure the liquidation of our allies' financial interests in the city.

As far as the religious question was concerned, I feared our church leaders might take a narrow, nationalist view. I had heard rumors that members of the Holy Synod had already proposed sending the ecumenical patriarch, along with the sultan, to Konya and installing a Russian archbishop in Constantinople. I do not know whether there is truth in any of this, but one had to expect all sorts of things. I was of the opinion that we should come to Constantinople as liberators from a long foreign yoke and preserve the full autonomy of its church, which at one time had baptized us. We should also provide financial assistance to the ecumenical patriarch, thereby freeing him from his dependence on local Greek bankers and solicitors. Our presence would thus sound the death knell of Hellenism, which had been using the patriarchate of Constantinople to promote its interests in the city. To improve future relations between the churches of Russia and Constantinople, we might reintroduce the institution of Apocrisarius—diplomatic bishop-representatives to fellow Christian churches, which had existed during Christianity's early centuries. The annexation of Constantinople ought to have an enormous impact on our religious life. Once an autocephalous Orthodox church had been incorporated into the Russian Empire, we would undoubtedly have to free our own church from state control. This would also necessitate the restoration of a Russian patriarch, in order to put the two churches on an equal footing.

As I write these lines in October 1916, this all seems like a faded dream. Will it ever come true? The entire meaning of the war for Russia still rests painfully on this question. In any event, I hope that my reminiscences of this historical time will be of some interest.

I met little opposition to my views in governing circles in Petrograd. None of our ministers had the slightest opinion on Constantinople. Besides, the game of "ministerial leapfrog" [*ministerskaia chekharda*], as Duma deputy Purishkevich aptly put it, had already begun, and no one was sure about his position. This also coincided with the considerable worsening of our military situation, which made the acquisition of Constantinople—even through our allies—extremely problematic.

Nevertheless, I thought it necessary to take the matter to the end, in case Divine Providence deigned to make this dream a reality. My notes were sent to the tsar. In a lengthy audience just before my departure to Serbia by way of the Stavka, the tsar gave his approval and agreed that my policy toward the ecumenical patriarch could bring about the election of a patriarch in Russia. When I pointed out the inevitable impact such an eventuality would have on our domestic religious life, the tsar keenly interrupted me.

"Why not? All the better. Nothing untoward can come out of it," he said.

He was pleased with my idea of visiting the grand duke at the Stavka in Baranovichi on my way back to Niš in order to discuss and coordinate future military and civil authority with him.[4]

In Baranovichi I stayed with my friend Kudashev, who occupied a small neat wooden house by the diplomatic chancery. Breakfast was in the officers' mess, a similar kind of building. I was impressed with the overall simplicity and efficiency. A sign forbidding handshakes, for which there was a significant penalty, hung on the wall. I greatly appreciated this rule, considering the sweltering heat of that July. Kudashev and I visited Chief of General Staff General Ianushkevich and Quartermaster-General Danilov, with both of whom I had had previous encounters. Ianushkevich had replaced Zhilinskii as chief of general staff in the spring of 1914, a few months before the outbreak of the war. He had earlier served as head of the general staff academy. His steady rise and subsequent brilliant career were, it seems to me, quite fortuitous, primarily owing to the fact that the tsar took to Ianushkevich at a military parade. Ianushkevich's most appealing quality was his eagerness to please (a quality that enabled Sukhomlinov and Maklakov to acquire ministerial positions). Grand Duke Nikolai Nikolaevich called him "a lady most pleasant in all circumstances." Actually, in a position of power, Ianushkevich was far from pleasant to everyone. He jealously guarded his standing and all channels of communication to the grand duke. The latter seems to have agreed that no matter should be left unattended by Ianushkevich. In general, there was little to disagree with in such a conduct of affairs, apart from Ianushkevich's personality. He had little patience with our allies. In his eyes, the English and the French were "swindlers, who put the entire weight of the war on us." He reiterated this belief in our present conversation in the Stavka. He despised the Ministry of Foreign Affairs and Sazonov. The feeling was mutual, which did little to help us achieve a common view on war aims and other matters.

During my stay in the Stavka, I tried to clarify an issue that had befuddled me for some time. I had heard that the old general, Baron Kaulbars, had been sent to Odessa with orders to form a staff and study the possibility of a march on Constantinople at the head of a special military detachment. I had heard that Kaulbars had retained his youthful audacity in his old age but was otherwise of limited ability. It seemed to me that the entire question of our capture of Constantinople was subject to more idle chatter than careful planning. Besides, I had no idea how my professional relationship with a petty tyrant like Kaulbars was going to work in case we took Constantinople. But how was I supposed to bring up such a touchy question in front of the military authorities, who had always been extremely protective of their interests? I tried a nationalist angle, telling Ianushkevich that my extensive social connections had enabled me to study public sentiment and become convinced that the question of Constantinople and the Straits was the single most important thing for us in the present war. In light of this, I considered it vital to choose very carefully the people responsible for the realization of this great Russian historic task. How would Russian public opinion view the capture of Constantinople by the German Kaulbars? People were already accusing Admiral Eberhardt of treason solely on the basis of his surname. My words made an unexpectedly big impact. Ianushkevich launched into a tirade extolling Kaulbars's virtues; the two were seemingly in cahoots. Among other things, he told me Kaulbars would probably be easily persuaded to let me approach the Holy Cross first, as if this were the winning argument with me! I refused to budge.

After my visit to Ianushkevich, I went to see the vastly more capable Danilov. "Black" Danilov (as opposed to Ginger Danilov or some other Danilov) was really in charge in the Stavka. He was a knowledgeable, intelligent person but unfortunately a theoretician. As such, he was out of place, since the position of chief war architect required different qualities and a different personality. Danilov represented the golden mean. He was easier to deal with, owing to his clear and concise speech. He was also against the appointment of Kaulbars.

An hour before lunch I was received by the grand duke, who lived in a simply furnished train car. Ianushkevich was also present. Everything he said was sensible and logical, leaving me with the best of impressions. Among other things, he stated that Ianushkevich had informed him of my misgivings regarding the High Command and that he would consider them in due course. For the time being, Kaulbars would remain in Odessa, until someone else took his place. The grand duke promised to do everything in his power and not in his power to achieve at least some of our ends independently. The grand duke also said he was aware of the importance of acquiring Constantinople by ourselves rather than as a gift from our allies. When the moment for decisive action came, he added, he would do everything humanly possible to ensure our military was up to the task. He completely understood my misgivings and the complications that might arise from conflicting agendas between the military and the civilian administrations.

Overall, I should have been most pleased with my visit to the military headquarters, were it not for the fact that things were not going well for us. I learned that we might have to give up Warsaw and begin a series of retreats. These setbacks undoubtedly made the military authorities more compliant than they normally were. Hence, the talks on Constantinople were decidedly low-key.

As he bid me farewell, the grand duke invited me to dine with him. The royal train, surrounded by spruce trees, stood on a side track. Nearby stood an elaborate yurt, a gift from the Kirgiz.[5] Next to the yurt, protected by a canopy on wooden stilts, were placed small tables each with four chairs—enough to accommodate thirty or forty staff and guests. The grand duke sat with Ianushkevich and Protopresbyter of Military and Naval Chaplains Father Shavelskii. I found him to be a very pleasant, intelligent, and sincere priest with a rather negative regard for the Holy Synod. It was said that he had some influence with the grand duke and to some extent with the tsar himself.

The meal was simple, with a bottle of white wine and a bottle of red wine at each table. Each table kept independent conversation. Occasionally, the grand duke would send someone a remark. After dinner the area suddenly emptied, and I returned to my dear host, Kudashev.

All in all, there were a good many people in the leadership, but not anyone consequential enough to unite the war effort. There was really no one to take on full responsibility at this historic moment. With his chivalrous soul and sense of responsibility, the grand duke—while not incredibly bright—could have been this person were it not for General Ianushkevich, who counteracted the qualities of the grand duke.

6

ALLIED PRESSURES ON SERBIA

The next morning my wife joined me for my return journey to Niš. We passed through Kiev, eventually arriving in Bucharest, where we had to stop because of the flooding in Bulgaria. Our brief stay in the hotel attracted the attention of the former Rumanian minister plenipotentiary in St. Petersburg Rosetti-Solescu, a loquacious, self-important man who had recently been able to secure rolling stock for the transportation of foodstuffs he was selling in Germany.

Nevertheless, he was keen on demonstrating his alleged Russian sympathies to all Russians who passed through Rumania. Along with his son, a pleasant young man who retained the characteristics of his education in the St. Petersburg Lyceum, he took us sightseeing around Bucharest. Bucharest had not changed at all. It was the same careless mosaic of swindlers, spies, cocottes, and noisy kiosks selling flour by weight, kerosene, honesty, and anything that could be peddled at wholesale or retail prices.

The train went through Bulgaria. Due to lengthy delays, I was unable to spend more than a quarter of an hour at the railway station with Savinskii, our representative in Sofia. We needed to discuss the impending advance of the powers in the Balkans. Savinskii promised to come to Niš during the next few days.

As for the unfolding general situation, after lengthy negotiations, Italy finally declared war on Austria in mid-April 1915. Speculation about the aspirations of the Italian cabinet abounded. This provoked a great deal of concern in Serbia, partly because Italy had managed to negotiate from us and from the Allies the handing over of Slavic territories. Pašić complained that he had been left out of the negotiations. When M. N. Giers, our ambassador to Italy, passed through Niš at this time, I arranged for him to meet with Prince Alexander and with Pašić to bring them up to date. I also wanted him to listen to what the Serbs had to say. They expressed their deep irritation toward the Italians in no uncertain terms, even bordering on the inappropriate. Thanks to the tactful Baron Schvitti, Italian minister to Serbia, who was able to skillfully parry with the appropriate interjections, none of this became an international incident. The irritation toward the Allies was also directed at us for treating Serbian interests so lightly. Understandably, this made a new Allied declaration to Serbia on the necessity of ceding substantial territories to Bulgaria inopportune. The secret negotiations with the Italians caught Rumania—and everyone else for that matter—by surprise. From the inception of the war the relationship between Bucharest and Rome seemed to be solid, with Rumania taking its cue from Rome in declaring neutrality.

Brătianu himself, who placed importance on this relationship, firmly believed that both countries would continue to remain neutral. The Italian minister in Bucharest had done his work well indeed. The Rumanians firmly believed that both countries would depart from neutrality simultaneously. Hence, Brătianu was unpleasantly surprised at the news of the Italian entry into the war. He was not averse to taking the same step, but at the same time he did not want to forego any possible territorial acquisitions, demanding Transylvania, Bukovina, and all of the Banat, with the Danube River as a future border between Serbia and Rumania, as the price for his country's entry into the war.

Just before my departure to Russia, I received permission from St. Petersburg to assure the wary Pašić, who was unaware of the full extent of Rumanian demands, that Serbian interests would be considered during negotiations with Rumania.

In the meantime, our allies were pressuring us to consider Rumanian claims. The significance of Rumania's entry into the war was overblown. Our own situation continued to deteriorate. By honoring our claims to Constantinople, the Allies made us subservient to their policies. Constantinople tilted the scale to such an extent that there was little we could do except concede to Italy's demands. Now we would probably have to do the same with Rumania. We adopted a most unfortunate tactic in regards to this issue. We seized upon trifles while agreeing to the essence. Time went by. As our setbacks increased, Rumania became less inclined to become involved without first obtaining as many concessions as possible from us. They gained Bukovina and the Banat to the Danube River without making a move so essential to us at this very moment. The ongoing negotiations with Rumania only served to underline the unfortunate absence of unity and cooperation between the Stavka and the Foreign Ministry.

At the time of my departure from St. Petersburg, I still did not know the outcome of these negotiations. Since we were yielding at every level, I voiced my opinion: let the Rumanians have what they want. The price: their immediate commitment. Alas, this very condition was unattainable. Very soon I personally would experience the results of these four-way negotiations.

During the time that I was in St. Petersburg in May, the Allied powers once again applied simultaneous pressure on both Niš and Sofia. They demanded that Serbia empower them to give Bulgaria territories as per the situation in exchange for Bulgaria's immediate entry into the war. They did not hide from Pašić that they considered Macedonia as a part of this general formula, with the parameters as defined in the Agreement of 1912. In exchange, Serbia would receive the coastline of the Adriatic with its outlying territories after the war. In any case, there would be a common border between Greece and Serbia.

Pašić categorically refused any consideration. He threatened to resign, stating that no leader in Serbia would take responsibility for acceding to such demands. As for the Bulgarians, they demanded more clarification. The result was a stalemate, albeit temporary. Soon enough our allies, especially the English, decided to push this matter to the end.

Public opinion in England was becoming increasingly irritated with the war effort in the Balkans. The naval catastrophe in the Dardanelles had already cost tens of thousands of lives and several warships. It brought home even more the fiasco of the expedition in the Straits. As a result, the English believed that without Bulgaria any initiative of this kind would be doomed.

They had to bring in Bulgaria before the fierce autumn winds rendered travel by sea hazardous for supply ships. Traditionally, the sympathies of the English public toward Bulgaria were strong, and most people accepted Bulgarian claims to Macedonia. Public opinion blamed the government for failing to achieve anything in the Balkans. The *Times* became the main forum for the growing opposition toward government inability to make gains in the Balkans.

Grey, sensing his loss of popularity, made the most unusual decision to send the former editor of the *Times*, Sir Valentine Chirol, on a semiofficial mission to the Balkans.[1] Brilliant, decent, intelligent, and with a solid reputation, he had been a correspondent in India, the Far East, and other countries. I knew him from before and admired his articles in the *Times*.

Chirol traveled to the Balkans with a secretary from the Foreign Office, who communicated with Grey in code. After his fact-finding mission, he passed through Niš. I had him over for breakfast several times, and we discussed the overall situation at some length. He spoke of the expedition in the Dardanelles with growing irritability, to the point where he insisted the whole affair had been initiated in a "criminally foolish" manner. It was clear that the English were prepared to do anything to extricate themselves from this cul-de-sac. However, his observations on the ground had not made Chirol an optimist. His conversations with Pašić and the crown prince had convinced him of the impossibility of gaining concessions from the Serbs. The situation in Bulgaria was not much better, as most Bulgarians seemed reluctant to accept the Entente's offer. He candidly acknowledged to me how he had imagined everything differently. He did not know how to get out of this mess, which he himself had helped to create in the first place.

Once again, on July 20, the representatives of the Entente countries received instructions to persuade Pašić of the importance of ceding Macedonia. They stressed the enormous sacrifices in the war effort on the part of the Allies to preserve Serbia's independence. For this, Serbia must in turn also understand the need for sacrifices for the common good. It was imperative to win Bulgaria over; however, this would be impossible without substantial compensation. If left unappeased, Bulgaria might even take actions that would seriously endanger the overall situation, and Serbia in particular. In light of these difficult circumstances, the Allies thought it necessary to ask Serbia to relinquish the uncontested zone of Macedonia at the end of the war in exchange for immediate Bulgarian military action in support of the Entente. In exchange, the Allied powers pledged to compensate Serbia in Bosnia-Herzegovina, along the Adriatic, and in other territories where Serbia's chief national, political, and economic interests lay. The Allied powers also manifested their intention to guarantee these territorial acquisitions at the end of the war only if Serbia agreed to suitable compensation for Bulgaria in Macedonia and Thrace. The note ended with the promise to maintain a common border between Greece and Serbia.

I read the text three days before having to present it to Pašić and telegraphed my misgivings to St. Petersburg. It was certain to be rejected because, basically, nothing had changed since the month of May. The only chance of success lay in a clear and specific delimitation of the territorial compensations Serbia could count on. I based the assertion on a conversation I had had with Iovanović. For my part, I naturally did everything I could to convince the Serbs of the necessity of concessions, even though I was doubtful anything positive could come out of this.

On July 23, the four Allied ministers presented Pašić with these demands. I had always spoken with him candidly, and this time was no exception. I told him in a friendly but stern manner that he would incur much greater responsibility by refusing the Allied note than by accepting it. It was a matter of Serbia's future and its relationship with Russia. I repeated what I had said to Iovanović earlier—the war demands commensurate sacrifices from every member of the alliance. National peculiarities and sentimental concerns should be relegated to the requirements of the war effort. If Serbia refused to sacrifice in this unparalleled war, which, after all, Russia had entered for Serbia's sake, what good was this alliance for Russia? Besides, winning Bulgaria over was very much in Serbia's own interest. Pašić looked nervous, answering that, in this war of life and death, Serbia would rather die with honor than commit suicide for fear of death. He thought it impossible to accept the Allied note, but he would nevertheless confer with the ministers, the party leaders, the crown prince, and the king.

On the next day Pašić informed me that the ministers and he were going to travel to Kruševac and Topola to discuss the Allied note with the crown prince and the king. He believed the following points needed clarification:

1. To determine Serbia's exact compensation for the territories it was asked to give up.
2. Whether the Allies considered the boundary as defined in the treaty of 1912 to be "sine qua non," or whether it could be modified.
3. How did the Allies define the common border between Serbia and Greece; how far would it be extended and where would it be?

I assured him that I would transmit his questions by telegram, requesting an immediate answer. I expressed the personal opinion that unfortunately the borders outlined in the 1912 agreement could not be altered. As for the other points, Russia would do everything it could for Serbia. Perhaps Pašić wanted to soften his stance by remarking that whatever Serbia did would be for the benefit of Russia. He went on to say that our close ties would only become stronger in times of adversity. He was mainly interested in Serbia's future share of Albania and Dalmatia and the delimitations in the Banat. He hoped that an agreement with Rumania was not yet signed. The Serbian government needed to secure Belgrade. The history of Serbia's confrontations with Austria reflected Serbian determination to protect Belgrade. They were not about to allow a new borderline bringing the Rumanians right up to the Danube. He talked about Bačka, Syrmia, and Croatia, and launched into a bitter complaint about the Italians.[2]

The ministers' trip did not take place right away, due to the arrival of the crown prince and acting chief of the general staff Živko Pavlović. Pašić grew visibly more intransigent after the conference between the civilian and military leadership. He insisted that the border of 1912 could not be accepted without alterations, but he still awaited our response to the points he had brought up.

My foreign colleagues came to the mission daily, and I managed to persuade them to ask their respective governments to specify territorial compensations for Serbia commensurate with its fancy. A substantial common border between Serbia and Greece could only be achieved if the two states divided Albania, leaving the port of Valona to Italy. Further we had to promise the Serbs Bosnia-Herzegovina, Syrmia, Bačka, Croatia, and Slavonia with the adjoining coastline. The question of the Banat was rather complicated, since nobody knew for sure whether we had already promised it to Rumania or not. If so, we had to inform the Serbs about the results of our negotiations with the Rumanians, since they considered Bucharest's entry into the war on the Entente side of the utmost importance. My telegrams to St. Petersburg emphasized that, should Italy's obstinacy make it impossible to clearly define Serbian compensations, the government would be unable to accept the Allied note, even if it so wished, because of the prevailing public sentiment and the attitudes of the army.

The question was actually quite simple. We were asking Serbia to make a very real sacrifice, giving up a region that had cost much Serbian blood. In exchange, we were making vague promises about territories not yet conquered, where Serbia's interests clashed with those of Italy. Furthermore, it was not a simple question of territorial acquisitions—it was a question of the national unification of the South Slavs. To make matters worse, Serbia was rightly worried about the impossible borders proposed in the Allied note. The common border between Serbia and Greece, which both countries valued as a deterrent against Bulgarian aggression, was in actuality a small corridor surrounded by enemies, which completely negated its strategic value. As far as Pašić and the Serbian military were concerned, the border with Bulgaria along the lines of the 1912 agreement was entirely unsatisfactory.

Serbian arguments did have one significant flaw—namely, that Serbs had voluntarily agreed to the 1912 border when they signed a military convention with Bulgaria. I reminded Pašić about this on numerous occasions, but he refused to take responsibility for this agreement, putting all blame on the late prime minister Milovanović, who had personally conducted all negotiations with Bulgaria at the time. A change of personnel could not free the state from all responsibility, of course, but Bulgaria's actions had nullified the agreement and justified the need to secure Serbia against Bulgarian ambitions.

Apart from that, the Allied promise of the entire Banat to Rumania was particularly painful. The entire history of Serbian relations with Austria had been overshadowed by the Austrian threat to Belgrade. Removing this threat only to replace it with a new, Rumanian threat would not do. Belgrade was the focal point and the center of Serbian culture. It was their capital. Hence, one of Serbia's cardinal war aims was to secure Belgrade. The Serbian people would never again agree to see it threatened by a neighbor.

Last but not least, there was the question of the Adriatic, and here, as in Albania, Serbia met with persistent Italian opposition. Italy seemed determined to annex purely Slavic territories and prepare for a future struggle against Serbia by insisting on a demilitarized Serbian Adriatic coastline along Bosnia-Herzegovina. It was clear that Italy wanted to prevent the emergence of a unified South Slav state under the aegis of Serbia, as well as to dominate the Adriatic. Rome was also not averse to cheap haggling.

The negotiations between the Allied powers and Italy about Serbia's compensations took place in these difficult circumstances. I have to give credit to my Italian colleague Baron Schvitti, who tried to bring the two sides together and avoid a further worsening of the conflict, although the Serbs continued to meddle in his affairs. For our part, we did everything possible to induce the government in Rome to compromise.

The situation was further complicated by the actions of the Bulgarian government, which, seemingly inching toward the Central powers, began military preparations along the Serbian border under the pretext of scheduled maneuvers. The Bulgarian minister in Niš did his usual thing of denying the most obvious facts and stated that there were no military preparations whatsoever. This only increased Serbia's doubts about its allies, which were pressing it to make useless sacrifices.

The powers proved unable to agree on a specific reply to the points Pašić had brought up. The main stumbling block was Italy's opposition to the size of Serbian compensations, which it considered excessive. The English minister received instructions to make a declaration on August 3/16, by himself if his colleagues had not received any instructions. I had not received any but, judging from the previous telegrams, knew that Sazonov would reluctantly have to accept Grey's correction of our text in favor of Rome. I joined the English and French in order not to increase the palpable sense of disunity in the alliance. The statement included the following points:

1. The city of Skopje and Ovče Pole must be defended by a strategic border yet to be determined.

2. In case Serbia accepted the Allied powers' stance on Macedonia, it would receive the following territories at the end of the war:

3. Bosnia-Herzegovina; Syrmia up to the rivers Drava and Danube, including Zemlin and Bačka; the Adriatic coast from Cape Planka to a point ten kilometers south of Ragusa, including the islands Zirone, Budua, Solta, Brazza, and Calametra, and the Sabbioncello Peninsula. If the Allies took over Slavonia, it would go to Serbia.

4. The Adriatic coast south of the ten-kilometer line by Ragusa would be divided between Serbia and Montenegro.

5. The coast south of the Drina River would belong to independent Albania.

6. The future status of Croatia up to the Dalmatian border, including Fiume, would be decided at the final conclusion of peace.

7. The coastline extending from Planka to the southernmost part of Sabbioncello, and from ten kilometers south of Ragusa to the Voussa River, would be demilitarized.

8. The Allied powers must insist on the border of the Agreement of 1912 in Macedonia, unless Serbia could persuade Bulgaria to make voluntary alterations.

9. The border between Greece and Albania would start in Macedonia, but the Allies could not specify its exact location at this point.

10. The powers would not demand for themselves any of the territories designated in points 3, 4, 5, 6, 7.

I added the following points on behalf of Russia: (1) we would assist Serbia in acquiring Croatia at the end of the war, (2) Serbia would receive the Slavic part of the Banat in case Rumania remained neutral, and (3) we would insist on a longer border between Greece and Serbia in Albania.

On the following day, August 4/17, the Italian minister was instructed to make an identical statement, with the exception of omitting any reference to Slavonia and making a small alteration to one of the other points.

Following the rule of seniority, I made my declaration after the English and French ministers. Although Pašić had already acquainted himself with the gist of the powers' statement, he was clearly nervous and agitated. He told me that the Allies facilitated his decision. Serbia would have to stand on its own, not only against Austria but against its own allies in defense of his country's lands and historical interests.

"That is, if they consider us an ally at all," he added. "Serbia is being divided and controlled like some African colony."

"What right do you have to make such statements against Russia after all that it has done?" I asked rather vehemently.

"I believe that Russia should never make impossible demands to Serbia," he answered.

Our conversation was short, as Pašić had to visit the king and was in a hurry to catch the train. However, he pointed out the biggest flaws in the Allied note—the vague description of the future border between Greece and Serbia, which could not be a deterrent against either Bulgaria or Albania; the reluctance of the powers to commit on Croatia; and the absence of any references to Slovenian-populated territories. There were aspects that irritated him, especially the lack of protection for Belgrade in the Banat and the demilitarization of Serbia's Adriatic coast. As far as that last point was concerned, even the Italian minister privately admitted to its unenforceability, stating that the Serbs would probably disregard it as soon as they acquired these territories. Pašić was most of all incensed at the lack of alterations to the Agreement of 1912. I finally suggested that, if Serbia did not negotiate, it risked gaining nothing by choosing between Macedonia and a South Slav Federation. "Then we'll choose Macedonia," he replied.

On August 20, the English minister asked Pašić to agree to the stationing of Allied troops along the Vardar River as soon as Bulgaria declared itself willing to join the Entente and attack Turkey. He added that the presence of Allied troops along this line would serve as a guarantee to Serbia that the final cession of these territories would take place concomitantly with the acquisition of the promised compensation. For my part, I wrote daily telegrams to Petrograd insisting that the Allies immediately move to the Vardar in order to keep the Serbs and Bulgarians away from each other. I believed this was the only way to avoid war between them. At the same time, we had to secure the main line of communication between Russia and her allies between the Danube and Salonika, including the port of Salonika itself. Unfortunately, the government did not view this with the same urgency as I did. The only thing they agreed with was the need to exclude Russian troops from the Allied force along the Vardar. I had two reasons to recommend this: (1) was to avoid clashes between Russian troops and Bulgarian brigands; and (2) in case of an Austro-German invasion of Serbia, then French and English troops could retreat to Salonika and sail home, but where would Russian troops go?

Before replying to the Allies, Pašić convened the *Skupština* (Parliament) and explained the situation. The Liberals, who had earlier refused to enter a coalition cabinet, were firmly opposed to any concessions. The leaders of this political party seemingly acted on the basis of personal motives and sought to gain popularity in the army through extreme chauvinism. In so doing, they stirred up plenty of problems for Pašić. As I have already mentioned, the growing mistrust of Bulgaria lay at the root of the problem, and it was not unreasonable. Unfortunately, at the time, we and our allies still had illusions about Bulgaria. Our representatives in Sofia kept these illusions alive, especially after the cautious English minister Elliot, who mistrusted the Bulgarians, was replaced by the Petrograd counselor, whose mission was to win the Bulgarian government over.

I once went to visit Minister of Transportation Drašković. One of the leaders of the Young Radical Party, this sincere and ardent young man was the most important member of the government after Pašić. He spoke about the upcoming decision with tears in his eyes, insisting that the sacrifice the Allies demanded from Serbia was pointless, since the Bulgarians would never join the Entente. They were merely waiting for the opportune moment to attack Serbia. I told him that Serbia had nothing to lose, as the promise of Macedonia was conditional on Bulgarian participation in the war against Turkey. Drašković argued that the only way to persuade the Bulgarians to join the Entente was by facing them with an ultimatum. In addition to this growing mistrust of Bulgaria, the Serbian reluctance to offer any concessions was due to their mistrust of the Allies; the Serbs were not sure the Allies would protect them from Bulgarian aggression.

I had forgotten to mention yet another joint Allied venture, which took place just before we delivered our statement. The tsar, the English and Italian kings, and the French president asked us to forward their private communications on the subject to the king of Serbia. They had initially intended to address these telegrams to the heir to the throne as acting regent.

However, they heeded my suggestion to tie the memory of such substantial territorial concessions to the name of the old king rather than the future monarch. Consequently, the four Allied ministers presented Pašić with telegrams addressed to the king on July 28.

The text of only two of these telegrams—the tsar's and the English king's—was identical. The Italian telegram differed substantially.

On August 18, Pašić handed each of us the king's answer. In the text addressed to the tsar, the king expressed his deepest gratitude to Russia in the warmest terms, acknowledging Russia's efforts on behalf of Serbia and pledging to do whatever he could as a constitutional monarch to appease the Allies. Pašić had a smile on his face when he told me: "Tomorrow I will give you the government's response to the Allied note. I think you will be happy with it." I do not know why the old man endeavored to mislead me. Perhaps this was a result of his clever nature. Although his words cheered me, I warned Petrograd that we should be wary until we had seen the official reply. As it turned out, I had every reason to be cautious.

On August 19, Pašić gave each of us a diplomatic note stating that Serbia was agreeing to a border as outlined in the Agreement of 1912 in principle, but with some adjustments and conditions:

1. Skopje and Ovče Pole must be protected by a previously determined strategic border.
2. Serbia must retain Prilep, due to its historical importance.
3. The joint border between Serbia and Greece must start from the heights of Perister and Sukha Planina and continue west to a specific point yet to be determined. The town of Bitola would probably remain outside Serbian territory, though.

The Serbs insisted that they had historical and national rights to the territories they were being asked to give up. It was clear that the Serbian government was hedging its bets and considered the sacrifice to be a temporary inconvenience. They also put forth the following conditions: (1) Bulgaria must immediately attack Turkey and help the Allies conquer Constantinople and the Straits, and (2) In addition to everything else, the Allies must promise the Serbs Croatia with Fiume, the western part of the Banat, and the Morava River valley. The Slovene lands should be free to choose their own allegiance. There were additional clauses, including the recognition of Serbia as a full Allied power, with the concomitant right to participate at the peace conference at the end of the war and free access to the Aegean for Serbian goods. The handover of Macedonia could take place only after Serbia gained control of its new territories and the rights of the remaining Serbian population in Macedonia were fully guaranteed.

I was bitterly disappointed with the Serbian reply. Although I had expected little from this affair the English had started, I had worked hard to achieve the seemingly impossible. I had kept my hopes up until the last minute, and now all was lost. Above everything else, I could not forgive Pašić his unnecessarily cunning remark that I would be happy with the Serbian note. Consequently, in retaliation, I stopped my daily visits to him and communicated only with Iovanović. Even though I went on suggesting to Petrograd how best to affect the Serbs, I had no hopes of success. My insistence on the need to dispatch an Allied force to the Vardar-Salonika line met with little approval. I expressed my views in a private letter to A. A. Neratov, a friend of the foreign minister, on August 23, 1915:

> I have tried to keep the Foreign Ministry informed about the difficulties the hitherto unsuccessful negotiations have been fraught with. For my part, I

did everything I could, endeavoring to bring about a successful resolution of the issue until the very end, even though I was aware there was only the slightest hope of success. I found the way the Serbian response was presented more shocking than its content, and I am sorry to say I failed in my mission. Although the border the Serbs propose is not what the Allies had in mind, one has to admit that they are indeed making a big sacrifice. We can ascribe the Serbian irritation to Pašić's unhappiness with the Allies, who discussed Serbian interests without even conferring with him. The handover of the entire Banat to Rumania, coming after Pašić had been assured Serbian interests in the area would be respected, was particularly painful. The Serbs now believe that the neutral powers negotiating with the two warring sides simultaneously are being rewarded for their cynicism and that only a firm Serbian stance against the Allies would allow them to make a profit from the war.

Pašić was especially sensitive on the Macedonian Question, as he firmly opposed the Agreement of 1912, which had been concluded by the late Milovanović. At the time, he refused to have anything to do with it. Coming to power after the death of Milovanović, he violated the agreement even prior to the outbreak of the Balkan War. On September 15/28, 1912, he informed Serbian diplomatic representatives abroad of his intention to annex Prilep and Okhrid. Pašić is ready to make certain concessions, but there were certain limits beyond which he was unwilling to go. This explains why he was prepared to tender his resignation if the Allies continued to press him. Iovanović told me Serbia should agree to an Allied—preferably Russian—delimitation of the border between Serbia and Bulgaria along the lines of the Agreement of 1912. However, he was outvoted on this.

As I write these lines, the Entente powers may well have decided on a course of action, in which case my observations, which I transmitted earlier today via telegraph, would be too late. I believe we can still influence with threats or promises. Whether Pašić stays or goes is immaterial; in any event, he will not budge. It is, of course, possible that an even more intractable man might come to power. We would have to change the conditions of our note if we want the Serbs to accept it. We have to bear in mind that Serbia's complaints are not entirely unreasonable. They are being promised territories as yet unconquered; besides, their acquisition would not alter the fact that they are expected to abide by impossible borders in three directions. The current war is still raging, and yet they are being faced with the possibility of three future wars—against Italy, Rumania, and Bulgaria. Serbia has to have at least one secure border. Since the handover of Macedonia to Bulgaria is the crux of the issue, we need to settle the question of the common border between Greece and Serbia and make sure Bulgaria does not gain an outlet on the Adriatic. The vague phrases in the Allied note about this are entirely unsatisfactory. Only the division of Albania between Greece and Serbia and a border running to the Adriatic would be tempting enough to persuade the Serbs to give up Macedonia.

I am sorry to say that we have given our allies a little too much leeway in the Balkans since the beginning of the war, especially given their regrettable lack of sufficient knowledge about the Balkan Question, whose resolution has been piecemeal. We needed Italy, so we made it offers of territory without conferring with Serbia or Greece. Then we needed Rumania, so we pretended Serbia did not exist. Lastly, we needed Bulgaria. Like it or not, we had to approach Serbia on this occasion, but we made a mistake yet again. We had to ensure Bulgaria's participation before talking to the Serbs or, conversely, ensure Serbia's willingness to give up the required territories before talking to the Bulgarians. I have sent plenty of telegrams to Petrograd about this. Instead of following my advice, they made two simultaneous statements that proved impossible to reconcile. Now nobody knows what to do, least of all the English, who were the main proponents of this course of action. Now we are facing a dead end.

How do we get out? I see no way out other than forcing Italy to cede Albania to Serbia and sending an Allied force to Macedonia. The only way to deal with the Balkans is to speak softly but carry a big stick. Otherwise, it would be impossible to influence Bulgaria. Give it as much as possible but pressure it to join the war on the side of the Allies. Otherwise, Bulgaria's neighbors will be offended, and Bulgaria will still end up siding with our enemies. Bulgaria will follow us only if we pair our concessions with very tangible threats.

As I write this, I fear my letter may be too late or, worse, I may have overlooked some important factor. Please do not be offended by my frankness. I think joint action between the Austro-Germans and Bulgarians is quite possible. This would mean the defeat of our Balkan policy and threaten enormous consequences . . .

Apart from this, I have a personal issue. What am I to do in case of an Austro-German invasion of Serbia, which would cut off my communications with Salonika and the Danube? Go to Montenegro along with the Serbian government? The Montenegrin roads are impassable, and I have been unable to ride a horse since injuring my knee as a young man. The prospect of Ipek in the late autumn makes Niš seem like heaven on earth. In any event, I hope God will spare us such adversity. My fate is entirely in His hands.

The situation was becoming increasingly tense. The Allied powers put pressure solely on Serbia, while attempting to cajole the Bulgarians. I believed this policy to be unsound and dangerous. On the same day I wrote to Neratov, I sent a telegram to Petrograd, expressing the need to unite Greece, Serbia, and Rumania and to tell the Bulgarians plainly that the Allied powers would no longer tolerate Bulgarian neutrality. To this end, the Allied powers would have to occupy the Vardar-Salonika line immediately. I added the following:

> The English have led the Entente powers to a dead end with their half-baked schemes. We have to find a way out of this impasse urgently. Otherwise, joint action between the Austro-Germans and Bulgarians will add a very real defeat to the moral failure of the Allies in the Balkans. The creation of a direct link between our enemies and Turkey via Bulgaria would mean the end of the operation in the Dardanelles. This, in turn, would enable Turkey to transfer significant forces to the Caucasian front. It would also mean we are unable to persuade Rumania to join us.

Alas, my telegrams did not receive the slightest attention. On the contrary— the English continued their game in Sofia, disregarding the fact that the Count of Mecklenburg had already arrived there in order to conclude the alliance between Germany and Bulgaria. The famous General Savov made a number of Germanophile statements in the press. All this was taking place while we suffered ignominious defeat after ignominious defeat, losing fortresses previously believed to be impregnable. It was, of course, this military situation rather than our diplomatic blunders that drove Bulgaria to our enemies' camp. At the same time, we had to refrain from behaving in such an undignified manner.

I sent several telegrams along these lines. "If we are unable to threaten Bulgaria while simultaneously assuring it of the exact territorial concessions it might expect from Serbia and, perhaps, Greece," I telegraphed on August 29, "we will not win Bulgaria over and will only alienate governments currently favorably disposed toward us. We must do nothing to weaken our position through statements that are not backed up by a threat of force." Two days later, on August 31, I telegraphed, "We must be careful about the preservation of Allied dignity. Our enemies have been taking advantage of every single Allied diplomatic blunder, raising doubts even in Serbia about Allied victory and about our attitude toward Serbia's interests."

Soon after receiving Pašić's reply to the Allied offer, I was saddened to part with my wonderful colleague Strandtmann, who was being posted to

Rome as first secretary to the embassy there. I was also glad for him and his family because he was leaving Niš for good and would not have to face the approaching storm. B. N. Pelekhin, formally first secretary in Montenegro, replaced him in Niš.

The news from Sofia was getting worse. As early as August 6, Savinskii telegraphed to Petrograd that a pro-Russian Bulgarian member of Parliament from Radoslavov's party had told him confidentially that Radoslavov had decided not to accept the Allied terms and was preparing to launch an attack on Serbia. Around this time, Zhekov replaced General Fichev as Bulgarian minister of war. Fichev, a temperate man, had been telling the Serbs they had nothing to fear as long as he was minister of war; he would rather resign than go along with a change of government policy. Naturally, this change of personnel appeared ominous to the Serbs.

Now Zhekov confidentially told the same member of Parliament that he would attack any country except Turkey. Savinskii wrote that the fall of Kovno had been a blow to our friends and a boon to the Germans, who were trying to prove to anyone willing to listen that the Russian army had been defeated decisively and that the Entente was lost.

German-bought newspapers were loaded with propaganda saying that Russia was rotting from within and would fall soon because of an impending revolution. I am utterly convinced that these declarations played a bigger role in persuading the Bulgarians than news of our actual defeats. I suspect they reasoned along the following lines: Russia will not be able to stay in the war much longer; there will be revolution; we will attack not Russia but Serbia, defeat it with the help of the Germans, annex all territories we require, establish hegemony in the Balkans, and then turn to Russia's new rulers, saying: "We fought against the old government, which you deposed. They are to blame for all evils and misfortunes." Ferdinand, who always feared and detested Russia, saw an opportunity to do away with his two-faced policy, openly throw his lot in with the Germans, and strengthen the monarchy with the help of Wilhelm. Savinskii wrote on August 8, and both he and the Russian military representative were being told by reliable sources that Bulgaria intended to join our enemies. These sources stated that King Ferdinand had visited Radoslavov and told him it was time for Bulgaria to make a decision and attack Serbia. To this end, he had authorized Radoslavov to change those ministers who were opposed. Nevertheless, this all seemed so incredible that, at first, Savinskii believed the Bulgarians were bluffing in order to extract bigger concessions from the Serbs and to convince the Turks to agree to a favorable adjustment of the border, which would provide a direct railway connection between central Bulgaria and Dedeagach.

I do not intend to write about what happened in Bulgaria. I was not fully apprised of the course of events at the time, and I do not consider this to be my task.

On September 1, the Allied powers made a written declaration in Sofia guaranteeing them the uncontested zone of Macedonia as per the Agreement of 1912, provided that Bulgaria concluded a military agreement with the Allies and promised to attack Turkey in the near future. If an answer did not come soon, then the Allies would assume that Bulgaria wanted no part and would consider their offer null and void. The note did not refer to an Allied occupation of the Vardar Line because "it was unpleasant to Bulgaria. If, however, this were not the case, the Allies would proceed to occupy said line immediately."

An answer never came. Instead, on September 8, Bulgaria began to mobilize. They reassured the Allies that this was to preserve armed neutrality. Even this late, our friends in Sofia continued to insist that it was possible to prevent a Bulgarian declaration of war if Serbia immediately ceded Macedonia to Bulgaria. Unfortunately, the Allied governments shared this view. On September 8, St. Petersburg instructed me to "appeal to Pašić's trusted reasonableness" and advise the Serbs to "avoid doing anything the Bulgarian government might interpret as a provocation and, if possible, refuse to engage in fighting." On September 10, I received another telegram from St. Petersburg urging me to somehow convince Pašić to immediately cede Macedonia to the Allies according to the Agreement of 1912.

When news of Bulgaria's mobilization reached Niš, the Serbs, strangely enough, felt relieved. Pašić commented to me that this should now clear the prevailing atmosphere in the Balkans. The Serbs were under the impression that the Bulgarian army was insufficiently equipped. Serbia was prepared to attack, whereas Bulgaria would take longer to mobilize its forces. They also underestimated the strength of the Austro-German forces earmarked for an invasion of Serbia. The French aviators attached to the Serbian army also supported this misapprehension. Izvolskii, our ambassador in Rome, reported to Sazonov that both Delcassé and Joffre mistakenly believed that the Germans had no interest in attacking territories in the Balkan Peninsula.[3] According to French aviators' reports, there were no military preparations in the Banat. Whatever bombardments there were at the present time along the Danube were to impress Bucharest and Athens and encourage Bulgaria to invade Serbia.

The actions of the Greek government seemed to vindicate Serbian optimism. Greece responded to the Bulgarian mobilization by also mobilizing. Prime Minister Venizelos asked the Allies for 150,000 troops, hoping that he might then be able to persuade the king to honor the existing alliance between Greece and Serbia. France and England promised to send forces if the Bulgarians attacked Serbia.

In the circumstances, Serbian representatives to the Allied governments urged the immediate dispatch of an auxiliary force. At the same time, they advocated a Serbian preemptive attack on Bulgaria. Neither of these suggestions met with much success.

Delcassé informed the Serbian ambassador that France was ready to send forces to Greece.

"This decision might provoke the Bulgarians to see reason yet," he wrote to Izvolskii on September 10/23. "I must therefore advise the Serbs not to take any initiative. If they do not heed this advice and do make that first step, then France and the Allied powers could change their minds."

Sazonov was much more direct. When the Serbian ambassador in St. Petersburg spoke of the advantage of attacking Bulgaria first, Sazonov said in answer:

> I would regard a Serbian initiative against the Bulgarians as a criminal act in the same way as an attack by the latter, which we want to forestall. Until such time, they are guaranteed the support of the Allies, Greece, and perhaps even Rumania. Together this represents a large-scale force. If the Serbs decide on an unalterable course of action, Greece and the Allies will not lend their support. Under such circumstances, even a victory over Bulgaria will not be a guarantee for the future. Serbia, weakened by its conflict with Bulgaria, will stand alone against the Germans, who will become overlords of the Balkans.

I received the contents of the above in a telegram from Sazonov on September 12. It was suggested that I convey this same message to Pašić "using the strongest words." On the same day, Pašić wrote to his minister to Russia:

> It seems that our allies do not clearly grasp the situation in the Balkans and do not realize the significance of Bulgarian mobilization. What the Allies fail to see is that Bulgaria has already joined Germany and Turkey. That fact is bewildering to us. This is not the time to hesitate, negotiate, and advise. It is time for quick and decisive action. A whole year of negotiations has failed to bring about a rapprochement, and it is quite clear we will not achieve anything now. Bulgaria will continue the charade of negotiating until its armed forces are ready to attack. We know Bulgaria and the Balkans, and we are suggesting measures that can help us reach our goals. If the members of the

Triple Entente continue with their previous Bulgarian policy, everything will be lost, and Bulgaria will succeed in duping us all.

Pašić went on to suggest the following:

> Present Bulgaria with a 24-hour ultimatum to stop its mobilization After this time period, occupy Varna, Burgas, and Dedeagach. Immediately dispatch an Allied auxiliary corps to Serbia, including at least one Russian division via the Danube. Persuade Rumania to a joint action with Greece and Serbia.

Pašić concluded with the words that "the Serbian High Command will not be held responsible for the military catastrophe, which will inevitably materialize in the absence of immediate, decisive actions. The government shares this point of view and urges the Allies to endorse the above suggestions." I realized the Serbs were correct in arguing that their only chance lay in preempting Bulgaria's mobilization, which put me in an awkward position. My colleagues and I urged the immediate dispatch of Allied forces to Serbia, whereas the Foreign Ministry continued to instruct me to demand the immediate cession of Macedonia to Bulgaria and refuse to countenance military action. I considered it my duty to pass this on to Pašić, yet I realized that all was in vain. I wrote numerous telegrams to St. Petersburg, Stavka, and our embassies in Allied countries, expressing the urgent need to help Serbia militarily, lest the Austro-Germans succeed in establishing a direct connection with Turkey and destroy Serbia. "Failure by the powers to make an immediate decision to come to Serbia's aid," I wrote on September 11, "will allow the Austro-Germans to continue defeating Allied countries one by one. The Serbian catastrophe might have the direst consequences for the course of the general European war."

When I brought up the handover of Macedonia to the Allies, Pašić told me it was too late for this. The possibility of concessions would only weaken the parliamentary opposition in Bulgaria.

On September 13, Pašić agreed to wait eight to ten days before doing anything. This way, he said, Serbia would know whom it could count on. He hoped that the Allies would come to a concrete decision regarding Bulgaria.

The Allies' suggestions achieved little.

"Our insistence merely stirs up resentment over here," I telegraphed on September 14, "since the importance of self-defense was paramount. It is impossible to accuse the Serbs of treachery for refusing to allow the Bulgarians to complete their military preparations, which are clearly aimed at Serbia. People here note bitterly that we are the only Allied power that has refused to dispatch even a small force or recognize that the Serbs had the right to defend themselves. I realize that, in this decisive moment, it is painful to accept that the Bulgarians are traitors. However, I consider it my moral duty to emphasize how dangerous hesitation is and how it only makes Ferdinand's government more secure. We need to issue an ultimatum."

In the meantime, the crisis was quickly worsening. Serbian optimism did not last long. Rumania was clearly reluctant to commit. Brătianu specified that if the Allies were to send four hundred thousand men to the Balkans, Rumania might scrap its neutrality and join them. In Greece, the gap between Venizelos, so straightforward and noble in character, and his two-faced, scheming king was widening. Fearful of Germany, the king found support in the military and in the conjecture that the Greek army would prove to be inadequate during a conflict.

The king's party wanted to keep away from the impending Balkan catastrophe. This attitude led to a highly selective interpretation of Greece's allied responsibilities to Serbia, whereby these could allegedly be invoked only in a purely Balkan conflict—that is, solely against Bulgaria. A simultaneous war against Austria and Germany seemed to alter the bases of the military alliance between Greece and Serbia.

King Constantine received the Bulgarian minister plenipotentiary on the day after the Bulgarians began to mobilize. The German military attaché in Athens had spent the time leading up to this in Sofia. Whereas Venizelos took on a clearly pro-Entente stance, Radoslavov insisted that Bulgaria had nothing to fear from Germany and Rumania. For his part, King Constantine maintained that Bulgaria would not attack Greece, which gave the impression that a rapprochement between Germany and Greece had taken place behind the prime minister's back. The king prevaricated and endeavored to dupe Venizelos.

There was a clash of natures between King Constantine and his prime minister. Venizelos was a man of ideals and achievement. He was an island unto himself. Fiercely patriotic, he pursued the idea of a Hellenic union and, until recently, a tightly woven alliance of Balkan governments. Convinced of the effectiveness of his ideals, he never strayed and believed firmly in their legitimacy. It was he who reconciled the Greek people with their future king and brought Constantine, then heir to the throne, back from exile. He did this for the good of Greece and not for any sense of loyalty to the dynasty. He himself was of the people, loving them with all his heart. The people were drawn to him, believed in him, and accepted his ideas. The king found this insufferable. He too made himself popular by putting the past behind and then gaining South Macedonia with Salonika and Kavalla and Epirus for Greece. Not being a nation of military prowess, the Greeks cherished the laurels of victory their armies had achieved under King Constantine as head of the army. The people regarded him as another Napoleon, crowning him with laurels. History will judge the price of this laurel wreath. During the war with Bulgaria in 1913, the Greek position was critical. It was the advance onto Sofia by Rumania and the peace accords that saved Greece. I had heard this from the most knowledgeable people.

The king basked in this glory, but Venizelos stood in his way. The Greek people did realize the input and wisdom of their prime minister. He was, after all, one of the architects of the Balkan League, bringing about at a later time the union of Serbia and Rumania following the duplicity of Bulgaria.

The antipathy the king felt for this popular man of the people was echoed by his wife. Being the sister of Kaiser Wilhelm, she remained German to the end. She still could not forgive the fact that she was forced to leave Greece with her husband, only to return at the mercy of this same Venizelos. That was demeaning.

Envy is truly characteristic of a superficial nature. King Constantine, in contrast to Venizelos, was far from being a prominent kind of person. Besides, he always admired Germany, especially its military. His wife, of course, fueled his emotions. I must say that Allied policy in the Balkans did appear to be tentative and was full of mistakes demonstrating more weakness than there was in reality. Germany, on the other hand, gave the impression of being stronger in its initiatives than it actually was. On the one hand, you had digression, discord, and indecision; on the other, organization, unity, and planning. Thus it was that Germany was able to make an impression on the Balkan countries. It was this very German magnetism that won Bulgaria over and clouded Rumanian judgment for a long time. King Constantine was also susceptible to it.

As I have stated before, he did not dare to oppose Venizelos openly. On the contrary, he gave him every possibility of initiating mobilization and of discussing reinforcements with the Allies. Venizelos believed his policy was gaining the upper hand and got a bit carried away in Parliament. He openly stated that Greece should remain true to its alliance with Serbia even if this meant a direct clash with Bulgaria, Austria, and Germany. As we know, the king disavowed him, and Venizelos resigned.

Luckily, by then, Allied forces had already arrived in Salonika; otherwise, the hesitation of the English would have ended all hopes of a future restoration of Serbia, which alone sustained the spirit of this unfortunate nation through the subsequent trials and tribulations. The ministerial crisis in Greece had a disquieting effect on the Serbs; it was difficult for them to contain their anger. They had to put up with it, in order not to increase the number of open enemies. They took to the hope of the impending arrival of French forces like a drowning man grasping at straws. They gave up the thought of preempting Bulgarian mobilization in the hope that Greece would join them against Bulgaria. Pašić advised the Serbian High Command to this effect.

Belgrade sustained vicious artillery bombardments. It was occupied by Austro-German forces. The Serbs fought back intensively. Even after the city was occupied there was fighting in the streets, in homes. Our hospitals in Niš were filled with wounded soldiers. One such veteran, a *komitadj*, handed a grenade to a nurse to keep, saying, "It might come in handy."[4]

Another feverish *komitadj* pulled a hand grenade from his pocket and threw it with all his might. Luckily, it fell into a pile of laundry in the corridor and did not blow up. Serbian soldiers almost shed tears at the mention of German artillery. They were most certain of themselves as soldiers.

"Were it not for the might of German artillery!"

"German soldiers could not have withstood combat with bayonets!"

It was only after the occupation of Belgrade that the Serbs realized they had underestimated the actual strength of Austro-German forces. French reinforcements, expected every day in Niš, did not arrive. In the meantime, Niš was decorated with flags to keep up morale. The impression, with which they forever left me, was that of a sickly, tentative smile. These flags, mounted on September 23, remained for ten days. No one wanted to take them down, not even when it became clear that the French were not coming.

Hopes for French assistance were sustained by the French minister, Bopp. An intelligent and reasonable man, he was also quite nervous and suffered from frequent mood swings. A staunch Serbophile, he detested the Bulgarians and hoped that France would save Serbia. He believed it his duty to keep up the Serbian morale and even presented himself to his government in this way, implying that all other Allied ministers were defeatists and fearful. This resulted in a scandal between Bopp and his secretary, who told my aide the French minister was passing on an exaggerated view of the situation. Naturally, I kept this information to myself and did not let it affect my excellent working relationship with Bopp.

As for myself, I strove to keep calm and controlled. I thank God for His help at this time.

I was able to remain calm to the very end in spite of the overwhelmingly difficult conditions. I was to pay dearly for this with my health upon my future return to Russia on leave.

We presented our ultimatum to Bulgaria on September 21, if I am not mistaken. For once we did not waver in our usual way, and our diplomacy took on a tone worthy of Russia:

> The Minister Plenipotentiary from Russia, associated with Bulgaria from the time of its liberation from the Turkish yoke, cannot remain in a country where preparations are underway for a fratricidal attack on an allied Slavic people. The Imperial Minister Plenipotentiary has received orders to leave Bulgaria with the entire mission and consular staff during the next twenty-four hours if the Bulgarian government fails to openly break off relationships with the enemies of Slavism and of Russia and dismiss from its ranks officers of those countries now at war with the Allied forces.

Unfortunately, just a few days before, Savinskii had come down with acute appendicitis and was immobilized. Upon receipt of this news, I sent one of our most experienced nurses to Sofia. By then there was no railroad connection between Niš and Sofia. The nurse was brought to the Bulgarian border by car and from there, by train. Despite some frightening moments along the way, the Bulgarians treated her very well.

The following event also took place during this difficult time. Various transport ships carrying supplies to Serbia from Russia went along the Danube under the supervision of Veselkin. He wanted to stop all deliveries at the beginning of September, but the Serbs begged him to reconsider. I supported their request, which was granted. In the meantime, on September 19, St. Petersburg informed me that our chargé d'affaires in Sofia had been instructed to deliver an ultimatum to the Bulgarian government. There was no time to lose.

Since I did not have a chance to confer with Veselkin, I immediately suggested to the commander of the convoy on its way back to Russia to intercept the next convoy sailing toward Serbia and persuade them to return to port. At the same time, I telegraphed Veselkin, explaining I had to speak directly with one of his deputies in the interest of time. I feared that the Bulgarians might detain the incoming convoy as it was sailing along their shores; in any event, it would be difficult for the ships to return safely to port later on. Regrettably, Veselkin was far too concerned with his own importance, and he telegraphed the commander of the convoy to disregard my order and continue on its way to Serbia. He relayed this to me, adding that, in the future, he expected me to contact him personally rather than one of his deputies. As I could not let the matter rest, I sent a detailed description of the whole affair to St. Petersburg, explaining that interdepartmental wrangling was ill advised in fateful moments such as these. Unfortunately, my fears came true. The Bulgarians detained several ships from the convoy, confiscated their supplies, and took our officers and crew prisoner, thereby initiating hostilities. I soon forgot about this incident, as I had far more important matters to consider.

During this difficult time, as the clouds gathering over Serbia became more and more threatening, there were rumors of growing Serbian annoyance with the Allies and with Russia. I was well aware of my weakened position. Obviously, the basic causes for the present situation in the Balkans were not our own mistakes no matter how great or small, or even the mistakes of Allied diplomacy but, rather, the military failures with which we were confronted. They made our army seem completely ineffectual and on the verge of disintegration. The situation was further compounded by Ferdinand and the attitude of his government toward Russia and Serbia. For us, the representatives of mediators and creators of unsound policies, our task seemed at times to be unbearable.

I have already expressed my frustrations at the diversity of the dispositions given to me. At this point, I should like to outline my personal relationship with S. D. Sazonov, the minister of foreign affairs at that time. I loved him fiercely and respected him. He, in turn, treated me very well. At times I even felt that he overestimated me. Our relationship began when he invited me to return to the diplomatic service as head of the Near Eastern Department. I accepted this most tempting offer with some misgivings. The prospect of service and civil obedience seemed somewhat disconcerting, as I had got quite used to my unfettered independence. Thus it was that at the height of the Balkan conflict, in the autumn of 1912, I became head of the Department of the Near East.

I would see Sazonov several times a day, for long periods of time. All relevant affairs—instructions to our ambassadors abroad, analysis of their reports and telegrams from abroad—were discussed by Sazonov, Neratov, and me. By developing respect for each other, by reaching common understanding and unity of thought, we established a solid working relationship. It is with gratitude that I look back upon those two years I spent working in the Ministry of Foreign Affairs. I could not conceive of a more ideal relationship than the one that pervaded the atmosphere of the office where we met every morning.

Sazonov was an intelligent and, above all, an educated person. There was nothing of the petty civil servant in him. His main strength and charm lay in his scrupulous nature. His was a straightforward and incorruptible Russian soul, honest and noble. These are the qualities that made his name in history.

He was not very discerning in the internal affairs of Russia. He viewed Russia through the eyes of his brother-in-law Stolypin.[5] After the death of Stolypin, Sazonov became more perceptive. He was a liberal conservative, eventually leaning to the left. It was this reputation of being close to the Kadets[6] that, in the end, became the reason for his dismissal from the government. In reality this sincere, open, and honest person was unable to become attuned to the majority of his colleagues in the cabinet. He was too much the nobleman and too European in his ways, finding it difficult at times to curb his irritation at their deceit and unscrupulous ways.

If he was able to keep his position for several years, it was because the tsar saw in him a devoted person worthy of his trust, whose loyalty was true and not self-seeking. In other words, he was dependable.

Sazonov would repeatedly say to me: "I want very much for you to get to know the tsar and to love him. If only you knew him, it would be impossible not to love him. The trouble lies with his entourage. We should do everything possible to promote good people near him."

He was well regarded by the tsar during their routine sessions. However, once the tsar departed from Russia to take command in the Stavka, that regard was lost. The tsar came under the influence of the empress, who visited him often during this time. The empress, in turn, was often influenced by various courtiers. Sazonov became the victim of these court intrigues.

Sazonov was respected throughout Europe for his moral principles. He was friendly—although, on the flip side of the diplomatic coin, this was not very apparent. This quality, however, was the key to his success. He gained the trust of the English, correcting their inherent view of an imperialist Russia bent on creating a worldwide "cossackdom."*

As the Balkan crisis served to underline our policy of peace, so it accentuated the belligerence of Germany. Being cautious, Sazonov grasped and trusted the legacy of Stolypin that Russia needed a long and lasting peace. Only in July 1914 did he finally acknowledge that it would be impossible to preserve the peace without losing face and that conflict was inevitable. As it was, the calamitous events of that July and the formidable reaction of society pointed to only one course of action, from which there was no return. History put Sazonov in the midst of events of world importance. He passed this test with flying colors, earning the motherland's justified respect. Such were the good deeds of a man I dearly loved. He had deficiencies of character, but so does everyone.

Sazonov was aware of being insufficiently prepared for the post of minister of foreign affairs. His only other posting of any consequence was that

---

* Trubetskoi coined the word *okazachits* defining this as a Cossack-dominated world. Tr.

of a counselor at the embassy in London. Although this was not considered an important posting, he nonetheless was privy to a wide political arena of international affairs. The rest of the time was spent in Rome, first as a secretary, then as ambassador to the Vatican. He had never occupied any of the eastern postings and therefore had no experience in local conditions, mores, or interests. Sazonov did not know the Balkans; neither did he have a grasp of the prevailing conditions or of the psychology of local leadership. Therein lay the crux of his mistakes. I must, however, stress that there were some achievements, the greatest one of which was drawing Rumania away from the Triple Alliance and persuading it to join our side. Admittedly, he overestimated Rumania's importance, but he was not alone in this.

I mentioned earlier that, soon after the start of the war, Sazonov readily understood that some kind of policy decision about the Straits was uppermost in the minds of Russian society. He capitalized on the mood in the Duma and secured Allied recognition of our rights to Constantinople and the Straits. This, too, was an achievement of his, although I must add that this diplomatic success did not garner much applause.

The very idea that Russia could increase its sphere of influence in Constantinople and in the Straits truly terrified Ferdinand and his entourage. Until now, he was certain that England would never allow Russia to attain this longtime ambition. However, once the Bulgarians—even those who were not necessarily enemies of Russia—realized that England would not oppose Russia on this, they became apprehensive and hostile. The Balkan conflict brought closer to Bulgaria the mirage of Constantinople. Bulgaria also feared that a neighboring presence of Russia would encroach on its independence, resulting in the end of Bulgarian dreams of hegemony in the Balkans. Our enemies fully exploited these sentiments with anti-Russian propaganda. As far as I am concerned, this recognition of our territorial rights to Constantinople and the Straits was fatal. We undermined the only means to an end, which would have been to do this through the Bulgarians. We now found ourselves in a vicious circle, which we could have broken had the war gone our way.

Ever since the spring of 1915, there were a number of setbacks that escalated into significant debacles for us, further motivating our enemies in Bulgaria. At this point, our allies exploited their magnanimity in conceding to us Constantinople, from which they themselves, by the way, were far-flung. During the talks with Italy and Rumania and on the Serb-Bulgarian Question, they demanded concessions. How could we balance these against the idea of Constantinople?

So it was, that, unfortunately for us and for the Allied cause, we lost control of the Balkan situation. This theater of conflict should have remained in our hands. Instead, it was monopolized by the French and the English who had no inkling of the actual situation.

England's obvious dilettantism in its military and political judgments in the Balkans cost her several ships and one hundred thousand army personnel in the Dardanelles alone. Grey, to make matters worse, showed characteristics of a stubborn and a narrowly pedantic propagandist.

When it came to territorial concessions, our allies conveniently shed their principles regarding the rights of nations. Like a clumsy tailor, they cut up lands into shapeless patterns. Later, as it became clear that Allied negotiations with Bulgaria were not going well at all, they stalled and hesitated, incapable of taking a firm stand. During this last phase we, too, were to blame for keeping the Serbs back from attacking Bulgaria while they had the advantage, although, in retrospect, I rather doubt that this would have changed anything at all.

There was no way that the Serbs could have forestalled an Austro-German march to Turkey. Neither could they have defended themselves against heavy artillery. On the other hand, who knows? Had the Serbs defeated Bulgaria, what would Greece and Rumania have done? Certainly the Serbs would have gained time for Allied help to arrive. All in all, we took on too much responsibility, which we really did not need.

I thought then, and I think now, that Sazonov was influenced by my replacement in the Department of the Near East, K. N. Gulkevich.[7] He was an unerring Bulgarophile who harbored illusions of winning Bulgaria over.

At times I was disheartened, realizing that my reports and suggestions, sent in telegram form time and time again, were being virtually ignored and tossed into a wastebasket. I wrote to Gulkevich and to Schilling, requesting that I be removed immediately since my opinion was obviously of no consequence. If I were to remain, then would they kindly change their attitude toward me?

I lost a lot of time over these worries and cares. My free moments were spent in the company of dear Bishop Dosifej, riding around the charming countryside of Niš. His Grace was my consolation and support. We rarely discussed politics, although the looming danger enveloping Serbia was certainly an unavoidable reality. He told me outright that it was his intention to remain with his flock no matter what. He was determined to share their sorrows, their fears and sufferings, and to defend them to the end. He emanated a pure, clear, and almost childlike soul. He certainly kept his decision.

One of my favorite excursions in the vicinity of Niš was to a little oratory in Grabovac. One time, the bishop and I were traveling in that direction, when we heard the sound of a record player come from the hill above the road. "A very kind young doctor who works at the hospital of Chele-Kule lives there," the bishop told me. "Would you like to meet him? He was educated in Russia and would be happy to get to know you. He is spending the summer in a tent up on the hill." This is exactly what we did. We got off the cart and walked up the hill, where a very young man wearing a Serbian uniform came out to greet us warmly. He proceeded to show us around his small tent where he slept on a bunk bed. There was a small field kitchen in another tent, where the doctor's batman also lived. A couple of straw chairs and a record player completed the setting. He was fond of playing records in the evening after he had walked home from the hospital. You could hear the sound of music clearly from the hill. Peasants returning to their villages would stop their oxen and listen to the impromptu concert for a long time, until the doctor got fed up with it and shouted there would be no more music that evening.

We started talking to the kind young doctor, who was a graduate of our Military Medical Academy. He was married to the daughter of Prince Andronnikov, a Russian émigré.

"Do you know, our host came back from the dead once?" the priest inquired.

"Really?"

"Ask him to tell you his story."

We did not have to ask the doctor twice to hear a very interesting story. At the beginning of the war, he worked as a doctor in the hospital in Valjevo, a hamlet located in the mountains in the northwest of Serbia, where Serbian General Headquarters was based at the time. Owing to the Austrian advance, the Serbs were forced to gradually evacuate this part of the country in the autumn of 1914. The Austrians treated the local population horrendously during their first invasion. There were refugees everywhere, including a fair number in Valjevo. When Valjevo was being evacuated in turn, the head of the military hospital, Genčić, noted that the young doctor had vanished, and he dispatched people to look for him all over the town. Being rather fond of the young doctor, Genčić sent the men to look again after they had come back empty-handed. They went to the hospital, which was apparently empty. Finally, they found the doctor lying in the morgue with the other bodies. They carried the seemingly lifeless body outside, at which point it began to show signs of life. In time, the doctor was able to make a full recovery. He himself had no memory of his convalescence, coming to only for a brief moment to find himself lying next to another man who was foaming at the mouth. The doctor assumed he was next to a dead man and lost consciousness for the duration of his illness. Describing what had happened to him as "resurrection," the doctor added that, because of the severe shortage of medical personnel, many patients had been left to their own devices at the height of the epidemic. There weren't enough graves, and the cemeteries were overflowing with corpses.

But these reminiscences of individual episodes make me digress from the main matter.

7

RETREAT

By September 20, 1915, it became clear that Niš would be unable to hold out much longer. I needed to apprise myself without delay of the Serbian government's plans for evacuation, so that we could leave together. I also needed to organize the evacuation of the Russian mission and of course the entire Russian Red Cross medical personnel.

The initial government plan was to make for Monastir. Being closer, it was the most obvious location for a base of operations while awaiting Allied reinforcements from Salonika and thus was less likely to be cut off. From there Salonika and Santi Quaranti were easily reached.[1]

There was never much cooperation between the Serbian High Command and the government. Throughout all the events during the course of the war, they watched each other with guarded jealousy. Numerous calamities had befallen the country since the beginning of the war—shortages of war matériel and foodstuffs, unheard-of epidemics, Allied pressure to cede Macedonia to Bulgaria, false hopes of Greek or Allied military support, and finally, underestimation of enemy forces. In the wake of these setbacks, the military and civilian government blamed each other, holding the other responsible. Unwilling to compromise itself, each remained reluctant to make decisions. Consequently, when the time came to act, nobody ventured to make a decision or take full responsibility. The chief of staff was the rather senile and ill General Putnik, who retained his position because of his legendary reputation and popularity with the soldiers. It was his second in command, Colonel Živko Pavlović, who took over.[2] Although young and capable, he lacked authority with the more senior generals and with the venerable Pašić.

Allied military representatives, echoing the prevailing mood of the High Command, openly criticized Pašić for his involvement in the operations of war just before September 1915. This widened the gulf between the High Command and the government even more.

The Military High Command blamed Pašić for influencing government policy and abiding by Allied demands not to initiate an attack on Bulgaria. They viewed this as direct interference on the part of Pašić. They held him personally responsible for the failure of negotiations with the Allies and with Greece.

After Greece reneged on its treaty obligations, Serbia was forced to change its plans. To sustain a war on two fronts was not within Serbian means. The only solution was for the armies to retreat southward to join the Allied armies and get closer to a naval base. It was indecision on the part of France that dealt the bad hand at cards. Initially promising to dispatch reinforcements to Old Serbia, it wavered, and the eagerly awaited help in Niš about which I wrote earlier never arrived.

By now any kind of immediate aid from the French was impossible. To move troops all the way from France to Salonika and from thence into Serbia was time-consuming. The English wavered, skeptical about sending forces at all. The Serbs had desperately wanted the Allies to gather and come to their aid. When Sarrail, reluctant to send flagging forces into the Serbian interior for fear of their being cut off, changed the directives, the Serbian High Command would not reconcile itself to the reality and finality of this decision.[3] When the French indicated that the Serbs come to them for reinforcements and concentrate more on avoiding being cut off, Živko Pavlović kept insisting that the French come to Serbian aid in order to hold off the enemy advance into Old Serbia.

Another factor was in the national character of the Serbian army itself. More than once it proved to be first-class, brave, and true. In its essence, however, it acted more as a militia. The Serbian peasant would give up his life to defend his village and surrounding territories. He could not fathom the notion of surrendering his land without a fierce opposition. The same could be applied to the native psyche.

More than aware of this, both Pašić and Živko Pavlović were reluctant to abandon Old Serbia, the cradle of the Serbian nation, to complete destruction and retreat to Monastir and the new territories, where neither the soldiers nor the populace had any local ties.

Activity in Niš was minimal.

In the meantime, as was to be expected, the Bulgarians proceeded to cut off the railroad connection to Salonika, making evacuation to Monastir no longer an option. The Serbs did not rule out the idea of uniting their forces with those of the Entente; however, they continued to insist on the latter coming to their aid. I myself had no inkling what the Serbs would ultimately decide. How could I possibly proceed with concrete plans of evacuation to Salonika? Our doctors, hospital, and organizations were needed more than ever in Niš. I also had to consider the effects of a withdrawal of the Russian mission upon a population already feeling abandoned.

I was in daily contact with the doctors. They were in high spirits and wished to continue with their work. The quarantine barracks organized by my wife had been taken down back in August, and a first-class permanent hospital for contagious diseases had since been built. Dr. Spasskii had just finished organizing the different wings. When I approached him about evacuation, he and his medical staff refused to leave, opting for the risk of Bulgarian occupation. Dr. Sofoterov too decided to remain. As for the personnel of the Moscow Red Cross, I decided that they should evacuate. Most were not professional medics, and the young women had been entrusted to my wife by their families. All of them, however, asked to remain until the very last moment and then join the general retreat. We had a truck provided by the Serbs as well as wagons pulled by oxen for supplies.

The Serbian Council of Ministers met daily, launching into pointless discussions about whether to stay in Niš or leave and, if so, where to go. Their endless chatter covered up their very real anxieties. Whatever decisions were reached were then reversed at the next meeting.

Eventually, the foreign missions were notified to pack the bulk of their baggage for transport on October 1 to an unknown destination. Initially, at least, they seem to have decided on Monastir; I even telegraphed our consul there to expect me. The date of departure was set for October 4. It was postponed for lack of train cars, which had been appropriated to transport the army. In the meantime, the Bulgarians disrupted the railroad system to Salonika, making evacuation to Monastir no longer an option. That was to be expected.

It was decided finally to make for Kraljevo, the first stage of evacuation. The government core would remain in Niš. This halfway measure was utterly unsatisfactory, as Kraljevo was located along a narrow railway line, and its geography meant it could only be a temporary base. Each minister had an excellent new car imported from America and could therefore retreat at the very last minute. We split ourselves into two groups: the foreign legations went to Čačak, the next town just after Kraljevo. We left the next day, October 7, by train.

Before my departure, I said good-bye to our doctors and nurses in the hospital. It was an emotional moment. No one knew whether we would see each other again. I gave everyone an icon and thanked them for their hard work and willingness to remain at their posts until the last minute.

We traveled in comfort during the first part of this trip, in the restaurant car. The rest of the train was all freight cars occupied by the more privileged Serbians. They sat on their baggage or on the roofs. As the train started to move, I felt a wrenching in my heart as I glimpsed for the last time those who stayed behind, among them the kind Bishop Dosifej. Along the way we saw the first Bulgarian prisoners of war. These prisoners had crossed over the border into Serbia, stating their intentions not to fight against Russia.

In Kraljevo I was quartered in the house of one of the local notables, a man by the name of Bunjak. He had a clean one-story house with a large living room and a study the family used as a guest room, as is the local custom. My Swiss cook, who prepared the meals of the entire Russian diplomatic personnel, also stayed with me. The landlords accommodated him in a large room with a separate entrance from the backyard, where we all dined twice a day. At the time, there was no shortage of food in the area, and our cook prepared excellent meals, which kept our spirits high. Occasionally, we received visitors from Čačak.

The Serbian government had dispatched a representative of the Ministry of Foreign Affairs, Gruić, to serve as a liaison to the Russian mission. His function was to keep us updated on the political situation, so that we could pass the information on to our government. The tone of his daily missives grew increasingly more depressed. On October 9, we telegraphed the following:

The situation on our eastern front is critical, due to the lack of sufficient troop numbers. The Germans are advancing slowly but steadily, thanks to their superior artillery. In the east, the Bulgarians have taken over parts of the railway line Timok-Vranja-Kriva Palanka-Kumanovo-Kočani-Veles-Štip and cut off our communication with Salonika. The military authorities believe we might be able to check the Bulgarian advance if 120,000–150,000 Allied troops arrive via Salonika within ten days, pending the dispatch of larger reinforcements. However, we fear Allied reinforcements might be too late. . . . If Germany and Bulgaria succeed in overwhelming Serbia, the Allies would eventually require a much larger force to defeat the enemy in the Balkans. We make a final plea to the Allies. We have done everything we can and, if our plea is not answered, we can do no more.

The last sentence revealed the signs of desperation; however, it could also be interpreted as a sign of Serbia's willingness to make peace with the enemy. The Austrophile Liberals and certain military circles close to the Serbian High Command raised their voices in favor of peace, as it was impossible to continue the struggle. On October 13, Pašić yet again urged the Allies to repair the communications between their forces in Salonika and the Serbian army. In case they failed to do so, he warned, we could expect "catastrophic consequences in a country which could not be expected to face calmly the dire situation it finds itself in."

In these circumstances, Serbian Minister of Finance Paču, an intelligent old comrade of Pašić and one of the leaders of the Old Radical Party, died in a small resort close to Kraljevo.

After attending his funeral in Vranja, Pašić came to Kraljevo on the joint invitation of the Allied ministers. He was remarkably calm and upbeat, and we could see that his unshakable belief in the success of his just cause positively affected the High Command and his entourage. I asked him frankly about the dangerous popular sentiment and grumbling in favor of peace. Pašić replied that Serbia would hold out to the end, even if it were to suffer Belgium's fate. Personally, he was most worried about the English hesitation to send troops to Salonika, which was detrimental to the Entente as a whole and its fortunes in the Balkans.

Eventually, even Pašić began to lose his nerve. Two days after his visit to Kraljevo, the entire government arrived there, albeit temporarily. The prime minister continued to hope that the Allies would liberate Skopje and restore communications with the Serbian army.

But then the situation became even more critical, due to a sudden shortage of food.

Supplies of wheat were concentrated in areas either already taken over by the enemy or about to be. Even Kraljevo, whose mild climate usually produced abundant harvests, was affected. The entire nation became an endless stream of refugees, unable to find any food or a roof to sleep under.

There was barely enough to feed the army. Pašić begged the Allies to rush food supplies to Salonika or to Durazzo, in case the army had to relocate to Albania.

I received only the scantiest news about the plans of the Allies. The few telegrams I received from St. Petersburg revealed little, insisting only that I persuade the Serbs of the need to hold out to the end and that the Allies "are carrying out all measures necessary to come to Serbia's aid as soon as possible." What these measures entailed, however, was anyone's guess. A dark autumn descended. One gray foggy evening, there was a huge explosion in Kraljevo. The damp wintry sky became a red glow, lighting up the entire city. Next to the station, the gasoline supply was burning furiously. It was assumed that the fire was started deliberately by some prisoner of war. Prisoners of war were hardly guarded at all. I do not refer here to the

14. Prisren, 1915. Forgotten Austrian prisoner of war.

15. On the road from Kraljevo to Raška, 1915. Repairs.

Austro-Hungarian officers in Niš of whom, if I recall correctly, there were a little more than six hundred. They had been sent to Durazzo and from there to Italy. The regular prisoners who were put to work repairing roads needed for the retreat were generally supervised by an aging member of the home guard, or "chi-chi." To feed the prisoners became increasingly more difficult. Many escaped and rejoined their forces; those who remained tried to make their way to Albania, dying on the road from hunger and exposure.

We left Kraljevo for Raška when the enemy was twenty-five kilometers away. We had two cars and four trucks.

Speaking of prisoners of war, I need to mention the Russian ones who, having escaped from Austria and Germany, made it to Serbia. Before the communication between Niš, Salonika, and the Danube was cut off, plenty of escaped Russian prisoners of war made their way through Serbia to France, Switzerland, and Italy. Their stories resembled fantastic adventures full of bravery and intelligence. One of them, a noncommissioned officer escaped from Austria, nearly got me in trouble. He spent a couple of days in Niš en route to the Danube, where he was supposed to board a steamship bound for Russia. Walking around town, he encountered an Austrian officer in full uniform—a Slovene prisoner of war who worked in the hospital—with a nurse. Without much ado, our NCO "arrested" him and took him to the police station in indignation. "How well you treat Austrian POWs," he said. "How could you let an Austrian walk about town freely with a lady?" Both the Austrian and the hospital complained about the behavior of our soldier, who nonetheless remained indignant. He had, after all, lived through serious trials trying to escape from these very same Austrians.

During the last days of our stay in Niš, an escaped Russian prisoner who had crossed the Danube to Serbia was escorted to the mission. The Serbian sentries had encountered him by the river and opened fire, believing him to be an enemy soldier in spite of his earnest protestation to the contrary. Once they realized he was really Russian, though, they began fussing. He only had a flesh wound, and he quickly recovered. He took one of the last ships to Russia. The Serbs awarded medals of honor to all our POWs.

I found the story of one Russian officer—a Latvian from General Samsonov's army, who had been captured near Soldau in Germany—particularly impressive. He had refused to accept the churlish behavior of the overseer, a German NCO, who frequently pushed the prisoners around. Along with three other officers, he planned his escape in secret. They decided to dig a tunnel behind the stove in the spring, when the stoves were no longer in use. They dug for three months, until the tunnel appeared deep and long enough. One night, one of the officers went to the end of the tunnel and lay in wait for the sentry to move away from the barracks. Once the coast was clear, he alerted the others by raising a white flag. However, they decided to expand the tunnel further and worked one more week. Suddenly, the Germans, who appeared to suspect something was afoot, made a thorough search in the next barracks. The officers realized they had to make their escape as soon as possible, even though the full moon made this hazardous. In the night of August 17, 1915, they told their fellow prisoners about their plan and made their way out in pairs. Our man was one of the first out. He and his friend took to the nearby forest, walking at night and hiding by day. They ate roots and grain. One night, they were walking along a mountain path, when some German army cyclists inadvertently encountered them. A desperate struggle ensued. "A ginger German grabbed me, and we both fell to the ground, struggling. I saw his revolver hanging on a chain around his neck and tried to use the chain to garrote him. He let go of me, and I pushed him into the ravine. I went up to the path, where my mate had been struggling earlier but found no one. I still have no idea what happened."

He continued on his own, living in constant danger and suffering from starvation and the elements. After eighteen days, he reached some sort of a column with a sign. It seemed the Swiss border was close. "I went to the column and tried to make out the sign in the dark. Then, all of a sudden, I saw a man with a gun approaching the same column. I was scared, but it was clear that he, too, feared me. I realized that after my long trip I must look terrible in the night. The young sentry looked as if he had seen an apparition. I shouted; the German, too, shouted and fired in the air, possibly to call for help. I ran down the hill and hid in a field of rye. I waited for a long time before crawling back up to the column. I needed to find out where I was. I read the sign and discovered I was at the Swiss border. I had met the sentry on the Swiss side, before unknowingly running to the German side. I was saved. I walked down the road to the nearest village, where I revealed my identity. I was taken to Berne, where I spent two weeks at the hospital before going to Paris. Now I am headed to Russia."

As I recall the details of this story more than a year later, I am touched by the man's lot.

How much he had had to live through!

A stream of refugees passed through Kraljevo. I also encountered a Russian team of sailors who had been mining the Danube. On October 18, it was decided that the government and we should move to Raška.

Since there were in all twenty of us, I had to leave almost everything I had behind. In Kraljevo, I was able to have a fine pair of *valenki* [felt boots] made for me. I also managed to find a woman's woolen sweater and some chocolates for the road. These acquisitions would stand me in good stead later on. We were joined along the way by our Red Cross medical teams and by Dr. Sofoterov, with the Russian nurses in tow. They had come by way of Kruševac.

There was a confusing situation concerning the medical personnel in Niš just as the last Serbian forces were about to leave the city. The Serbian military hospital invited everyone to leave, and part of the remaining Russian medical personnel decided to follow this advice and move to Kraljevo. By this time, it was becoming increasingly clear that the retreat to an unknown destination would be excruciatingly hard, with little prospect or finding food or lodgings along the way. In light of this, I suggested that the Russian medical personnel return to Niš, and I telegraphed to St. Petersburg about the need to ensure their welfare was being looked after by a neutral government after they had fallen into captivity. At this point all semblance of order vanished.

Two nurses told the Serbian hospital authorities that they were willing to continue working and asked to be reassigned. They were told in no uncertain terms that Serbia needed Russian soldiers, not nurses. Admittedly, an enormous catastrophe had befallen the Serbs, which made them angry and irritable. Even under these extreme circumstances, however, the humble foreign-born volunteers who had dedicated themselves to their charitable work deserved at least a modicum of respect and attention. I instructed Dr. Sofoterov to look after their needs during the retreat, regardless of whether their legal papers were in order. This was no time to be punctilious.

We began to hear rumors about the Bulgarian occupation of Niš. There had been three lawless days between the Serbian retreat and the Bulgarian entry, when plenty of burglaries had taken place. Apprehensive of Bulgarian atrocities, Bishop Dosifej went out to meet them in full ceremonial garb. The Bulgarian commander allegedly dismounted and asked for the bishop's blessing. Things were quiet at first, but two days later the bishop and a trusted deacon were taken away to Bulgaria, to a monastery near Plovdiv. The following year, the bishop posted an open letter to Strandtmann in Rome, in which he sent me his regards. This is all I know about his whereabouts up till now (November 27, 1916). I decided not to write, in order not to put him in any danger. The route from Kraljevo to Raška between mountains was incredibly picturesque and the road not too bad. We passed crowds of refugees of all ages, position, and nationality. The indispensable Mamulov, sitting next to me, pointed out parliamentary deputies, civil servants, merchants, priests, teachers, well-to-do peasants; all of them on horseback, in oxen carts, in wagons, or simply walking. I recognized French doctors, English suffragettes; there was the ill-fated Admiral Traubridge striding along with some of his sailors. There were Russian doctors and nurses and Slavic refugees from Austria, who had come to Serbia at the beginning of the war. The air was filled with shouting and conversations in all sorts of languages and dialects. A common bond of humanity united them until the moment came for food or lodging, when it was quickly forgotten.

Raška was a tiny hamlet, like a swallow's nest, leaning against the foot of a mountain.

We were billeted with a pleasant young woman whose husband was in the army. She came from Bosnia, and in spite of her antipathy for the Krauts, her spotless apartment reflected Austrian etiquette. Determined to receive us with the maximum hospitality possible, she treated us in the morning to real Viennese coffee with cream. On my bed was a lace coverlet, the kind that Serbs use only for newlyweds or for some very special occasion. I was afraid to ruin it but was told that she would be offended if I did not sleep under it. She seemed to enjoy looking after us.

Upon our awakening and before breakfast, she brought us some delicious jam with water, as was the custom.

The house where we stayed was in a small square in the center of town. Cars and carts quickly filled the square as people arrived to spend the night.

There were several narrow streets going away from the square, and that was the whole town. We, diplomats, could not stay long in Raška, and it was with deep regret that we had to leave this lovely hospitable town, of which all of us retain the most pleasant memories. We had to make room for the Serbian High Command.

Our charming hostess insisted that we take two jars of jam with us so that the Krauts would not get them. When I gave each of her children a gold coin, she became red as a lobster from the idea that I was paying for my hospitality.

Raška was the last town within the borders of Old Serbia. The territories beyond twenty-five or thirty kilometers had been taken over by Serbia from the Turks in 1912. There was no time for improvement of roads.

To make matters worse, the autumn rains washed away parts of the winding road along the Ibara River. The going was rough. Automobiles were able to get through to Mitrovica somehow, but trucks struggled. A vehicle with the Greek chargé d'affaires tipped over on a curve. All the passengers were thrown, fortunately without injury, except for the manservant of the Italian ambassador, whose leg was broken. Poor Baron Schvitti, not being in the best of health himself, became totally dejected. This manservant had been with him for many years, and he just could not bring himself leave him behind. He arranged to transport the man to Prizren, where he would be looked after by the Catholic archbishop. The Greek chargé d'affaires, a self-important man, was offended to the depths of his diplomatic ego at being placed in a vehicle together with the manservant.

I had been in Mitrovica back in 1908 and compared it to what it was now. At that time, it was controlled by the Arnauts, who walked the streets armed from head to foot.[4] They were clean shaven with a warlock on top of the head. In all of Mitrovica at that time, only the Austrian and Russian consuls wore hats. At that time, I could not leave the city limits even for an excursion without a cohort of guards on horseback. The Turkish governor feared reprisals should something dire befall me. Although tobacco sales were forbidden in Turkey, it was sold openly in the streets of Mitrovica. The policy was not to upset the social order in Albania. The Mitrovica of 1908 was a throwback to the times and mores of something like the Zaporozhian Sich. Albania was a lawless place, and Mitrovica was a robbers' headquarters.

The first thing I noticed upon entering the town was that the architecture of Mitrovica had not changed. The only addition was a large stone military barracks the Young Turks had built shortly before the outbreak of the Balkan War. There were the same old Turkish homes with wooden grating in the windows and rotund second stories. I saw the same narrow dirty streets with open marketplaces; aged Turks in white turbans smoking water pipes and gazing indifferently at the noisy scene, oblivious to potential customers. This is where the comparison ended.

New rulers had replaced the previous ones. I did not recognize the once proud Arnauts.

Where had these young men—fiddling with their knives, pistols, and rifles—gone? Now the fire had gone from their eyes, and they kept their heads down. Does the erstwhile overlord tread so carefully?

This change was not simply due to the Serbian conquest of the area from the Turks—it was the consequence of the savage Serbian retaliation to the Albanian uprising at the end of the war, when entire villages disappeared from the face of the earth, and not even children were spared. How strange it was to see proud Arnauts now laboring under the orders of an unhappy shouting Serb.

Mitrovica was quickly filled with soldiers and refugees, and it became difficult to get around. I was placed in a home once occupied by the first Russian consul. He had been murdered by Arnauts just outside the city limits for interfering in their mistreatment of Serbs. My host was a Serb who cherished the memory of the late consul. My lodging was comfortable and a good size, but there was not the pleasant cleanliness of Raška and Kraljevo. Every room had bedbugs. I undertook drastic measures and moved my quarters to an unoccupied part of the house, which at one time had been a reception hall and was now a storage space for furniture. A portrait of the tsar and of Queen Victoria still hung on a wall. I bought a small iron stove in the marketplace.

The food situation was more problematic, even though the diplomats took their meals in the best so-called restaurant in town, which proudly bore the name The Bristol Hotel. There were really only two dark, rather squalid rooms befitting a poor village inn, where we were served a greasy roast pork dish every day. The only waiter was a soldier from the territorials who, tiring of responding to repeated shouts of *vojniče* [soldier boy] from disgruntled customers, quit. His place was taken over by a young lad, which only made matters worse. What could we do? To enhance our meals, I brought out champagne that I still had with me from Niš.

My foreign colleagues would gather in my room daily. We felt helpless. Whatever we gleaned in the way of news only added to our pessimism. To dispel our thoughts, we played bridge. My invariable partner was either Sir Charles Des Gras or the Rumanian military representative.

The military situation was such that to remain at length in Mitrovica became impossible. As before, there was no concrete decision where to go.

The Serbian government was still hoping for victory over the Bulgarians, with support from the Allies, and a movement southward to Monastir. In the meantime, winter was approaching. Rains completely ruined the roads. There were prisoners of war still available to repair roads, but which road—to Monastir or to Montenegro?

At this time, I received a visit from the Montenegrin minister plenipotentiary, Lazar Miušković. King Nicholas was concerned with our hopeless circumstances, especially those of the Russian minister, and desired to give me a medal of honor. I replied that I was most touched by the concern of the king and honored by this distinction. Could he possibly send us the horses and vehicles he had received the previous summer from Russia? I explained that, even though the Serbian government had not reached a decision yet, it might be a good thing to organize transportation now. Miušković proved most responsive. He sent a telegram to Cetinje, in response to which the king sent former Minister of Finance Popović to assess the situation.

Clearly, no matter which route we took, we would have to travel on very bad mountainous roads and paths. We would need to travel on horseback and hike on foot. I decided to start training myself. Because of a bad knee, I had not ridden a horse for twenty-three years. Furthermore, I had vertigo.

For my first excursion, I walked up Mount Svečan. This mountain is especially picturesque with its wide ravine opening from below providing a view of the white houses and minarets of Mitrovica at the foot of the mountain. The mountain itself rises as a sharp cone. At the very top there are ruins of an ancient fortress and castle where the king of Great Serbia, Stefan Dečanski, was choked to death.[5]

I went with Colonel Novikov, V. V. Semiannikova, and Sonia Gorbovaia. Halfway there, I felt sick and had to turn back. Whatever happened, I had to overcome this.

The next day I took the same route on horseback, riding an ill-behaved nag. Mamulov, my irreplaceable companion and now professor of equestrian sports, went riding with me. Popović the Montenegrin accompanied us as well. He wanted to see how I would cope and what I would need in the future. We went along steep winding trails, sometimes making our way along riverbanks. Little did I know that this was to be a foreshadowing of what was to come. Mamulov and I took excursions every day after that.

In the meantime, the commandant of Ferizovići Station, whose duty it was to organize transport for the diplomats, preferred to commit suicide. We did some serious thinking. Since the horses from Montenegro had not yet arrived, Mamulov and I decided to acquire horses from neighboring

Albanian villages. Initially, the Albanians treated us suspiciously, supposing us to be Serbian spies and fearing that their horses would subsequently be requisitioned. We displayed our money and demonstrated that we were willing to pay their prices. This worked well, and in no time at all we had a caravan of eight or nine horses. We had to leave behind our trunks and larger baskets. At the suggestion of Popović, we ordered longish wooden crates that could be attached to both sides of the saddles.

Finally, a decision was reached to evacuate all those in Čačak to Monastir via Prizren; that is, the secretaries and the Belgian minister with his family. The Belgian minister had to vacate the premises that he occupied, to make room for Pašić, who was expected to arrive in Mitrovica any day. In fact, there was so little accommodation that the good-natured Sir Charles was billeted with some local clerk from the Serbian Ministry of Agriculture and ended up sharing his double bed with an inspector from the same ministry. The latter gentleman, sensitive to this unlikely situation, made a point of retiring early. He feigned sleep whenever Sir Charles came into the room. At daybreak, he would be gone.

Gruić, the Serbian representative, turned out to be completely inefficient. At our request, he was recalled. The government sent us the former Serbian minister to Sofia, Čolak-Antić, a sensitive, kind, and well-educated person, but somewhat bemused. He knew little about the intentions of the Serbian government and the High Command and was therefore unable to provide us with any kind of important information.

Rumors reached us that the enemy had taken Niš and Kraljevo. The Serbian army was about to be cut off from three sides and surrounded. From the letters that Iovanović sent me from Raška, I was able to ascertain that the bitter recriminations that had plagued the relationship between the Serbian civilian and military authorities continued to be the order of the day. The High Command was laying all the blame on Pašić, who had insisted that the Allies would come to Serbia's aid within three weeks of the Bulgarian invasion. There was no direct communication between the Serbian High Command and the French general Sarrail. All correspondence went by way of Paris-Salonika. Rumor also had it that Russia was reneging on its pledge to help Serbia. I could do nothing do dispel these rumors, since I received no communiqués on that subject from St. Petersburg. My only contact with St. Petersburg was by telegraph to our embassy in Rome, from where it would then be sent on—a slow process.

The best I could do was to get to Raška, where I met with both Pašić and the heir to the throne. I came out of these meetings with the sense that both would fight to the end. However, their resolve wavered between despair and hope, depending on the military situation. We diplomats were adamant about remaining with the government. Finally, on October 30, the government arrived at Mitrovica. That very day, we received news that the Serbian army under the command of Vojvoda Stepan Stepanović had managed to slow down the Bulgarian advance. The army thus avoided the imminent threat of being cut off and surrounded.

This respite was momentary. Shortly after the arrival of the government to Mitrovica, I learned that the Bulgarians had taken Giljani and could surround Kočani. It was imperative to leave for Prizren tomorrow at dawn. To do that, I needed confirmation. Armed with a flashlight, I made my way to Pašić's headquarters, where I met up with the French minister. We waited for Pašić, who was discussing matters with the crown prince. Upon his return, he confirmed that Giljani had fallen and that fighting was already taking place at Ferizovići Station.

That same night we sent the horses on to Prizren. At 8:00 a.m., we boarded the train to Lipljan. Pašić and the government, along with the entire Serbian High Command were already on the train. From Lipljan we made our way to Prizren by automobile.

Prizren is the most picturesque and charming of all the towns I passed through during the retreat. It had kept its Turkish character. As usual, it was situated at the foot of a mountain that had a citadel and a konak. What made this town unique was a fast mountain stream, aptly named *Bistrica* [Clear] flowing through the middle. The cluster of houses on one of the bridges reminded me of Florence. For a Serb, Prizren evokes memories of history long past. King Nicholas of Montenegro once wrote a poem, which every Serb knew by heart:

"There, there, behind those hills! Prizren!
I behold thee."

I stayed at the Russian consulate. Among others there was the French military attaché Fournier.

Although he was critical of the Serbs for their indecisiveness and for not retreating directly southward to join the Allies, he felt the tide could still be turned, even at the last minute, if General Sarrail were to take decisive action. He told me that he would be telegraphing just that to Paris.

We did not get to stay long in Prizren. I was not even able to see the town properly, due to the fact that it was snowing and I was under the impression that I would get another chance. I found a full edition of the *Thousand and One Nights* and spent my time engrossed in the book. My colleagues came to see me. Sir Charles realized only after the fact that the woman with whom he was lodged was actually a midwife, which explains the knocking on her door at all hours of the night.

On the third day, Pašić summoned all of us diplomats and told us that we would have to make our way to Montenegro immediately. The road to Monastir was in Bulgarian hands. He had not given up all hopes of retaining Skopje, even though the news from the front was far from positive.

Failing that, his plan was for us to eventually meet in Salonika. He himself would travel by way of Durazzo (Durrës). As for us, we would have to go first to San Giovanni di Medua. We suggested it might be better to wait until the situation cleared up. Pašić insisted that we evacuate immediately—if things took a turn for the worse, all hell would break loose, and foreign diplomats might become endangered. I inquired what he intended to do. He told me he had Albanian friends who would guide him along pathways to Durazzo.

"From there, I'll get to Salonika."

All was said and done. The very next morning on November 7, we left Prizren for Đakovica.

Iovanović joined us, together with his wife and twelve-year-old son. I appropriated a carriage from the consulate. We harnessed a pair of pure-bred racehorses belonging to a wealthy Serb who was anxious to get them at least to Dečani. The road was very muddy and difficult to maneuver. I pitied those magnificent horses straining with all their might.

When we reached the White Drin, the river bordering Serbia and Montenegro, we had to go over a rather awkwardly constructed, narrow stone bridge. We went by foot urging on the horses. We pulled them by the bridles for fear that they might topple over into the river below because of the steep incline of the bridge. I remember this day, November 7, because it marked one month from our departure from Niš.

We spent the night in Đakovica, very much an Albanian town, as guests of the Kmet who greeted us warmly and fed us very well.[6] The following morning, it was off to Dečani, which we were anxious to reach by nightfall. The roads were in such bad shape that I walked the twenty-five kilometer distance. We passed through the occasional village, where we invariably encountered deserted streets, with two-story gray stone houses surrounded with fences, without any windows looking out to the street. Each little house thus resembled a fortress, from which the owners could open fire at any possible attackers. These houses and all of Albania, as a matter of fact, reminded me of the cruel Middle Ages. Albanian mores originated during Turkish rule, when their overlords found it difficult to transport heavy artillery to this mountainous area and, in any event, were interested more in recruiting these Muslim brigands in the struggle against the infidels rather than in subduing them. Serbian soldiers and guns had quickly quashed the rebellion at the end of 1913. As we passed through the Albanian mountains two years later, the memories of Serbian reprisals were still very much alive in the local population. Once they realized the erstwhile invaders had become helpless refugees, we found ourselves in a difficult situation. Even earlier in Mitrovica, the Montenegrin minister had asked one of the people I was buying horses from what his nationality was. "Until today, I was a Serb," he replied. Clearly, he did not intend to remain a Serb for much longer. We passed through one last large Albanian village before finally reaching Dečani. . . .

One of my dreams had come true. The Dečani Monastery was one of the most important Serbian historical relics, a monument of the times of Serbian greatness prior to the Battle of Kosovo. Located in an area where Turks and Albanians had ruled for centuries and where there were minarets aplenty, this magnificent marble monastery built in a strict fourteenth-century Byzantine style was particularly striking. The surrounding mountains had become staunch guardians, hiding it from the enemy's gaze.

During the last decade of Turkish rule, Dečani Monastery came under the protection of Russia. A group of Russian monks were brought in from Mount Athos, starting with Father Cyril and Father Varsofonii.

Surrounded by wilderness and exposed to bandits, Albanians, Serbs, and Montenegrins, they made the best of their situation. Father Varsofonii, an exceptionally brave and ingenious man, was able to keep his nerve even in the most precarious of situations and successfully negotiated with the rival national groups in the area. Back in the spring of 1915, my wife sent a small medical team, which included doctors and six nurses with medical supplies, to the monastery at the request of Father Varsofonii. Shortly before the autumn invasion of Serbia, we considered recalling some of the medical personnel, leaving three people to attend to the most urgent cases. Most of the patients were Albanians from the area, which became important when the monastery was threatened by fifteen hundred Albanians from a different tribe eager to take back land they considered theirs that had been returned to the monastery after the Balkan War. Fortunately the Albanians, who lived next to the monastery and who were benefiting from this medical care, appeared at the monastery to defend it. The siege lasted a week until the Bulgarian forces came to its relief.

I had been eager to visit the Dečani Monastery from the beginning of my stay in Serbia. I talked to Pašić about this; since he had never been to the monastery either, we agreed to make the trip together. As fate would have it, Pašić never got to see Dečani, and I arrived at the most tragic time for Serbia.

The monastery was even more spectacular than I had imagined. Huddled up against the mountains, Dečani had preserved its original edifices as well as the atmosphere of an age long gone. The high fence was not merely an ornament or a reminder of the past—it still served a very real purpose in protecting the monastery from enemies. The huge churchyard was filled with various buildings, which opened their doors to numerous pilgrims during holy days and to numerous refugees in times of crisis.

The main church had been fully preserved. It was most remarkable for its architectural style, magnificent in its austere simplicity. It also had a beautiful iconostasis and columns. The beautiful services performed by the Russian monks completed the picture, making an impression on Russians and foreigners alike.

The monastery was crammed with travelers. Like us, they were looking for protection and shelter. No one was turned away. There we all were, meeting once again: English suffragettes, Serbs, Frenchmen, Russians, Slovaks. I recognized some royal carriages with oxen standing nearby. When night fell, the vast monastery courtyards became alive with campfires, blotting out the full moon. It was magic.

The next morning, after the liturgy, the abbot led me to a hidden room. He wanted my advice about three objects, which he was intending to bury because of their historical significance. There was a golden seal belonging to King Stefan Dušan and given to the monastery along with a deed of patrimony, a chalice belonging to the same king, and a pitcher once belonging to Prince Marko.[7] Everything else in the room was not as significant. The abbot decided on a site not far from the garbage dump in the hope that no one would suspect anything.

The old king's marshal of the court thought it a good idea to leave the king's robe and crown, which he had brought with him on the road, at the monastery. I do not know whether he ever did or not.

We said good-bye to the hospitable abbot, Father Varsofonii, who sent us off to Ipek with thick fresh cream on bread, cheese, and other goodies.

It was already evening when we arrived in Ipek. I drove up to the patriarchate where I was to stop. It had been built in the thirteenth century, which made it older than Dečani. I was well received by the metropolitan, who had studied in Russia. Unfortunately, he had earlier given the Russian monks in Dečani a hard time, even though he could not have replaced them with Montenegrin monks.

The patriarchate was at the edge of town, which was a good thing, because it was easier for us to continue on horseback the very next morning. The date was November 11. About half an hour after we left Ipek, the road became a meandering mountain path. My horse was a splendid mountain pony, smart and calm. I let her choose her own way, trying not to notice that, as with all mountain ponies, she preferred to walk along the very outer edge of the steep and narrow mountain path. The view was breathtakingly beautiful; the air crisp and fresh. Above us loomed majestic mountain peaks, below were gushing torrents. We stopped often to drink the crystal clear water of mountain streams. Sadly, my splendid little mountain pony contracted pneumonia and died.

Shelter for the night was some rudimentary inn or *han*, a wooden structure not made to be heated. Our circumstances were primitive to say the least. It was winter, and there was snow in the mountains. At least we were able to obtain hay for the horses, even if it was at an exorbitant price. In places, the road was either completely destroyed or nonexistent. We clawed our way up and down the mountain on all fours pulling our horses by the bridles.

We rode our horses downstream. By the time we reached the next shelter or *han*, we were totally exhausted.

I recall my first night in one of these cabins aptly named *Belukha*, probably because this part of the mountain range was covered with snow the year round. One had to virtually crawl to reach the entranceway. The horses slipped and fell to the ground, getting up only with the greatest difficulty. I would never even have made it there were it not for the able help of two Czech doctors. We were ushered into a room with ten people: English, French, and Ioco Iovanović with

16. A *han* or cabin. The dead horse is Trubetskoi's "splendid little mountain pony."

his wife and son. The cold dark room was bereft of any furniture, and we all had to make ourselves comfortable on the floor. There was hardly enough hay to make oneself a pillow, and I collapsed in exhaustion. The British secretary, Killing, whose horse had just fallen into a ravine, brought me a cup of instant broth. This revived me. I must say that both he and Sir Charles Des Gras were most solicitous to me over the course of our journey. Sir Charles told me later that he regarded me as a younger brother, whom he was bound to help. As long as I live, I shall forever cherish the deepest feelings of gratitude toward him.

Traveling in such difficult circumstances simplified everything in a way. Mrs. Iovanović, without any embarrassment, requested toilet tissue from her husband. As she left the room, she asked Sir Charles whether in his opinion she could find an appropriate spot. He was unable to reassure her. As it happened, we all had to go out onto the road.

Mt. Čakor was the most important destination along our journey. Once we had reached it, we took out a bottle of homemade slivovitz from Dečani and sat down to lunch. Čakor marked the boundary between Montenegro's old territories from its new acquisition, and I had never been more pleased to drink liquor. Our meal was briefly interrupted by a couple of gunshots coming in our direction from beyond the mountain. Perhaps the Albanians were taking potshots at us.

The remainder of the journey through Old Montenegro, however, was less than comfortable. We reached our next destination, the Velika Inn, fairly early in the afternoon. The English had already arrived. Mamulov and I decided to push on. We urged Sir Charles and Killing to join us; they were too exhausted, however. Much later, in Corfu, Sir Charles confessed that he felt unhappy and abandoned by everyone. He even felt rancor toward us. Had we only known his feelings, we would certainly have remained in Velika. Ultimately, this would have been a wiser decision.

On our journey, we would ask how far we were from a certain place, much as we would in Russia. In Russian villages, one peasant would say four versts, another six or eight. The same thing happened in Serbia and in Montenegro, the only difference being that they measure distances in hours—the Serbs say *sat*, derived from Turkish, and the Montenegrins say *Uhr*, derived from the German. We had traveled quite a distance from Velika and considered spending the night in a village. We were told that Andrejevci was but an hour and a half away.[8] Three hours later, we were no closer to our destination. Nightfall caught us on a steep trail; to the left a mountain of evergreens, to the right a deep ravine with the sound of a waterfall somewhere far below.

We decided to make camp in the forest. We unsaddled the horses, cut some wood, and started a campfire. We rested with our feet toward the fire, using our saddles for pillows.

Shortly, we ate and felt much better. Lying on my back, I gazed at the stars, inhaling the clean mountain air. I felt fortunate that I did not have to sleep in a cold and filthy shelter.

My reverie was interrupted by the sudden appearance of Albanian shepherds. Our Montenegrin guides suggested that we should leave immediately, because they could come back with reinforcements and attack us. The moon came up as we continued on our way. By then it was about 1:00 a.m. A scout who had been sent on ahead returned and informed us that Andrejevci was not far. The moon was bright, and we were able to see the footpath except when the path curved in such a way as to block out the moon. It was at just such a moment that the path suddenly ended and instead became a rivulet with protruding rocks. We slid our way down the rest of the mountain, dragging our reluctant horses behind us by the reins, as it started to snow. Finally, we managed to reach Andrejevci and spent what remained of the night at the mayor's home. I remember vividly the decorations in the guest room. There were postcards depicting a young man wearing a green smoking jacket next to a lady in pink. Such postcards can be found in most Montenegrin homes, and they are a clear reflection of what Montenegrins consider to be high culture. Among other things, the fine embroidery hanging on one of the walls of the mayor's home depicted a large scale tipped sharply to one side. On the high end of the scale was a heart. On the low end, a bag with the number *10,000* embroidered on it. Above the scale were the following words: *sadašna ljubav* or "contemporary love."

We said good-bye to our hospitable Kmet and continued on our way. This time we had two wagons drawn by Russian horses. We sat on top of our luggage and felt very much like kings. We met up with Sir Charles and Bopp and offered them a ride on the second wagon.

Again, the roads were washed away in places, rocky and slippery. It was hard to believe that wagons could take such abuse. Thankfully, the capable Mamulov took command of our expedition in difficult moments.

It is not easy to convey the joy we felt when, on the second day after leaving Andrejevci, we saw automobiles parked in front of an inn. These were the very same vehicles the king of Montenegro had dispatched, along with provisions, to take us the rest of our journey. To celebrate, I produced my last bottle of champagne, placing it lovingly into a pile of snow. To me, as we sipped the champagne, the cars seemed imaginary, an event in a novel, not real life.

Sir Charles, Bopp, and I got into an automobile together, traveling at top speed. I had heard that traveling by car through Montenegro was quite an experience, but I was not easily impressed after all the trials and tribulations of our anabasis. King Nicholas had spent a great deal of energy and money building first-class roads in this part of Montenegro. However, since the roads had been constructed before automobiles, they were narrow and wound sharply, something the experienced local drivers did not consider. Be that as it may, the vistas were grandiose.

According to legend, when God created the earth, a bag of rocks carried by an angel ripped open, and all the rocks fell onto Montenegro. I recalled this legend inadvertently while I was traveling through this aptly named country of endless cliffs and giant boulders. I wondered how people managed to live in this inhospitable place. The people, especially the women, were beautiful and walked with a proud elegance.

We arrived in Podgorica, our last stop before Scutari, late in the evening. Although we had a truck at our disposal, only Mamulov was brave enough to travel along the dark road at night. When he told me about the trip later, I was under the impression that this had been one of the most astonishing moments in our hard journey. Along the way, he encountered the same Austrian prisoner of war who had assisted the Russian doctors in Niš, on horseback. The coming truck frightened the horse, which fell into the ravine along with its rider. Luckily, the ravine was not particularly deep, and both the horse and the rider were fine. During our stay in Podgorica, I was accommodated in a summer house with no stove belonging to a local man of means. We suffered from the cold as there was not a woodstove to be gotten anywhere. We ate at a local hotel, where the food was tolerable, together with the former minister of foreign affairs, now provincial governor, Plamenac. A scion of one of the most notable Montenegrin families, this young man bore the mark of King Nicholas's peculiar governing style. He combined the elegant veneer of a fluent French speaker with the typical Balkan rogue.

Consequently, we had to put up patiently with many an exercise in dubious oratory at the dining table. During his tenure as minister of foreign affairs, he had had a liaison with Princess Xenia, a self-important lady whose influence over the old king enabled her to interfere successfully in affairs of state. Plamenac was forced to resign in the wake of the Montenegrin occupation of Scutari in the spring of 1915 against the express will of the Allies, Italy in particular. This seemingly took place with Austrian encouragement. The two countries were at war on paper only and did little to harm each other. The Austrians preferred to see Scutari in the hands of the weak Montenegrins rather than the Italians, who might be able to set up formidable defenses in conjunction with their naval base of San Giovanni di Medua.

The hesitant policy of King Nicholas became most evident in the Scutari Question. He had grown accustomed to promoting his personal welfare, along with that of his little country, by cautiously negotiating with all states. Hence, he could not bring himself to discard this vacillating attitude even during the Great War, which in the Balkans had clearly taken on the guise of a struggle to the death between Teuton and Slav. He seemed to be in cahoots with Austria, even though he was nominally at war with it. The growing mistrust of Italy among the South Slavs, who saw it as a potential successor to Austria in the Balkans, further complicated the issue. A skeptic by nature, King Nicholas doubted our ability to destroy Germanism in the current war and intended to remain on the best of terms with friend and foe alike. The king's policy, clear for everyone to see, contributed to the increasing demoralization of the people of Montenegro at the time of the Serbian retreat. The situation only grew worse, as the defeated and hungry Serbian army pillaged the already meager Montenegrin supplies.

While in Podgorica, Bopp, Des Gras, and I decided to make a side trip to Cetinje to thank King Nicholas for his help. After our difficult retreat, it was especially pleasant to find ourselves surrounded by the usual comforts we found in the Russian mission in Cetinje.

Cetinje is, for all intents and purposes, a village with several medium-sized buildings. One of these served as King Nicholas's palace. The king received us as we were, I in high boots and a gray jacket. He was most pleasant, happily avoiding any serious political discussion. He emphasized to each of us individually the need for food and supplies, which were rapidly dwindling from their having to feed the hungry and beleaguered Serbian army. Fond of effective phraseology, he said, "J'ai pu lutter contre la Monarchie [Austria], mais je devrais capituler devant la boulangerie" [I was able to stand up to the monarchy, but I should surrender to the bakery].

At the palace, we met up with Baron Schvitti, who had made his way directly to Cetinje. Having been Italy's ambassador to Montenegro before Serbia, he was a *persona grata* with the king and was his guest at the palace. We were supposed to return to Podgorica that same day, but instead we remained at the Russian mission in Cetinje for the night, succumbing to the vision of a warm comfortable bed, a bath, and breakfast. The summer house in Podgorica now seemed even colder and more uncomfortable.

On November 18, we departed for Scutari. Pašić and the crown prince had already arrived there by a different route. We were supposed to travel by car for half an hour to Lake Scutari, where we had to board a steamship.

The lake was covered in deep fog as we approached, and the Montenegrin captain refused to sail. His old ship had sustained substantial damage over time and, being the only one of its kind servicing the lake, it seemed unreasonable to risk it in such adverse weather. The young Russian medical personnel traveling with us were in high spirits, laughing loudly at everything, to Bopp's chagrin. We had to wait several hours until the fog lifted and it became safe to sail. I had never seen so many geese in my life.

Unfortunately, the fog descended again, and we arrived in the port of Scutari without even noticing its surroundings.

We were met by the only available carriage in the city, an antediluvian wreck, which took Mamulov and me to our lodgings. We were given an apartment previously owned by an Austrian doctor, who had fled the city after its occupation by the Montenegrins. The apartment was spacious and clean. There were stoves, but there was no fuel. It was a long time before I removed my overcoat.

8

SCUTARI

We arrived in Scutari on November 18. Under other circumstances, I would have enjoyed the pleasant sight and sounds of this unique town with its Albanian architecture and the surrounding colorful countryside. Except for the high street with its numerous shops, the city's streets are narrow and dominated by the typical stone walls of Albanian two-story houses with bars on their windows and fruit gardens in the backyards. One can see plenty of little boys and girls playing in the alleys. There are always throngs of people on the high street, primarily Albanians but also a few Montenegrins. Women wear colorful clothes, especially on Sundays—leather trousers under heavy skirts, shirts and jerkins embroidered with gold and silver, and mantles with high collars. These elaborate, expensive garments make it difficult to move around, but they are quite common nonetheless.

During the Balkan War, Scutari had been occupied by Montenegro. Montenegro was subsequently forced to evacuate it at the insistence of the Great Powers, which feared Austrian presence. Thus, the city found itself under international control, headed by a Colonel Phillips from Britain. During this time, pavements appeared, country roads improved, and the city in general was given a face-lift. Many streets were renamed to reflect the nationality of the patrolling troops; for example, I lived on Kiel Street, next to Goeben Street, where German sailors could be found earlier. Ernest Renan Street had been named after a French battle cruiser, and so on. With the presence of foreign garrisons, you could find stuff in the stores of Scutari that was unavailable in Cetinje; in general, Scutari was a much richer and more important center than the tiny Montenegrin capital.

The marketplace was located closer to the lake, in the older section. Government offices stood in the central part, along with the homes of wealthier Albanians. Hovering over the city was an ancient citadel with a spectacular view to Lake Scutari. On a sunny day, one could even watch the Drina and Bojana Rivers emptying into it. The climate in Scutari was mild, although we chanced to be there at the coldest time of November and December. They say that roses start to bloom at the end of January.

Scutari was so charming that twenty years ago a wealthy Englishman by the name of Padget built and lavishly furnished a large house with the intention of settling there permanently. Everyone in Scutari knew about the Villa Padget! It was a gray-stone house, complete with two towers and beautiful wooden doors, which kept its Albanian outlook. The towers proved particularly useful once enemy aircraft began flying over Scutari. Inside, it resembled an English manor. The spacious living room, which boasted a huge Venetian mirror and a large fireplace, was most impressive. When I went to the house to see Des Gras, who was staying there, I met Padget himself, who had never actually lived in the house. Having been appointed to the British Provisioning Commission, he had made his first trip back to Scutari after buying the house. He performed his duties with considerable diligence.

Within a week of our arrival, Scutari filled to capacity with refugees and soldiers. Stores were emptied, and food became scarce. This sleepy town with its gardens and Turkish walls turned into a town of lawlessness. From the start, the Montenegrins resented the incursion of the retreating Serbian armies. King Nicholas was unhappy about having to shed his two-faced political dealings and make commitments.

Seeing Serbia's debacle and wary of provoking Austria, he feared for his own country. Neither did he want the Serbians to remain in Scutari for long. Because of their presence in Scutari, he could not communicate openly with Austria.

With the arrival of the Serbs in Scutari, there appeared two rival administrations—Serbian and Montenegrin. At the head of the latter was Vojvoda Neguš-Petrović, the king's uncle, a little old man wearing a Montenegrin folk costume and an ill-becoming pince-nez. Frail and ailing, this typical representative of the Montenegrin royal court—half gentleman, half rogue—seemed incapable of doing much. The young commander of Montenegrin forces in the area, General Vešović, was more energetic. He traveled around town with an entourage of heavily armed gendarmes. The Serbs set up their administration in the old Turkish headquarters. The presence of these two administrations, which regarded each other with mutual suspicion, only contributed to the increasing chaos in the city.

The retreat of the Serbian army through Montenegro to Scutari was completely unexpected. When I parted with Pašić in Prizren, he told me he intended to go to Durazzo, along with the army. When the decisive moment came, however, things worked out differently.

Apparently Pašić, who was still somewhat justifiably counting on Allied help, told his armies to make for the coast any way they could in order to avoid capitulation. For this reason, the unexpected retreat was not well organized. Pašić felt that, since the Allies controlled the sea, they would be in a position to send supplies and troops to Scutari and Medua.[1] The English and the French had in fact promised to supply the Serbian army as early as October, when the Serbs had not abandoned their territories altogether. The Italians also seemed willing to acquiesce to the Serbian request for help. At the time, the Serbs had doubted the possibility of dispatching supplies through Medua, indicating their preference for Durazzo. Later on, they remembered the Allied insistence on Medua and decided to retreat to this port.

At the time of our arrival in Scutari, a few ships did indeed sail into Medua with provisions and other goods ordered by the merchants of Scutari. The Serbian government bought them all up. No sooner did they start to unload the cargo, however, but Austrian warships bombarded these miserable supply ships, destroying everything, to the enormous detriment of the Serbs. We could hear the bombardment from Scutari.

This setback seriously affected the Serbs' mood. Their initial plans had been to remain in Montenegro and Albania. Once news spread of the availability of Allied supplies along the coast, the argument went, Serbian soldiers would make their way there without further delay. A reorganized Serbian force of 150,000 troops would then be able to attack from Albania in coordination with an Allied advance north of Salonika.

In the meantime, Serbian diplomatic representatives informed Pašić that there were growing Allied doubts about the feasibility of the Salonika expedition. The English were particularly reluctant to commit. The military correspondent of the *Times*, Colonel Reppington, published several articles in which he decried the proposed Salonika expedition as an unnecessary diversion of troops and efforts from the primary western front to the secondary Balkan theater of operations. His recommendations carried much weight in England and were seemingly vindicated by the disastrous Dardanelles operation, which, among other things, had prompted the Austro-German invasion of Serbia.

The dilettantish Dardanelles fiasco could not prove the unfeasibility of the proposed expedition to Salonika, of course, but it strengthened English doubts. The Serbs were far from happy to hear this.

On November 22, the representatives of the Allied nations received an extensive communiqué from the Serbian government. In essence it stated:

> *Serbia, from the moment of the Bulgarian mobilization, acquiesced to the request of the Allies not to take the initiative in attacking Bulgaria. The Allies promised to send 150,000 troops to Salonika. At the cost of heavy sacrifices, Serbia kept its commitment to the Allies to the very end. After two months of conflict against an enemy two and a half times its size, the army made a desperate attempt to meet up with the Allies by way of Skopje, despite the fact that the Allied commander in Salonika did not consider a combined attack to be possible. Now, after the debacle, Serbian armies must hide in the mountains of Albania and Montenegro, where they will rearm and reorganize to continue fighting the enemy. Having fulfilled its obligations honestly and to the very end, Serbia surely has the right to inquire of its allies: Is there any truth to the rumors that the Allies intend to leave Serbia on its own and relegate the Balkan front to secondary importance?*

On November 26, I sent a telegram to St. Petersburg. I had no idea of who was the new minister of foreign affairs after the dissolution of the Duma, nor for that matter, who would be signing the answer to my telegram. It went as follows:

> *Hunger is imminent. There is murder and theft on public roads. Among the Albanians there is ferment that can erupt at any time into an uprising. The Austrians have free rein on the sea, disrupting supply convoys and making the Allies look weak. I am given no instructions or guidance that would enable me to fend off the potentially dangerous mood of hopelessness. The people believe capitulation is inevitable. I urge you to respond to the Serbian communiqué asking whether the Balkan War is over and whether the Serbs can count on the bringing in of food.*

That same day I chanced to meet the crown prince, who came to see Ioćo Iovanović. His verbal appeal, which I telegraphed as well, was heartrending.

"I did all that I could," he told me. "I proved my willingness to fight to the very end, and I shall continue to do so. I beg you to give me bread for my army. I brought the men here. I am responsible for them, for those dying of hunger. The mood would change with the first truckload of flour. If I've lost part of the army, then the best survived. A little bit of bread and a bit of rest is all that is needed to give my army the chance to advance. Make it possible to give people some hope; they deserve better than death by starvation."

The heir to the throne became exceedingly irritated when the subject of the Italians entered into our conversation. By not lifting one finger, it was as though Italy rejoiced at Serbia's misfortune. He expressed the hope that we could precipitate a response from Rome, as well as from France and England.

I sent many more telegrams like these two to St. Petersburg. After his arrival at Scutari, Military Attaché Artamonov dispatched the same telegrams to the Stavka. No replies came. I had not received any sort of communications from the ministry in three weeks and had to telegraph to the embassy in Rome to find out who the new minister of foreign affairs was. Finally the Ministry of Foreign Affairs sent news from my family; I was relieved to find out they were safe and sound.

Throngs of soldiers arrived in Scutari daily. Some came as part of surviving military units while others came on their own. All were dressed in rags. Their plight was desperate. They were paid in Serbian currency, which was useless, having no value whatsoever. Tattered and hungry, they roamed the streets of Scutari, pale shadows of themselves, eyes feverish. Not knowing exactly what to do, they died in disbelief without a struggle. All of them until recently had been well-to-do, proud farmers. Having lost everything, they had sunk to the depths of poverty. I recall a boy-soldier who broke down when I offered him some bread. He had not eaten in two days. In his emotional outcry was tension, physical weakness from all that he had endured, gratitude, and at the same time shame, for having to accept my offering of bread. Often, a starving soldier would die from a bowel obstruction after eating.

If the people had no food, then the horses had nothing to eat at all. There were hundreds of dead horses all over the town, in streets and squares. With no one to take responsibility and with no means of transport to remove the carcasses, they were left to rot. It was worse when the horses were stripped of their skins and left behind. Eventually someone came up with the idea of throwing the carcasses into the rivers and lakes. After that, we ceased catching and eating fish.

Even we, the foreign representatives, were badly off. We staved off hunger only because we had our own flour. The poor soldiers would buy a small loaf of maize bread for the exorbitant price of ten dinars or more. We often saw them picking up dirty onion peels from the street to supplement their meager meals. Coal was scarce and phenomenally expensive.

17. Scutari, 1915. Serbian encampment.

Then the military aircraft from Cattaro appeared.[2] Flying very low over the town, they dropped bombs upon the town center, where we lived. Everyone was caught off guard at first, and a panic ensued. Eventually, watches were organized; the large bell in the main bell tower would sound at the approach of the warplanes, and the people learned to hide in shelters. Our residence, along with the main administrative buildings, was right in the town center. All of their windows were smashed, and it was impossible to replace them.

Pašić worked at his desk in a coat and hat. It was December, and the weather was cold. The window in my bedroom was also broken, but I taped it with paper and bundled up at night. When the morning came, the idea of getting out of my warm bed made me shudder. Whatever there was in the way of wood was for cooking purposes only.

The raids were carried out in the mornings. My colleagues and I would begin our day by walking to the edge of town and organizing an excursion to the citadel, where Montenegrin gun batteries were placed. We would hear the warning bells along the way; by the time we reached the fortress, we could actually see a small enemy aircraft. The Montenegrin guns opened fire, as did anyone in the city with a revolver or a rifle. These otherwise useless barrages were almost as dangerous as the Austrian bombs, since most shells fell back into the city. The pilots did not pay much attention to these shots, flying low to drop their bombs.

On the eve of Catholic Christmas, a bomb landed not far from the Catholic cathedral, leaving behind quite a few casualties. Pro-Austrian Catholic Albanians said, "Austria loves Albania, but not the Albanians."

The Catholic archbishop undoubtedly had some kind of direct communication with Austrian headquarters, because toward the end of our stay in Scutari, the bombings almost ceased.

We would return home for luncheon, and after a secondary raid, we would meet at 2:00 p.m. to assess the situation, exchange news, compose and send necessary telegrams. Afterward, I would attend meetings with Pašić or Iovanović. I would be met with the same question: Did I know anything new about Allied intentions? I had no answer.

At this time, Chief of General Staff of the Serbian Army Vojvoda Putnik was brought to Scutari on a stretcher. Weak and very old, he no longer had the energy and capacity to reorganize the entire Serbian army. He was given a substantial leave of absence.

Everyone was pessimistic about the possibility of prolonging the struggle. The Serbs had to leave behind military equipment, destroying whatever they could or throwing it into ravines as they retreated over the mountains. Many of the soldiers had no rifles at all. Others exchanged their guns with the Albanians for bread, thus creating new dangerous possibilities. Essad Pasha in Durazzo notified Pašić that Austrian and Bulgarian emissaries were creating ferment among the Albanians, possibly cutting off future communications between Scutari and Durazzo.

At the beginning of December, we began hearing rumors about a possible uprising, which threatened to cut off Scutari from San Giovanni di Medua. The Austrians also began military preparations. In the circumstances, it became impossible to even think about reorganizing the Serbian army on the spot.

The French military staff urged the Serbs to leave Scutari and move south to Durazzo, where it would be easier to reorganize. Medua was too close to Cattaro and could easily be subjected to Austrian bombardment. As a port, it was too small to accommodate large seagoing vessels. Under such circumstances, rearming seemed impossible.

The Serbs responded that their army lacked strength to undertake a new march. The steep pathways that passed for roads between Scutari and Durazzo were dangerous and virtually impassable after all the rains. There were two possible routes—along the sea and along the mountain. The former passed through a series of swamps, where horses used to drown. The latter was too narrow. A handful of Albanians could easily rout a part of the army. In addition, there were no means of crossing the overflowing rivers. In view of these considerations, the Serbian government insisted that ships be sent to Medua to evacuate the army either to Durazzo or to Salonika, where it could then reorganize.

At the end of November, King Nicholas's son Prince Mirko arrived in Scutari for a visit with his first cousin Prince Alexander.[3] As with all of King Nicholas's sons, Prince Mirko was somewhat of a ne'er-do-well. His beautiful Serbian wife, née Konstantinović, left him because of his disorderly ways. At the time, Mirko made himself out to be a friend of Serbia and openly complained about his father's "Austrophilism" and attempts at a separate peace.

King Nicholas kept extending invitations to Pašić for discussions, which Pašić kept postponing in the hope of receiving answers from the Allies about their Balkan plans.

Prince Alexander went to Cetinje instead, on what was ostensibly a family visit.

During his absence, in view of the bad news from Essad, Pašić requested confidentially that we convey to our governments the urgency of sending convoys to Medua to evacuate the government and its civil servants presently in Scutari to either Durazzo or Valona.[4] As for the heir to the throne, Pašić did not know whether he should evacuate with the rest of the government or prefer to make his own way along with an escort.

Prince Alexander knew nothing of this. Apparently, upon his return from Cetinje, there was an unpleasant clash between them. A very dejected Pašić subsequently explained to us that the government could not abandon the army, especially since the army blamed the government for the present situation. On December 2, Pašić pointed out to the ambassadors that there were but two options: to evacuate at least forty thousand troops to southern Albania or wherever the Allies decided, or to capitulate. It was extremely painful for Pašić to make such a statement, which would have spelled the end of his hopes and led to Serbia's political suicide, leaving it to the mercy of its enemies. Pašić, of course, meant to create an effect and force the Allies into specific action on the subject of evacuating the unfortunate Serbian army.

On the following day, December 3, we received a new communication from Pašić, which informed us of the desperate situation of the army and called for help one last time. After a difficult retreat in the hope of reinforcements, the Serbian army had reached the limit of its endurance. It was disappointed not to have found the expected supplies, clothes, or war matériel here. The enemy was closing in quickly, and the exhausted Serbian army was in no condition to halt the Austro-Bulgarian advance, which threatened to encircle it completely. There were two ways to avoid capitulating. The first, which was most desirable and certain, was to evacuate the army by sea from Medua to a place designated by the Allies. The second was for the Italian army to take on the defense against the Austrians and the Bulgarians. A land retreat was impossible, as it would result in the loss of at least half the remaining military personnel, thereby negating completely Serbia's few remaining military capabilities. In light of these considerations, the Serbian government must ask the Allies to evacuate no more than fifty thousand Serbian troops. It would be impossible to avoid the impending catastrophe if the Allies failed to come to Serbia's aid in this fateful moment. The Serbian people had done everything to continue the fight to the end.

We greeted December 6, 1915, normally a big holiday in Serbia and Montenegro, with heavy hearts. St. Nicholas's Day was also notable for being the name day of the tsar and of the king of Montenegro. The Orthodox church in Scutari, which had been under Russian protection, was full of people. The Serbian and Montenegrin authorities were also present. After the conclusion of the religious service, the priest gave a speech about the suffering of the Serbian people and how he had hoped it would come to an end at the enchanting shores of the Adriatic. Instead, the Serbs had found only starvation. He finished with a call to prayer for salvation. By the end of the service, everyone was crying.

I have already mentioned the growing Serbian disaffection with the Allies. At the beginning of the retreat, the Serbs had hurled plenty of accusations at Russia. Once it became clear that we could not offer any immediate military assistance and that Serbia's fate depended almost entirely on the actions of the Western allies, the Serbs realized how different Russia's attitude toward them really was. While the French and English appeared sympathetic and promised to send help, it was obvious they regarded the Serbs solely as a military asset in the larger struggle. Given the desperate situation in which the Serbian army had found itself, it would be unable to take to the battlefield any time soon. In the meantime, evacuating it required the diversion of considerable resources.

The indifference and the nearsighted diplomacy of the Allies was nothing compared to the treatment of Serbia by the Italians. The latter's heartless attitude offended even the English and the French. During these most difficult times for Serbia, Italy could have sent at least a minimum amount of aid, considering its geographical position and proximity to Serbia. The "difficulties" of bringing in supplies and provisions to Serbia via the sea were vastly exaggerated; Italy refused to accept any Serbian refugees and undertook no measures to support the Serbian army from potential attacks by the Bulgarians as it retreated south.

Worst of all was the Italian treatment of Serbian troops making their way to central Albania. Prompted by the Allies, the armies retreating with the old king made for Valona, from where an evacuation was possible. The Italian general, however, threatened military action should the Serbian armies cross the Skuba River.

The Serbian army had recruits within its ranks who were fifteen-, sixteen-, or seventeen-year-old boys, taken along to escape the enemy. These recruits, exposed to all the hardships of the retreat, remained unprotected. The Italians treated them as prisoners of war, surrounding the compound created for them with barbed wire, not allowing them to leave the compound without permission. Out of ten thousand recruits, only twenty-five boys were permitted to gather wood at a time. These stories may have been slightly embellished, but they capture the Italian attitude toward Serbia perfectly. Instead of offering aid and assistance in times of adversity, the Italians merely attracted Serbian hatred.

"The Italians are dangerous not as enemies, but as friends," became the saying among the Serbs, a reflection of their scorn and hatred.

The Italians treated King Peter appallingly in Valona. As soon as he arrived there, they offered to let him board an Italian warship to Brindisi, where he could stay in a palace. The offer was couched in terms that did not take no for an answer. The king acquiesced, but once in Brindisi, he checked into an inn and declared he would immediately sail for Salonika, in order to join a small number of Serbian troops who had retreated south through Monastir.

In a telegram to M. N. Giers, our ambassador in Rome, Sazonov labeled this attitude as monstrous. He bade Giers to put pressure on the Italian cabinet to change this unexplainable attitude toward Serbia. The question of Valona had been resolved with the agreement of April 13/26; therefore, Italian fears for this region were completely unfounded.

In an addendum, the tsar wrote in his own hand, "That's right!"

I must say that the Serbs never gave up hope for a personal intervention by the tsar. Nicholas II did take the plight of the Serbs personally and did indeed appear to have some influence on the Allies. On December 5, Prince Alexander sent the following telegram to the tsar:

> With hope and faith that My forces on the Adriatic coast would be rearmed and reorganized by the Allies as promised, I brought them over the roadless mountains of Albania and Montenegro. There are no possibilities here for their reorganization. They cannot survive. They will come to a tragic end. In these oppressive moments and at this time I am turning to Your Imperial Majesty,

upon whom I can place my last hopes, with a request for assistance from Your Imperial Majesty, to reorganize and enable My army to join the Allied forces. To this end, the Allied navy must transport My northern army from San Giovanni di Medua to a safer place, preferably in the area of Salonika, not too far from the Serbian border. There is no way that an exhausted and starving army can possibly make a march along mountain paths used by goats, from Scutari to Valona, as per the intentions of the Allied Supreme Command. It is My hope that Your Imperial Majesty will take this, My entreaty, into consideration and that Your Imperial Majesty would be willing to prevail upon the Allies to save the Serbian army from an undeserved, yet looming catastrophe!

Signed: *Alexander*

On December 8, 1915, Prince Alexander received a telegram from the tsar in response to his direct appeal. It was, in all probability, written by the tsar himself.

It was with the deepest concern that I followed the retreat of the heroic Serbian armies through Albania and Montenegro. I wish to express to you, Your Royal Highness, MY [capital letters] outright admiration for the way you managed to overcome your difficulties along with your able leadership. I have ordered the Minister of Foreign Affairs to prevail upon the Allies to guarantee their presence along the Adriatic shore. I hope now that the courageous military forces of Your Royal Highness will be able to leave San Giovanni di Medua.

I firmly believe that they will recuperate soon from their deprivations and once again take part in the struggle against the common enemy. Victory and the rebirth of Great Serbia will obliterate for you, and for the brotherhood of the Serbian people, all your past sufferings.

Signed: *Nicholas*

The imperial telegram, arriving at the most disheartening moment for the Serbs, was a bright ray of sunshine penetrating the gloomy darkness of an underground cellar. The heir to the throne, Pašić, all the ministers, could not hold back tears of joy. For three days they mulled over this telegram. It gave them the encouragement and moral support they all needed so badly. I myself and Mamulov became quite emotional when we read similar messages forwarded to me by Strandtmann, who by now was in our embassy in Rome. What a difference it makes to know that someone has you in his thoughts!

18. Map of line of retreat.

9

THE EXODUS

M ost of the details of our day-to-day existence in Scutari are now pale and undefined. There remains only the memory of horrible suffering in a desperate situation.

Supplies began to trickle in by mid-December. We all pleaded with the Serbs to march the army south by road. Our entreaties obviously had some effect: the Serbs themselves realized the futility of waiting for the arrival of large transport ships to Medua to bring out the army.

The able-bodied decided to walk to Durazzo. Others who had gold, the only currency accepted by the Albanians, also made their way to Durazzo independently. All the foreign medical missions, including our hospital staff, were evacuated by sea to Italy. I heaved a great sigh of relief when news reached me from Rome that they had arrived safely.

Around December 20, Pašić finally received a reply to his query regarding the future of Serbia. After all this time, Pašić received not one but four replies, each very different from the other. The Russian version, of course, pleased the Serbs the most. We reconfirmed our decisions and commitment to gain territories for Serbia. The other replies were vague, although the language did remain most cordial.

At about this time, the French government offered to bring the Serbian army to Bizerte, a move opposed by French Chief of General Staff Joffre.[1] Corfu was being considered instead. It was much closer and on the way to Salonika, the future base of operations for the Serbian army. However, nothing was yet decided, only that the army must not remain in Albania. As for evacuations, the Serbs left those decisions entirely to the Allies.

Much remained unresolved, and so we waited. To pass the time I organized daily games of bridge at my place from 5:00 to 7:00 in the evenings. Sir
Charles was my partner as always.

We took long walks. I actually even read the newly translated works of
Marcus Aurelius, edited by Kotliarevskii, which he had given to me in Niš.[2]

In Scutari I also met the wife of the powerful Albanian bey Prenk Pasha.
He himself lived in Cetinje under government surveillance if not outright
house arrest. The Montenegrins feared his influence with Catholic Albanians
and wanted to keep a close eye on him. Prenk's house in Scutari was a typical
Albanian mansion, with a large backyard and sentry towers, from which
there was a magnificent view. Prenk was apparently an older man, while
his wife was quite young. She spoke Italian and understood some French.
A simple girl, she would burst out laughing at the slightest hint of a joke. I
was interested in examining her collection of traditional Albanian folk costumes, to which she gladly consented. There were fabulous scarlet-and-blue
velvet costumes embroidered with gold, which drew a vivid picture of life in
the not-so-distant Albanian past.

An episode still vivid in my mind was the trip by Pašić to Cetinje to discuss Serbo-Montenegrin relations. The following is a report I wrote to the
minister of foreign affairs from Corfu regarding this question.

> *Corfu, January 31, 1916. No. 2.*
> *Most Respected Sir, Sergei Dimitrievich:*
> *During our time in Scutari, the relationship between Montenegro and Serbia*
> *weighed heavily upon the situation in which the Serbs found themselves. It is*
> *worth discussing, since the exceptional situation of wartime has revealed much*
> *that was not evident under normal, peacetime circumstances.*
> *I noticed a dichotomy in Montenegrin sentiment toward the Serbs.*
> *Ordinary people were sympathetic to the idea of a union with Serbia. The*
> *Balkan War served to manifest the quality of the Serbian army, unlike the paltry*
> *laurels of Montenegro. The Serbian government itself and its national policies*
> *were regarded as stable. These Montenegrins were determined to fight to the*
> *end. No compromise with the Austrians.*
> *On the other side were civil servants and army officers, with King Nicholas*
> *at the head. People with his way of thinking do not want the subservience of*
> *Montenegro to Serbia. Obviously, they fear for their positions, which they may*
> *have to relinquish should a union with Serbia be achieved. Dynastic and per-*
> *sonal interests are paramount, as the Montenegrin civil servants and officers are*
> *naturally fearful of losing their positions to Serbs in case of a union. Personal*
> *traits of character and false pride should be addressed as well. Each Serb and*

Montenegrin considers himself superior to the other and will exploit each other's weaknesses while justifying his own.

Invariably, the ramshackle retreat of the Serbian armies did little to charm the locals. Discipline was gone. It goes without saying that hungry soldiers snatched up whatever they could find. The carnage they left behind did little to bolster the morale of Montenegrins sympathetic to the notion of a "Great Serbia." If anything, it enhanced the idea of an independent Montenegro with expanded territory, a policy dear to King Nicholas. To occupy Scutari was the first step to a Greater Montenegro.

The idea is quite justifiable in that Lakes Scutari and Bojana provide the most natural sea outlets for Podgorica and Cetinje. Unfortunately, because the Allied powers had to take Italy into consideration, Montenegro lost its claim to Scutari. Austria was most favorably disposed to Montenegrin presence in Scutari, seemingly as a bulwark against the Italians. Despite the best efforts of the Austrian consul in Scutari, however, Austria lost the advantage of Montenegrin presence in Scutari.

Under such circumstances, the occupation of Scutari influenced the future policy of Montenegro and its relationship with the Entente powers, which became suspicious of King Nicholas's intentions. Our allies lost trust in the purveyance of supplies to Montenegro.

The relationship between Italy and Montenegro also deteriorated.

King Nicholas, true to himself and to his personal agenda, sought to balance the power between Austria and the Allies to his own advantage.

After the Serbians, having left everything behind, retreated to Montenegro and Albania, King Nicholas concluded on his own that in order for Montenegro to avoid a similar catastrophe, he should seek possible advantages. He pinned his hopes upon Austria's agreeing to a cease-fire and handing him Scutari, for which he was quite ready to dispense with Lovčen and Sandzak.[3] Thus, a wedge between Serbia and Montenegro would be established, ending any chance of a union, reiterating Montenegro's independence and preserving his dynasty. The king could also claim at this point that he was able to save at least a small part of Serbian culture from the ravages of war. The king expounded on these considerations to me while we were biding our time in Scutari. He was obviously trying to determine Russia's reactions to his policies while securing Austria's approval at the same time.

In the meantime, as King Nicholas pondered upon the cessation of hostilities with Austria, the Allied navy stopped protecting convoys of supplies bound for Montenegro, leaving them at the mercy of Austrian submarines, which torpedoed them right into Medua.

In the circumstances, the continuation of the struggle became increasingly difficult, as the king emphasized on several occasions. Italy, in the meantime,

*offended that it was not given control of Scutari, made no attempts to aid
Montenegro, even though it was in Italy's best interest to keep the Austrians
out of Lovćen. The English did the same. There was certainly nothing that we
could do, and the French reaction was much too slow. General Mondesir visited
Cetinje and Lovćen just two days before the Austrian bombardment began. The
procrastination of the Allies justified to some extent King Nicholas's desire for
capitulation.*

*This then was the backdrop for the meeting in Cetinje between Pašić and
King Nicholas on December 10.*

*During those few days, the details of this meeting became for us a distraction
from the tragedy all around us. We confabulated upon which of these two crafty
old men would get the upper hand. I visited Pašić immediately upon his return
from Cetinje. He looked pleased. His account of the meeting was so vivid that
I visualized exactly how he went to the king the morning after his arrival; the
greetings; the initial pleasantries guarded at first, then warming up; each pre-
tending to believe the other. After this Oriental-styled meeting, King Nicholas
came right to the point. Is the Serbian army capable of continuing to do battle,
and, if so, on what will this depend?*

*Without hesitation, Pašić answered that the army was in bad shape.
Exhausted and with no military supplies, it could not be depended upon to
withstand a major attack. The Serbs were counting on the Allies. They, in turn,
would not allow the army to disintegrate and would create an opportunity for
the army to leave Albania.*

"Well . . . what if the Allies don't help?" asked the king.

*This was a rather painful question because three weeks had passed without
any replies to the Serbs from the powers. Pašić reiterated his conviction that the
Allies would never abandon Serbia.*

*"Well, suppose they do. What will you do then?" the king asked insistently.
Pašić assured him that this was impossible. In the unlikely chance that this did
happen, there would be enough time to make the appropriate decisions.*

*By then breakfast was served. The king ushered Pašić in to meet his family.
"Meet another optimist, just like me," said the king as he introduced Pašić to the
queen.*

*That evening, as Pašić recounted various episodes during his trip through
Albania, the king said casually,*

*"Actually, you never did clarify what you would do should the Allies abandon
you." Pašić more or less repeated his earlier statements. The next day, the same
question with the same answer.*

*"It was obvious," Pašić said to me, "what he wanted. Should I have replied
that an abandoned Serbia would have to capitulate, the king would use my*

words to propagate his opinion that it is useless to fight on. Had I said 'no capitulation' he probably would have complained that the stubborn Serbs had lost their minds; better not join them in this act of badness."

Pašić had spoken with the passion of his convictions and got the better of the king. Serbia had lost everything; its future depended on the Allies. Montenegro, untouched by the war, had lost nothing and yet hoped to gain everything.

Events in Montenegro took on a faster tempo after this visit. The king instigated a ministerial crisis through Parliament. He controls the Parliament, using it for any sociopolitical issues that require a reference to public opinion.

The ministerial crisis was supposed to prepare the Montenegrin public for the seemingly inevitable peace negotiations with Austria. Soldiers and officers, assuming that an agreement had already been reached between Montenegro and Austria and preferring to avoid further bloodshed, made a halfhearted defense. The short-lived bombing of Lovćen and the occupation of the seemingly impregnable heights by the Austrians were not of great significance. Such was the opinion of Chairman of the Council of Ministers Lazar Miušković.[4] This was the course of events until a last-minute rupture.

It seems that the Allies and the Montenegrins themselves went too far in their suspicions of King Nicholas. They assumed that the king had already come to a secret agreement with Austria. Some even claimed to know the text in detail. Until now there had never actually been an agreement of any kind with Austria, just casual talks. The old king depended upon their possible reality.

Austria too suspected the king and was reluctant to believe him. It made impossible demands and conditions that the king could not accept. What happened then is very unclear. The king traveled to France. Peace was concluded by those whom he had left behind. Two-faced politics again! But you certainly will know more about this than we do in Corfu.

Presently there are thirty Montenegrins here, including three generals and over fifteen hundred enlisted Herzegovinians, who deserted to Montenegro at the beginning of the war. They have been evacuated to a separate island. According to G. Boisson, the French chargé d'affaires and Bopp's replacement, the only thing that they and the Serbs have in common is the desire to keep as far away from each other as possible.

I am not speculating about what the future holds for Montenegro and its relationship with Serbia. I simply feel it exigent to chronicle here the meeting of these two nations and their two leaders during this crucial time, as Serbia marches on to its destiny and King Nicholas remains at a crossroads.

Please accept my, etc....
Signed: *Prince Trubetskoi*

I ended the above letter at the point of the Austrian advance on Christmas Eve, December 24.

On December 26, the newly minted president of the Council of Ministers Lazar Miušković arrived in Scutari. As the former Montenegrin minister to Serbia, he wanted to say good-bye to Prince Alexander and Pašić.

Miušković paid me a visit. His conversation turned into a bitter tirade against the lack of Allied help. I sensed a possible capitulation. In view of this, I replied that I would not advise him to sit on two chairs at once; that would bring about the total destruction of his country.

Miušković continued to shift the responsibility for whatever would happen onto the Allies. A telegram came from his king, and he left the same day.

On the fourth day of their advance, the Austrians occupied the allegedly impregnable heights of Lovčen, and on December 29, King Nicholas sent some emissaries to the Austrians. Austria demanded the surrender of all Montenegrin forces and all Serbian forces on Montenegrin territory.

That day, during a meeting of foreign diplomats, French Minister Bopp suggested going all together to Pašić to discuss the unfolding events. We could expect Austrian activity along the coastline any day now, in which case we would be completely cut off and taken prisoner. We needed to leave Scutari immediately, and the Allies needed to send vessels to Medua in order to evacuate the government and the diplomats.

We agreed with Bopp's plan, and we all went to see Pašić. He acknowledged the seriousness of the situation. He was adamant that the Allies should send the navy immediately to bombard the coastline. As for our departure, until at least thirty thousand soldiers were safely evacuated from Medua, the government could not depart. We begged Pašić to reconsider. At the current rate of evacuating three hundred troops per day, it would take more than three months for the operations to be completed. Given the gravity of the situation—which Pašić acknowledged—time was of the essence, but he refused to budge.

We all came back to my place and continued to discuss our situation. Everyone agreed that our responsibilities would terminate upon capitulation. There was no need to become prisoners of war. If the Serbian government wished to stay, then our respective countries should send rescue boats for us. My reply was that I could not join them because, from the very beginning, my instructions had been "to share the fate of the Serbian government."

My colleagues argued that our governments did not realize the gravity of the situation. In the past, they had been too slow to react and inefficient. The situation was such that, if we were to be taken prisoners, they would hold us, the ambassadors, responsible for not forewarning them of our dangerous situation. What they said was true, and I agreed to add my signature to our collective telegram. We stated that we would be willing to risk imprisonment if that were necessary, providing the governments made that decision for us. If, on the other hand, they reached a decision for us not to become prisoners, they should send rescue vessels to Medua immediately.

In view of the urgency of the situation, we asked the Italian ambassador to transmit this telegram on our behalf by radio to the duke of Abruzzo, commander of the Allied fleet in the Adriatic Sea, requesting that he pass it on to our representatives.

In the morning of December 31, Pašić sent for all the ambassadors. The government had discussed our situation and had concluded that we were indeed in danger of imprisonment.

Would we immediately telegraph our respective governments to get warships to Medua tomorrow, January 1, to evacuate the heir to the throne, the government, the members of Parliament with their families, and the diplomats?

"What were you thinking about yesterday when we talked to you about the same thing?" Bopp asked bitterly.

"Do you really think that it is so simple to organize all this within twenty-four hours?" Pašić shrugged in response. He had actually been of the opinion that the government should have evacuated Scutari a long time ago, but he had been unable to act on this, due to opposition from the crown prince.

We had no choice. We gathered once more at my place, and the Italian ambassador sent a transmission on our behalf to the duke of Abruzzo to send warships to the rescue. Medua lay fifty-two kilometers from Scutari. It meant that we had to leave that very night to reach Medua by the evening of January 1.

Previously, on December 27, all the ambassadors received gifts of provisions from the Italian and French governments except for Des Gras who, along with the other English, was staying at a villa that Paget had built long before. The promised packages had been delivered to the Italian minister. We had been keenly awaiting them for over a month. As we gathered round, we felt like children opening gifts on Christmas Day. We tried to guess the contents of each individual parcel as we opened them one by one with greatest joy. Sir Charles, appearing at this moment, took in the scene with a feigned expression of indifference. We all gladly shared our "hoard" with him. We received ham, rice, macaroni, butter, bacon, biscuits, wine, cognac, jam, apples, oranges; so much of everything! There was enough for each of us for two months, and we had but four days! We distributed most of what we received.

Earlier, at my urging, Strandtmann and our Russian Red Cross in Rome managed to acquire a hundred hospital beds. They arrived in Scutari just before our forced departure. During the retreat, we had left behind all hospital supplies in Montenegro, where the need for medical aid was enormous. These beds we donated to the local hospitals. One of our medical team of nurses remained on duty, leaving Montenegro only after it capitulated. Some of the clothing and food went to teachers who were hard up.

In the medical supplies sent from Niš to Medua, there was a crate of first-class cognac and wine. Here, the liquor more than served its purpose.

A boat from America to Medua carrying immigrant Montenegrins bent on helping their native Montenegro in the war (effort) and other passengers was sunk very close to Medua. Most passengers drowned. Apparently, the reason they drowned was that they had their life savings on their persons, refusing to give them up. Be that as it may, some did make it by swimming toward shore, where they were picked up by English sailors in lifeboats. In charge of the Port Authority was no other than Admiral Traubridge, that same person who had allowed the *Goeben* to make it through (the Straits) and who consequently was "exiled" to Belgrade.

Traubridge had noticed my name on this box of hospital supplies carrying the cognac and wine. He had it opened and used it as medicine and body rub on the survivors, saving lives.

There is some consolation in that thought.

New Year's Eve was spent organizing and packing until 3:00 in the morning.

We departed Scutari at 7:00 in the morning of January 1 on horseback. I shall never, ever forget that day or that journey, the most exhausting of all our wanderings.

The weather was awful. A cold sharp wind whipped our faces. Rain was followed by snow. The road was in terrible condition, full of ditches and potholes. The scene was much the same: refugees, soldiers, exhausted and cold, rested at the roadside. Freshly made graves with crosses lined the road on each side in anticipation that Prince Alexander and the foreign diplomats would be passing by. We had to dismount to avoid trampling over carcasses of horses left right where they fell. I honestly consider the fifty-three kilometers from Scutari to the coast as the Way of the Cross, for all the suffering the Serbian people had to face.

I was so exhausted I was barely able to move. As we approached Medua in total darkness, blinded by the snow, we heard voices of soldiers walking toward us, the other way. Apparently, their evacuation was postponed because of us.

As we made our way toward the harbor and saw the flickering lights of the ships that would take us away, we came across a refugee camp of more than four thousand people awaiting evacuation. Most had been there for almost a month, camping under an open sky. There was no shelter from the wind, rain, or cold and hardly any food. Women built makeshift tents for their children from skirts. Frequent Austrian bombardments only aggravated their situation. An occasional boat could only board from 300 to 350 refugees at a time. People jumped into the water, desperately grabbing at the boats in hopes of being taken aboard, only to be pushed away. There were incidents of miscarriages, even insanity. It took numerous telegrams, much tenacity and cajoling before they were finally evacuated.

While we were waiting, Traubridge came by to invite Pašić, Des Gras, Bopp, and myself to dinner. Occupied with spoon-feeding tea to the minister of education, who was doubled over with colic, Pašić declined. The three of us blindly followed Traubridge to some sort of barn, which he had transformed into a temporary dining room. The strong and icy wind threatened to tear off our overcoats. Poor Bopp's cheek became greatly swollen, making him even more unhappy. The pleasure of a delicious beef Wellington almost obliterated the memory of our recent discomforts, and Traubridge was an accommodating host. We left at 10:00, rejoining Pašić.

There was only one steamship in Medua, which was being fixed up for us. We thought that we might have to put off our departure until the next day. Traubridge left. Just as we were about to give up, Traubridge returned, inviting only the ministers and ambassadors to go with him. The secretaries and everyone else would have to wait until morning. We followed him down to the shoreline. Twelve to fifteen of us squeezed somehow into a launch. There was no room for any baggage whatsoever. The going was very rocky. Our vessel, the armed Italian merchant ship *Città di Bari*, was waiting for us at anchor at quite a distance.

It was exceedingly difficult for me to part with Mamulov. I had no way of knowing whether he would make it to this boat, never mind the things. Traubridge promised to do what he could to reunite Mamulov with me. Another hour or two passed by. To my greatest joy, there he was! And with all our things! He and the efficient Greek chargé d'affaires managed to get all personal belongings to the diplomats on board. I heaved a big sigh of relief at the sight of Mamulov. I felt bad for Pašić and his colleagues, who did not even carry a change of clothes. Their things arrived a week later. At this moment, my one thought was that I would no longer need to walk long distances, nor would I need any longer to comply with my fate. I was at peace at last.

19. Medua, 1915. Evacuation to Corfu.

Our boat was bound for Brindisi. General Mondesir, who was in charge of the reorganization of the Serbian army, would apprise us of our final destination, as well as that of the army: Bizerte, France, or Corfu. There were many of us in the dirty, brightly lit cabin: ministers, army generals, and representatives of different countries. As I sat next to Pašić, I watched the lights of Medua suddenly vanish through the porthole. The stormy sea rocked us back and forth. We were overwhelmed. We had departed from the shores of Albania and left Serbia far behind! Ours was an exodus of a nation keeping faith that the Eastern star would guide it back to its homeland. I was witnessing a great historical drama and one of the most tragic.

The first person to speak up was Marinković.

"A year ago, some novelist writing about this experience would have been criticized for unlikely fiction, 'qu'il a manqué de mesur' [that he missed the point]."

Pašić sat deep in thought. He appeared to be more energetic than his seventy years. Finally, he said, "Yes, we lost everything. We saved only an image of Serbia."

Such words should be relegated to the finale of some great drama, as the curtain descends in the theater. It was not an actor expressing his sufferings, but the leader of men involving his people in this sacred image of their homeland, a shining beacon of hope, steadily lighting the way.

10

Corfu

Our ship maintained a zigzag pattern to avoid enemy submarines. We arrived at last in the port of Brindisi at 5:00 in the evening on January 2. Mrs. Pašić was there to meet her husband. She was a kindly person, most respectful of her husband, and somewhat intimidated by him. How wonderful it was to witness the loving reunion of these two dear old people.

That same evening we, the ambassadors, left for Rome. The Serbian ministers remained in Brindisi in order to proceed on to Corfu, the final destination of the Serbian army. How supremely happy we all were as we disembarked. We were once again in civilized surroundings, away from danger. Our trials and tribulations were left behind! Even to sit in a filthy station awaiting our train was almost pleasant.

Taking advantage of train connections in Bari, Mamulov and I made a quick side trip to the magnificent Russian Orthodox Church of St. Nicholas, still in the process of construction and funded by the Palestinian Society.[1] The priest in charge was none other than the former choir director of the embassy church in Constantinople, my good friend, Father Kulakov. He and his entire family greeted me as if I were their own. What a pleasure it was to reminisce about Constantinople and to feel the permeating warmth of the hospitable, good Russian family! It was a glimpse of home, and we decided to visit Bari once again before our departure to Russia.

A small incident occurred on the train to Rome. It was very hot in the night, and I decided to get up and turn on the fan. It was difficult to see in the dark, so I pulled the first handle I discovered. There was loud screeching, and the train immediately ground to a halt—I had pulled the emergency brake!

I called the train conductors and explained my predicament. They accepted my explanation, and we resumed our trip without any further incidents.

I had hoped to get some respite in Rome—perhaps even enjoy a short holiday—but it was decided in St. Petersburg that I should proceed on to Corfu without delay. The Italian government was rushing its ambassador to Corfu as well. Bopp, ill and fatigued, did not have the strength to go with us and left for Paris instead. Schvitti departed on his own to join the Serbian ministers. Sir Charles and I, along with the faithful Mamulov, traveled back to Brindisi and boarded a minesweeper for Corfu on January 7. The sea was calm, and we enjoyed sailing close to Valona. We reached the port of Corfu in the evening, where we saw a great many Allied, primarily French, warships—battle cruisers, minesweepers, and so on. We disembarked and set off toward the city on foot.

I was to spend two restful months at the Hotel St. Georges, occupying a corner room on the third floor. When I woke up that first morning, I sat for hours looking out of the window, taking in the breathtaking sights and sounds of my surroundings. The hotel was located at a square where military drill took place. Directly in front of me stood an old picturesque citadel. To the left, there was a beautiful palace. The azure sea enveloped everything in a gentle glow. Overwhelmed by a sense of calm and happiness, I felt the soft breeze blow across my face. There was nowhere to rush, nowhere to go. I cabled my wife that I had found myself in an earthly paradise!

The days were pleasant in their blissful monotony. I thoroughly enjoyed my long walks along the waterfront and into the interior of the island, through the gardens, villas, and olive groves. The golden oranges and mandarins seemed a reflection of the sun, and the pale oranges resembled moonlight. The pleasant odors and bright colors were those of the bountiful South. From the edge of the island, there was a breathtaking view of a romantic little islet on which Arnold Böcklin had based his painting *Isle of the Dead*. I had no idea how he used this magnificent isle resembling a bouquet of flowers in the middle of the sea for such a somber theme.

Occasionally, we went for longer drives around the island. Among other things, we visited the famous Achilleion Palace. A French officer guard took us around the wonderful park, which has an excellent view of the sea. However, I found the architectural style quite tasteless. Empress Elizabeth had intended to build a monument to Achilles, portrayed as he lay mortally wounded in the heel. Kaiser Wilhelm, who acquired the palace after the death of the Austrian empress, did not like this one bit. He decided to "correct" history and duly erected a colossal statue of Achilles, which seems to threaten the island and the entire world. In other words, Achilles had joined the Prussian army. The monument bears the inscription: "From Wilhelm, to Achilles."

We also visited the Serbian army camps organized in the interior of the island, between olive groves. When the decision to withdraw the Serbian forces to Corfu was made, there were no proper facilities to accommodate such a large number of people. Although the days were warm even for January, the nights in Corfu were cold, which, when added to the general exhaustion of the troops, resulted in high mortality.

At first, the evacuation of the Serbian armies was precipitous and disorganized. There were no barracks or tents set up as yet. They had to disembark on Vido, a small island opposite Corfu, where the French had hospitals and some medical personnel for physical assessment; 150 soldiers died per day, their bodies simply thrown into the sea from the shoreline. Eventually, a boat would come to remove the dead bodies and cast them farther out into the sea. By the time I visited Vido, the worst was over, and the mortality rate was next to nothing. Most of the victims were the boy recruits. Luckily, no epidemics broke out of the type that had ravaged Serbia the previous year.

The decision to evacuate was too long in coming. I must admit, however, that once it was made, the French took charge and did an excellent job. Small French steamships took the evacuees from Medua to Valona and Durazzo. From Valona and Durazzo, large transport ships sailed in convoy with French and Italian warships to Corfu. Consequently, not a single transport ship was sunk. The French provided war matériel and, along with the English, food. To evacuate 150,000 people, to clothe them, feed them, and once again transform them into a fighting force was no easy task. The French, helped by the English and Italians, managed to turn these beleaguered, starving soldiers into some kind of an army. By the end of February, the evacuation was complete.

Every morning I used to walk from my hotel down to the port, which bustled with activity. Considering the great variety of cargo boats and other vessels, the unloading of supplies and equipment was precisely engineered and well organized by the French. English trucks, under the efficient command of French General de Mondesir, transported supplies to the Serbian encampments. Personally, I found Mondesir to be somewhat aloof and pompous. He was disgusted with the Serbian laissez-faire attitude and disorganization. It was fortunate for the Serbs that his aides, taking everything with a grain of salt, were able to persuade the general to let the Serbs well alone and not undertake any severe measures. Bojović, who replaced Putnik, and the new Minister of War Tersić, were appreciative of the French effort and did their best to establish a solid working relationship.

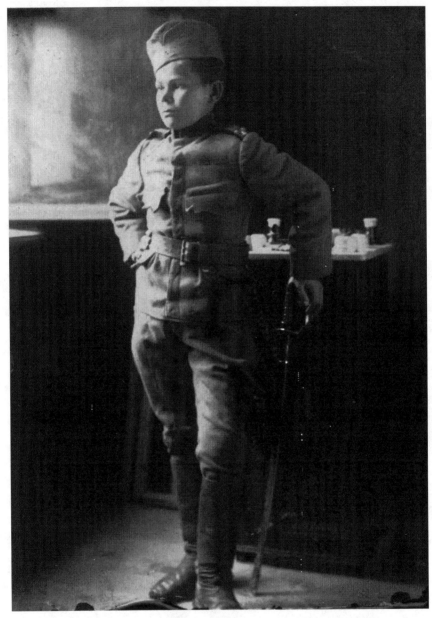

20. 1916. Voluntary Serbian teenage recruit. Postcard.

Apart from Mondesir, there was the energetic, fascinating Admiral De Gedon,[2] who came from a distinguished and aristocratic family. This family had achieved great heights in French naval history and had a ship named after them. De Gedon was a pleasant and charming man. He had seen much over the course of his career in the navy and used to tell extremely interesting stories of his endeavors. In contrast to the pompous Mondesir, he was straightforward and to the point.

The new ambassador from France, Bopp's replacement, was Boisson. Before the war he resigned from diplomatic service and was called to military duty. He served in the Dardanelles where, after being wounded, he returned to diplomacy. A person of great wealth and a Protestant, he was self-disciplined and intelligent. He, De Gedon, and Mondesir met every day to coordinate their various agendas.

The last boat to arrive on Corfu was that of Prince Alexander, who had been very ill and suffered from gallstones. The prince was given an honorary salute. French snipers, in Corfu for a rest, and Serbian battalions formed a ceremonial guard of honor. How handsome they were, those young Serbian soldiers, as they proceeded with their ceremonial march. A senior colonel wiped away tears. These young men embodied the future resurrection of Serbia itself.

Time on Corfu seemed to have slowed down. Unfortunately, the weather took a turn for the worse, with rains and heavy winds reminiscent of the Italian sirocco. To amuse ourselves, we often had breakfast and lunch at the house of a Russian Greek by the name of Logofetti. At the outbreak of the war, this wealthy shipping magnate who usually resided in Taganrog found himself in Corfu, where he had a magnificent villa. Both he and his English wife were ardent Russian patriots, even if they spoke a somewhat peculiar form of Russian. As they had no children of their own, their niece lived with them. Their hospitality knew no bounds, and they never tired of asking me to move in with them. Naturally, I did not want to abuse their hospitality; still, we often visited them, and I even used to take a bath before lunch. We played bridge in the afternoon.

I also got to spend plenty of time with the crown prince Alexander. Still young and lonely, he yearned for his homeland. We took long walks, discussing anything that came to mind. His mistrust of me faded, except in those fleeting moments when he feared we might be tempted to abandon the faithful Serbs for the treacherous Bulgarians.

I often recall the Church of St. Spiridon, belonging to the Count Bulgaris family, where the relics of this great saint were kept. This landmark church came under the patronage of Russia at the time of Catherine the Great, which explains the emblem of the imperial eagle over the portals. There is a chalice attributed to Benvenuto Cellini. The enormous chandelier of gold was made in the eighteenth century.

Before long, the prince and Pašić traveled to the mainland in pursuit of continuing Allied support. There was not much more for me to do here. I took advantage of this opportunity and was permitted to take a leave. I expected to be away for no more than four months.

Pašić and Iovanović went a few days earlier. I left Corfu on March 2, 1916, for Brindisi, together with the prince and Mamulov on a French minesweeper. The weather was pleasant enough. The commander: a most gallant fellow. Suddenly, an alarm sounded.

"Un sousmarin! [a submarine!]"

The reaction was instant. The crew went into overdrive, shouting "un sousmarin, un sousmarin" with spontaneous enthusiasm. In a matter of minutes our minesweeper was ready for the inevitable encounter with the submarine and made directly for the periscope protruding from the water's surface. Two more minutes went by. The periscope turned out to be a buoy. The sailors did not disguise their disappointment, a disappointment certainly not shared by the civilian passengers.

I later experienced a similar false alarm in the English Channel. I was standing by a small gun, which fired twice when the crew claimed to have seen a periscope. The first shot was a near miss, but the second one hit the bull's-eye—an excellent achievement given that we were sailing at twenty-two knots. These two occasions convinced me how brave French sailors were and how they relished a dangerous situation!

Once again it was necessary to change trains in Bari for Rome. This time, Mamulov and I decided to make a quick visit to the (Catholic) basilica to venerate the relics of St. Nicholas.

Our kind Albanian housekeeper, Maria, had exacted a vow from me to light a special candle to St. Nicholas.

"You will come to no harm because he will protect you," she had said.

We traveled across all of Italy, from south to north. From the very first moment of our arrival in Italy, I was surprised at how little the war reflected in everyday life. The only indication of something out of the ordinary was the presence in Bari of *carabinieri* (police) requesting to see our documents. The other was the unusually low hotel prices in Rome, obviously due to a lack of tourists. For the second time, I was deeply touched by the hospitable Strandtmann family, who greeted us with such warmth.

11

EUROPE

I f the war was little felt in Italy, the opposite was true in the empty streets of Paris. The absence of men was obvious. It took us at least half an hour to find a porter upon our arrival at the railway station. We chose the Hotel Continental because of its central location and proximity to the Tuileries, which looked particularly charming in the early spring. I spent ten days in Paris. I needed time to order a new wardrobe, but most important, I was interested in the results of the Allied conference just getting under way. The Serbs expected much from this conference, especially from the discussions concerning the upcoming Salonika expedition.

At this point, no one really knew the actual tally of Allied forces in Salonika, though people estimated approximately 220,000. The reorganized Serbian army was expected to be over 100,000. To everyone's consternation, a telegram from Prince Alexander in the autumn of 1916 indicated that these numbers were vastly exaggerated. He was "obliged" to dispel Allied illusions. He determined that in reality there were no more than 120,000 Allied and Serbian bayonets in all. Such gross error was typical of Allied coalition planning. I understood then why General Sarrail had been unable to undertake any kind of action.

Back in March 1916, however, we had the mistaken notion that by summertime there would be 330,000 bayonets in Salonika, an unrealistic number for a successful military venture according to the crown prince. He calculated that the forces in Salonika should be increased to a half million soldiers; otherwise, a large number of troops would remain inactive. An army this size could wage a much more successful campaign in the Balkans, defeating Bulgaria and taking Constantinople rather than pursuing a campaign in Europe, where victory was hard to come by. As he outlined this plan to me, the prince emphasized that Russian interests were taken into consideration. I felt gratified. This not only coincided with my personal opinion, but it could conceivably become policy.

I encountered Zhilinskii in my hotel. He concurred with this point of view. As emissary of the tsar to the French General Headquarters, he promised to raise this point at the conference. I was convinced that a turnaround in the Balkans would have a decisive impact on the European war, especially if we could persuade the Rumanians to join us and invade Bulgaria, concomitantly with an Allied advance northward from Salonika. As for Izvolskii, our ambassador, I already knew that he held the same view.

How unfortunate for us that our representatives were able to pursue but a fraction of this attractive possibility. Joffre was critical of the Salonika expedition. In his time, Delcassé had promised 150,000 soldiers to the Greeks and Serbs, much against his better judgment.

Briand, who later replaced him, favored a more energetic policy to include the Balkans. Thanks to him, our delegates were able to obtain a promise from Joffre on the eve of the conference not to cancel this expedition.

With the arrival of delegates from England and Italy, private meetings were set up between the Russians, the French, and the English, who were represented by Kitchener and his chief of staff, Robertson. The English were of the opinion that there were too many unengaged soldiers in Salonika and not enough men for an advance. Instead of rationalizing the need for more forces in Salonika, however, they were set upon recalling their army personnel. This was met with a strong rebuff on the part of Joffre, disinclined to carry the burden on his own. Our delegates emphasized the moral blow that a partial recall of the forces from Salonika would have. The matter came to an end with the decision not to recall the forces from Salonika at the moment.

The Italians declined at this time to send forces to Salonika. The general consensus was that they could easily have done so: they had less than half of their total military at the front lines. We were expected to send a brigade to Salonika.

The conference proceedings were meant to ratify the earlier private discussions.

Rather unexpectedly, however, the leftist French delegate Bourgeois suggested drawing up a joint resolution on war aims, which implicitly referred to Poland. Izvolskii feared the recognition of certain Polish rights might serve as precedent for international law, and he did not shy away from telling Briand as much. Briand tactfully avoided bringing up the issue.

The Polish Question gave our representatives in Allied countries a difficult time. I had to tackle it the very first day after my arrival in Rome from Albania, when the former deputy in the State Duma and leader of the National Democratic Party Roman Dmowski came to see me in my hotel. I had seen Dmowski on several occasions, the last of which had been at the beginning of the war. At the time, Grand Duke Nikolai Nikolaevich's proclamation already existed in draft form, and Dmowski knew its content thanks to his friendship with Wielopolski, who had translated it into Polish. Dmowski then told me his rather far-fetched dreams of territorial expansion, which included Posen and Danzig, the latter being necessary to provide Poland with an outlet to the sea. He was of the opinion that the more Prussian territories Poland acquired, the nearer it would draw to Russia, as the efforts of the Polish people would be squarely focused on the struggle against Germanism. The question of Poland's constitutional makeup, while important, was only secondary to Dmowski and had to be subordinated firmly to the question of national unification.

I agreed with these ideas and principles, and they became the basis for the grand duke's proclamation. When Sazonov and I were working on it, we realized we would have to mention the question of Polish national unification, which Russia alone could resolve—Germany could offer the Poles nothing comparable. This was important in that it would determine the future political orientation of the Polish state, much like the Treaty of San Stefano determined Bulgaria's political orientation over the following decades.

The Dmowski whom I met in Rome was very different from the reserved, detached politician I had known earlier. His very first words revealed bitterness and disappointment with Russia. He could barely contain himself as he explained how much Minister of Interior Maklakov's policy had wronged the Poles. Russian administrators seemed determined to treat the grand duke's proclamation as a "scrap of paper" that in no way affected them. The situation grew considerably worse once the retreat began, resulting in irreparable damage. According to Dmowski, the Russian troops burned the towns and villages, looted the countryside, and forced the population to retreat with them. Apart from being exceedingly cruel, this policy was utterly useless, since the army took only old men, women, and children— young, healthy men hid in the forests and returned to their pillaged homes afterward. "The Poles cannot think about the possible return of Russian troops without a sense of dread and horror," Dmowski concluded.

Our enemies benefited from the growing Polish resentment of Russia. The famous social democratic leader Piłsudski organized Polish legions in Austria and promised to raise an army of 700,000 after a Polish proclamation of independence. The Austrians looked into the matter and seemingly decided they could raise as many as one million Polish recruits. Along with the Germans, they decided to take matters into their own hands and bypass Piłsudski. In any event, they remained doubtful of the loyalty of Polish soldiers. The Germans forced many able-bodied Poles to move to the interior of Germany in order to free up German workers for the army. They succeeded in bringing 150,000 Poles to Germany by promising these starving people food and good wages in Germany. According to Dmowski, there were three facets to Germany's Polish policy. First, the Germans refused to recognize Poznań as a Polish region. Second, their treatment of Russian Poland was quite liberal, aiming to demonstrate the superiority of German to Russian rule. Third, the Germans encouraged Poles to claim Lithuania as their own. Even though they offered to introduce Polish as the language of administration in Vilnius, however, they failed to tempt the local Polish population. True to their arrangement with Russia regarding the ethnographic borders of Poland, the Poles of Vilnius elected to retain Russian as the language of administration.

Nevertheless, Dmowski considered the German temptation to be very dangerous. On the one hand, there were the horrific memories of Russian rule; on the other hand, the promise of independence, even if it was a clever trick. The very thought of seeing the Polish flag fly and a Polish king rule could inspire the impressionable Poles. Dmowski told me that he feared for his people. He himself knew that yielding to German temptations would be fatal for Poland, but the suffering Poles might not realize this. He concluded by saying the only solution was for the Allies to come up with a joint proclamation on Polish independence. In this way, Russia could bolster its faltering prestige and make sure that it did not force one million Polish soldiers to join Germany.

I replied that, having just left Albania, I knew nothing of the Russian government's plans regarding Poland. As a private individual, however, I was of the opinion that the Polish Question was an internal Russian matter and had nothing to do with the other Allies. I did not think the Poles would benefit from its internationalization either. Nobody had lifted a finger to help the cause of Polish independence. At the same time, Russia would feel bound by a promise it alone had given to the Poles much more than a forced international concession. Russian dignity would not accept such a solution. "Russian dignity!" Dmowski exclaimed. "And what would you say about Polish dignity after all Poland has suffered at the hands of your government?" He further hinted at the danger of Polish recruits in the German army. It seemed to me there was an element of blackmail, though perhaps this word is a bit too strong.

After I had informed Giers of my conversation with Dmowski, he told me that the Poles were working hard to win sympathy in Rome. Russian

diplomatic representatives thought it imperative to make a public statement regarding Poland as soon as possible. This was the only way out of an
increasingly dangerous impasse. Izvolskii talked to me at great length about
the dangers of growing French sympathy for Poland, as did our ambassador
in London, Count Benckendorff, even though the English were traditionally
a lot more reserved than the French. The two ambassadors asked to relay
this to Sazonov after my arrival in St. Petersburg. I did just that, but Sazonov
already knew perfectly well that a decision had to be made.

My ten very educational days in Paris left me with a lasting impression.
I hardly recognized Paris, that fun-loving and frivolous city. An underlying
seriousness, an awareness of the significance of events, pervaded the streets.
There was little movement of any kind even in the boulevards.

As I mentioned earlier, there was a noticeable absence of young men,
except for some Swiss waiters. The street lamps, covered with shades to hide
the light from aeroplanes, cast a dim light. Gone were the familiar elegance
and fashion. In the restaurants and theaters there was no trace whatsoever
of jewelry or expensive toiletries. Coattails disappeared from fashion. The
new norm was to walk back to the hotel from the theater, as cabs were
nowhere to be seen. The military attaché in Paris was the young and energetic yet somewhat boisterous Colonel Count Ignatiev. His was the enormous responsibility of overseeing military orders on our behalf in France.
Considering that he was totally unprepared and completely on his own, he
created a formidable organization bursting with activity.[*]

Ignatiev offered me a tour of the factories built with our money and
working exclusively for us. I readily agreed to such an opportunity. Ignatiev
put a Frenchman, Colonel Chevalier, at my disposal who took me on a comprehensive tour from one end of Paris to the other.

What I saw was really impressive. At one munitions factory, where I met
Mr. Citroën, there were five thousand workers of which two thousand were
women. He took me into his office and opened an album for me to look at.
The first photograph was that of a vegetable garden surrounded by fields.
It was labeled April 1915. On the next sheet, there was a skeleton wooden
structure in place of the garden, labeled May. Next there was August, with
finished buildings, and by September, missiles ready for use. At the time of
my visit, the factory was producing ten thousand shells a day exclusively for

---

[*] He was also in charge of counterespionage in Switzerland. In this time of conflict, countries
invested enormous and uncontrolled sums of money in espionage. He bought up military supplies and
built munitions factories. He hired a talented engineer from Odessa by the name of Sitrone. To sound
more like a Frenchman, this fellow moved the e around and changed his name to Citroën.

Russia. I do not have much experience of factory production, but there was no doubting the competency and efficient use of labor.

Both men and women worked with exact precision. The women were especially efficient. Up to twenty women at a long table passed shells to each other with incredible dexterity and speed. Each shell was thoroughly inspected.

Apparently, most of them had been seamstresses before the war and thus were accustomed to fine needlework.

After the revolution, Ignatiev returned to Russia and handed over to the Soviets all the funds that had been placed in his charge. Moscow gave him the rank of general. This remarkable and distinguished gentleman was then put in charge of receiving important visitors to Moscow. As for Citroën, he lost a fortune in Monte Carlo. He went from being a major industrialist to a servile director of a factory left behind by Ignatiev.

I toured a plant that manufactured a type of heavy vehicle tractor able to surmount trenches and scale up and down steep inclines. In another, I witnessed the testing of machine guns.

The bustle of activity was efficient. It reflected that inherent Latin process of logical thought that was the essence of France, where every possibility was pursued with innate practicality, clarity, and talent for organization. To my mind these factories and plants testified to the great concentration of effort by a people driven by the present uncertainty.

This was during the second month of the siege of Verdun. Already then, Frenchmen—illumined by a halo of everlasting glory—began to question whether they had enough manpower to endure. Would Russia, with its seemingly endless manpower, perhaps come to the aid of its ally?

There were a number of well-chosen officers from our general staff in Paris. Some had come on military business; others were attached to Zhilinskii's military mission. Most arrived directly from our front lines with the prejudicial notion that the French army was not active enough and that the burden of war rested on our shoulders.

As they witnessed the enormous toil in the interior and the organization of the front lines, that prejudice was quickly eradicated, and these same individuals almost turned into French zealots. At this moment in time (March 1916), they felt that the French front was significantly more important than the Russian front because of the massive German presence. Our officers maintained that only upon their arrival in France did they realize how the war should be waged. They regarded our methods to be primitive in comparison. Joffre's careful preservation of human life was, according to them, a major achievement, even if Russian society regarded this somewhat critically. Every maneuver was carefully worked out and nothing was left to chance.

In order to relieve the German pressure at Verdun, we undertook an attack around Baranovichi. I saw the telegrams Zhilinskii was receiving from the Stavka. The young colonel who brought them to me was utterly dejected, saying we had not learned anything. Our artillery was ill prepared when we began the offensive. After our first successes, we suffered enormous losses. We retreated to our initial positions without gaining anything. The loss of these lives was demoralizing. Our military representatives in France reported on each operation with great detail. Unfortunately, the Stavka retained its derogatory attitude toward the French and refused to believe we could learn anything from them. Even Chief of Staff General Alekseev shared this opinion.

In the opinion of Zhilinskii's aide, sending the French thirty thousand soldiers per month as requested would be in our interests. Such a plan, however, could never work. We did not have enough officers. Russian soldiers without our officers would become *chair à canon* [cannon fodder] in French ranks. There was no possibility of that.

The French also wanted workers from Russia for their factories, since their own workers were working for us. They could not quite believe that we had a labor crisis in Russia. How to explain the actual economic situation, the general mismanagement in Russia, and the misappropriation of funds both in the interior and at the front? To put it mildly, the French war economy was intensive, and the Russian war economy was extensive.

I visited the embassy quite often and found that Izvolskii had aged. He and his wife greeted me warmly. Izvolskii eagerly expounded on his "political philosophy." He was a clever and experienced politician, knowledgeable in his field and quite out of the ordinary. As minister of foreign affairs, he had served Russia well. A good relationship was established with Japan, significant at the start of the European conflict. He worked out the entente with England. He reorganized the ministry and brought in talented people. He was all in all a good person, albeit somewhat vain. Even though people undervalued him due to his vanity, Izvolskii was one of our best diplomats. I listened intently and found his "political philosophy" to be "practical politics" and a reflection of his abilities.

He was inclined to associate with aristocracy, preferring the company of the older and less interesting circles of the Faubourg St. Germain. Because of this, of course, he did not have much social contact with the ruling democratic republicans of France. It was up to Sevastopoulos, the embassy counselor, to consolidate these connections.

Greek by birth, Sevastopoulos was capable, intelligent, and clever. However, he was not easily accepted into diplomatic service. The posting of attaché to the embassy in Paris was as far as he could be expected to go in the service. Before long, however, he became the counselor to the embassy in Paris, a most desirable position. He tactfully cultivated friendly relationships with leading republicans and intellectuals, who were of much greater interest to me than some dukes and duchesses or other. Thanks to his soirées, I had the pleasure of meeting fascinating people, such as Jack Berard, one of the rising stars in Parliament; the playwright Robert de Flers; and the journalist Hebette. It was also there that I saw old man Cruppi and his wife.[1] I had met them in the summer of 1915 in Niš, which they visited as part of Cruppi's tour of the Balkans and Russia in the capacity of representative of the *Matin* newspaper. Cruppi had once been a minister of foreign affairs briefly and now served as a member of Parliament. His wife was an extremely intelligent and cultivated woman who was interested in music and the arts. They had left Niš together with my wife, who helped them in any way she conceivably could on their joint trip to Russia. Consequently, Cruppi and his wife were eager to extend the same courtesy to me during my stay in Paris.

Another interesting person I met was a certain Mrs. Shimkevich, a Russian Jewess who had moved from Moscow to Paris in her youth and subsequently married the famous painter Carolus-Duran. When her husband left her for another woman, she contemplated suicide. Thankfully, the Cruppis looked after her during this time of ordeal, and she started a new life, making a number of new connections in political and media circles. Her quick wit and good looks made her literary salon very popular, to the point where Briand and other statesmen became frequent visitors. She knew positively everybody who was anybody.

My conversations with these people left me with two impressions of French political life.

The first was their deeply felt commitment to the war. Gone was any trace of French frivolity.

They explored ways in which to organize the country better. Their dissatisfaction with the present regime was obvious. That was my second impression.

"The parliamentary system has become obsolete," said one member of Parliament.

"Just wait until the soldiers, *les poilus* [combatants], return from the front. They'll show us," said another.

"Excuse me, gentlemen," Cruppi interjected. "I've heard so much about the hopes for a parliamentary system in Russia, that ours cannot be as bad as it looks."

And so it was that I peered into the world of French politics. Back in Russia, I often recalled these conversations whenever I heard sharp criticisms of our administration: criticisms that, no matter how justifiable, gave rise to mistaken illusions.

My ten days in Paris flew by imperceptibly. I accepted an invitation by the Serbian crown prince, who stayed in the same hotel as us, to join him for his trip to London. I had successfully avoided the official events and receptions in his honor. It was difficult enough to return to the hotel surrounded every day by crowds gathered in a demonstration of solidarity.

The Channel crossing went without a hitch. The weather was beautiful. We were escorted by cruisers. Above us were dirigibles on the lookout for submarine boats. There was the matter of a buoy that was fired upon because it was mistaken for the periscope of a submarine.

Upon our arrival in London, the crown prince was received with ceremonial fanfare, which I watched from the train window. He was met by the English crown prince along with the entire English cabinet. An honor guard stood at attention. A rumble in the distance was superseded by cheering crowds.

Sazonov sent a telegram urging my return. I was able to spend only two days in London. My stay, unfortunately, was too short to make any kind of solid impression.

At first glance, it seemed that the war affected London and the English much less than Paris and the French. There were noticeably more men of military age in the streets. In the Ritz Hotel, where I stayed, the gentlemen sported coattails, and the ladies wore diamonds.

Champagne flowed. This was in part because the English are a lot more conservative in their tastes than the French, which makes it difficult to change. The main reason, however, was that the enemy was less than a hundred kilometers away from Paris, whereas the English were separated from them by a body of water. Only the occasional zeppelin threatened the peace of London's residents.

I paid a visit to our ambassador, Count Benckendorff. I had never met him before but had learned to respect him from his correspondence with the ministry. He came from an aristocratic family close to the imperial court and was a diplomat of the old school. Being half-foreign, his Russian language was lacking, and all mail and telegrams were written in French. Wiry and small in stature, he amazed me with his lively energy. His speech was rapid, interspersed here and there with some astute observation of people or situations. He had an uncommon flair, a sixth sense, giving him the ability to perceive the reality of a situation and its outcome. English political circles had confidence in him as an aristocrat and a gentleman, especially since he had been in London for so long. The king trusted Benckendorff and, on one occasion, even told Sazonov that, if he were to lose Benckendorff, all England would be in mourning. Russia owes him a great deal. This half foreigner did much to overcome the prejudices and suspicions of the English toward Russia. I expressed to Benckendorff my thoughts regarding the Salonika expedition and the significance of a Balkan campaign for the European arena. At Benckendorff's request, I paid a visit to Nicholson, a colleague of the secretary of state for foreign affairs to whom I repeated the same. Although Nicholson agreed with some points and generally showed enthusiasm, I sensed his misgivings.

As for Salonika, he replied, "Yes, but where do we find more soldiers?"

Meanwhile, the general opinion was that the English did have divisions they could send to Salonika, without endangering the western front.

On that same day I left for Newcastle, where we embarked on the *Jupiter* to Bergen.

On board we met the Russian journalist and literary critic Chukovskii and Joshua Wilton, a correspondent in St. Petersburg.[2] Both were on their way back from an intensive tour of France and England by Russian journalists. They were in England at the invitation of the British government. I also made the acquaintance of a well-known statesman involved in bringing together the Church of England and the Russian Orthodox Church. Chukovskii was the nicest gentleman, very talented and witty. The long journey to St. Petersburg flew by thanks to his endless high spirits and every possible joke. We stopped overnight in Stockholm.

I clearly heard Russian spoken in the streets. I was told that there were forty thousand resident Russians, many of whom were draft dodgers. The situation in Sweden was a bit problematic. The army and the aristocracy did not hide their pro-German sentiments, in spite of the general mood of apprehension. Fortunately, Parliament and democratic circles opted for peace. It was the opinion of many that springtime could possibly bring some unpleasantness. The railroad line was guarded by some Swedish military. A few spots had wire fences. All in all, these minimal preparations did not appear to be very serious.

12

RUSSIA

I arrived in St. Petersburg late at night on March 26 and was met by my brother-in-law, A. C. Bouteneff.[1] My wife had been ill with pneumonia. This was the reason for the telegram from Sazonov urging my quick return. Fortunately, she was feeling much better and insisted that her brother bring her along to St. Petersburg. She was waiting for me at the home of my niece, S. P. Lamsdorff.

I am not going to take the time to describe here what it felt like to come home after all my wanderings and anxious thoughts that, at best, I would be taken prisoner by the Austrians. I would prefer to dwell on subsequent and final events bringing me to the end of my notes.

Sazonov gave me leave to go home to Moscow. My whole family was there.

Moreover, my sister-in-law arrived with her husband, Konstantin Onou, from Holland to say good-bye.[2] They were on their way to America, where he was to take on the post of counselor to our embassy in Washington until the appointment of an ambassador.

A few weeks later, after Easter, Pašić and Iovanović arrived in St. Petersburg. I returned at this time for an audience with the tsar. Earlier I had written a letter for Sazonov to send to the tsar, in which I outlined my conviction that the war should be waged in the Balkans, with our forces in Rumania and the Allied forces in Salonika.*

---

* This letter, for whatever reason, is not contained in the published 1983 Russian version of the book. It was tucked away at the very end of the original manuscript. Trubetskoi refers to it as a continuation of the above. I feel that it should be included here. Tr.

During his stay in Petrograd, Pašić undoubtedly hoped to clarify Russia's views of the more pressing issues in Serbia. In essence, they were the following:

> What annexations could Serbia count upon in the future? And what actions will be undertaken in the Balkans by Russia and the Allies within the general framework of the war?
>
> As far as the question of Serbian annexations is concerned, in December of this past year, it had been determined that promises made by us will be honored. Furthermore, Bulgaria was promised annexation of lands by the Allied powers on condition that it comes over to our side with the stipulation that if it does not, the promises are not binding.
>
> Such is the present situation from a formal standpoint.
>
> In actual reality, when all of Serbia is presently occupied by Austro-Bulgarian armies, we need to focus on liberating it and certainly cannot consider whatever future compensations there might be. It would be enough to determine what we would be able to do for Serbia if circumstances permit.
>
> There is no doubt that it would be in our interest to expand Serbia at the cost of Austria, creating a strong Slavic government on the Adriatic to counterbalance Germanism.
>
> The Macedonian Question is far more complicated. Before Bulgaria entered the war, the Allies insisted on Serbia surrendering Macedonia to Bulgaria according to the Agreement of 1912. The powers hoped for Bulgarian cooperation in order to tailor an agreement between both governments along ethnic principles.
>
> It is impossible now to dwell on this due to the actions of Bulgaria.
>
> It is my deepest conviction that the fundamental reason for Bulgaria allying itself with the enemy can be attributed to its fear of Russian expansion in the Straits. Above all, the idea of taking over Constantinople never left Ferdinand's mind. He, as well as those around him, realizes full well that if Russia were to establish itself on the Straits, it would mean the end of Bulgarian dreams of hegemony in the Balkans.
>
> If Bulgaria resists the idea of a strong Russia in the Balkans, then I ask, would it be in our interest to wish for a stronger Bulgaria after its criminal siding with our enemies? On the other hand, if we pursue the question based on ethnic principles, then the answer would be that Macedonia, in its ethnic structure, cannot be called a purely Serbian or a purely Bulgarian region. It's as though its Slavic population were made of dough from which one could fashion either Serbs or Bulgarians. Therein

lies the reason for the fierce conflict between the two peoples, each following in its own convictions.

Even if at present no real foundation exists for returning the border to 1912 to the detriment of Serbia, it would be more prudent to confine our exchanges with the Serbs to vague well-wishing, in light of the ongoing course of the war in the Balkans and the possibility of a coup in Bulgaria.

In view of the above, I feel that we should limit ourselves now to a declaration to the Serbs of our sincerest desire to do everything possible to restore and possibly strengthen Serbia, while avoiding the Macedonian Question.

As to the ultimate aims of Serbia, the question before us is how to achieve them and, before anything else, the Salonika expedition. In his conversations with me in Paris and London, the Serbian crown prince expressed the following:

"The hope for a quick and complete success in the European theater of war seems dismal. The German loss at Verdun points to difficulties and sacrifice common to both sides as the Allies advance. The Balkans is a totally different matter, where the possibility of keeping Bulgaria subdued is quite real. The war and political ramifications of that would be enormous, especially if we were to cross the Danube.

"Such policy is of great interest to Russia and Serbia, bringing positive results of the war ending with control of the Straits. Only then could we induce Rumania and Greece to join our side. An advance in the Balkans could become the beginning of an advance for us in the European theaters of war."

I do not undertake to judge to what extent the Serbian heir to the throne is correct in his surmise, but it should not be excluded from further considerations concerning the war in the Balkans. Looking back it seems to me the significance of the Salonika expedition was somewhat overlooked by our allies.

The matter was basically concluded at half measures. This seems to me a continuation of blundering tactics in the Balkans on the part of the powers from the very start of this war.

There are 220,000–230,000 Allied troops in Salonika. If the Serbian forces get there, the total will be 330,000–340,000 soldiers. The numbers are too great for a defense only against Bulgaria's armies and not enough for an advance. They are not enough to bring Greece and Rumania to our side.

It may be educational to look at Germany in retrospect. In order to bring Bulgaria over, it did not pause to send sufficient forces to the

Balkans for a serious blow. Having achieved what they wanted, they recalled a larger part of their forces from Serbia and sent them elsewhere. Should not the Allies, in order to make allies of Greece and Rumania and to resolve the Balkan and Turkish Questions favorably, do the same?

According to the Serbian crown prince, there needs to be an army of 500,000 concentrated in Salonika. That would mean adding an army of 200,000 to the numbers already there. The English could lend such an army if pressured to do so and if they were to overcome their prejudices against the Salonika expedition. These forces at their disposal could be used elsewhere.

Of course I do not know whether we in turn could take on any actions against Bulgaria, providing an advance were to be put aside in the European front where we would temporarily continue to occupy a defense position.

A possible advance over the Danube would obviously have a deciding result with the Salonika expedition. In any case taking into consideration our developing success in Asia Minor, increasing the forces of the Salonika expedition would seem to be an important priority so that any significant advance against us in this theater of war would be routed.

Such are my general considerations, which I have allowed myself to bring to your attention.

One answer or another to the above questions is deemed essential to the formation of a general plan that can become a base of discussion for our representatives to the Allied governments and to the Balkans.

Accept . . . etc. etc.

Prince Trubetskoi

I more or less repeated this to the tsar, sharing my impression that the Allies did not place much significance in a wider field of action. They were concerned with the European fronts, which they felt to be more important. Certainly, the conference in Paris was a reflection of this when it decided not to increase Allied strength in the Balkans, thereby undermining what for us was so essential.

"That's for sure," the tsar interrupted me. "Success in the Balkans would force Rumania out of its neutrality and bring us closer to resolving the question of the Straits. What do you want me to do? I personally wrote the king of England a letter on this subject. With my permission, Alekseev wrote two more letters. The English won't listen to reason and do not want to send forces to Salonika."

I replied that, from my meetings in Paris and London, it was my impression the Allies would reconsider their policy about Salonika once they knew of our decision to attack Bulgaria from the north.

"We had a ready army in the autumn," said the tsar, "but, at that time, Rumania did not allow us to pass through its territory. Now the army is fragmented. Some of it has been sent to the Caucasus, the rest to other fronts. It would take another month or two to organize a new army. I shall do so if the Allies demonstrate a willingness to increase the army in Salonika."

"Your Majesty," I replied, "allow me to express my opinion regarding this question. I think that we should not leave the initiative up to our allies. We have two options. Either this is not of the utmost importance, in which case there is nothing to discuss, or we give serious thought to our campaign in the Balkans, take matters into our own hands, hit Bulgaria hard from the north, and demand that the forces in Salonika be increased, so as to launch a simultaneous attack from both ends."

"I say it to you once again," said the tsar. "This question is of the greatest importance to me, and I shall keep track of it. Kitchener is expected here shortly.[3] Unfortunately, he himself is against an expedition from Salonika. I've heard that he is losing his foothold in England."

As we know, Kitchener's ship hit a mine on its way to Russia. He perished in the explosion.

The conversation touched on Bulgaria.

"There were errors made in Bulgaria," said the tsar.

"Yes, the Allies made a few mistakes," I answered.

"And that is your opinion as well?" the tsar replied in a somewhat tart manner. I was caught off guard with that question. It appeared he was pleased by my subtle criticism of Sazonov. Just the day before, Sazonov was telling me that the tsar's attitude toward him had changed.

"Your Majesty," I said, "of course there were inevitable mistakes made from our side. That is a matter of course. However, I believe that Bulgaria's entry into the war against us did not result from diplomatic failures but from other, profound reasons. Simply put, Bulgaria did not want our entry into Constantinople."

"Why not? Wouldn't Bulgaria be better off as our neighbor?"

"They don't think this way."

"Well, yes. Ferdinand . . ."

"It is not only Ferdinand," I continued. "If he were alone in his thinking, we could have managed something. Ferdinand, however, relied on the support of those who were complicit in subterfuge. The Bulgarians understood very well that, if Russia were to occupy Constantinople, it would be the end of their hegemony in the Balkans. They would not be able to dominate their neighboring countries."

"Yes, of course," the tsar agreed. "I have cut Bulgaria out of my heart."

"Yes. But to change this situation, we need to hit Bulgaria hard. This comes back to my report to you."

My audience with the tsar was rather lengthy. Minister of Communications Trepov, who was waiting to be seen after me, became angry that he had been unable to report anything. Also in the waiting room were Minister of Finance Bark and Palace Chamberlain Voiekov, who was reputedly very influential. I had had to spend considerable time in the waiting room myself and was able to observe how insignificant both of these ministers were and how they tried to win the favor of the even less significant Voiekov. The whole thing was most unpleasant.

And so, in 1916, my diplomatic service came to an end. After a trip down the Volga and Kama, I returned to our estate in Vasil'evskoe, where we received the astounding news of Sazonov's dismissal and the appointment of Stürmer to the Ministry of Foreign Affairs.[4]

My first reaction was to resign from the Foreign Service. Sazonov persuaded me not to do so. The promotion to the control of foreign affairs of a person who knew nothing and had a bad reputation was absurd and could not possibly last for long. This appointment was calamitous for us. Sazonov's downfall was the Polish Question. He had been pushing for a wide autonomy for the Poles, something the tsar seemed in principle to agree with. Sazonov insisted that, if nothing were done, one fine day the tsar would read in the newspapers that the Germans had given the Poles much more. Any subsequent Russian concession to Poland would then appear to be forced and insufficient.

Sazonov had pleaded with the tsar not to assign the Polish Question to Stürmer, as he had different ideas. The tsar therefore instructed Sazonov to have Krirzanowski work on a draft project. Thereupon, Sazonov left the Stavka and took a medical leave of absence for a few days in a sanatorium in Finland. It was there that he received the news of his dismissal. In a personal letter to Sazonov, the tsar wrote that, after long deliberation, in view of Sazonov's long-standing conflict with the chairman of the Council of Ministers, he was letting Sazonov go, albeit very regretfully. His trust in Sazonov, as always, remained unwavering.

Sazonov responded by expressing his gratitude to the tsar for removing him from those responsibilities that he was finding difficult to assume due to a difference of opinion between himself and some of his less sincere colleagues. It was this very quality of sincerity, which the tsar saw fit to mention, that had engendered conflict with his colleagues in the cabinet.

Sazonov's dismissal astounded the Allies. The French and English put in requests, through their military representatives to the tsar, for his reinstatement. They manifested their incomprehension of his removal. The tsar replied that he understood how they felt but that Sazonov's health prevented him from carrying on. Why the tsar decided to resort to such an obvious lie, which everybody could see through, I do not know. I think the tsar's not untypical lack of courage played its part.

For everyone, the appointment of Stürmer was more depressing than Sazonov's dismissal.

I saw Stürmer for a few minutes in August. Feeling poorly, I decided to take a medical leave and travel to Kislovodsk. In view of this, I went to see the new minister and inform him that he should appoint a new minister plenipotentiary to Serbia if my absence from Corfu was inconvenient. Stürmer had no opinion on the matter, but his aides had informed him there was no need for him to urge my departure for Corfu, since I would have nothing to do there. His pomp and outer appearance made a bad impression on me. Tall, fat, with a scraggly beard, he was quite repulsive. His beady eyes were cold and nasty, with that typical expression of a self-important bureaucrat who wants to cover up an intellect devoid of any thought. Whatever courteous manners he may have had, they did little to enhance his image.

There was a general lament in the ministry. Everyone mourned Sazonov's departure. As for Stürmer, who spent half an hour a day at the ministry, the consensus was that he was essentially a boor, incapable of grasping any kind of new development. He took interest only in his personal advancement, his worldly affairs, and so forth. He was indifferent to the problems confronting Russia. I do think, however, that accusations of treason were unfounded. He was just too politically illiterate to promote his own agenda. Until his appointment, he knew less of foreign affairs than the average reader of a newspaper. He considered that Salonika had always belonged to Greece, so how did Allied forces turn up there? He also thought that the German ambassador continued to reside in Rome.

To cover up his general ignorance of things, he developed a tactic of silence during meetings with Allied representatives. During his four months as minister of foreign affairs, Russia lost what was left of its prestige. Our allies could not help but view us as an Oriental state, where all sorts of harebrained schemes were the order of the day.

I have an interesting story about Stürmer to tell, which took place upon my return from Kislovodsk in early October, when I decided to find out whether I should travel to my post in Corfu. I did not go to see Stürmer himself, as I figured he would discuss the matter with Neratov, who was de facto foreign minister. During my stay in St. Petersburg, I came across S. V. Tu-kholka, my old friend from Constantinople. Tukholka was a big eccentric, an idealist, and a wonderful person all round. Fate had taken him all over the Orient, where he served as a consul and devoted himself to the study of the occult and dark magic. He published several widely read brochures on the subject. Shortly before the outbreak of the war, he met a palm reader in St. Petersburg and married her.

Tukholka now invited me to dinner. His wife extended me a warm welcome. I had never before seen a palm reader or fortune-teller, but she looked exactly how I had imagined. Her age was impossible to tell, as was the color of her wild hair and the glow on her cheeks. Her dark blue eyes were especially unusual. She politely offered to read my palm. Although I was never favorably disposed to fortune-telling, I decided to give it a go. She asked me to write down two questions on a piece of paper and then fold it in four. My first question was: Will I have to travel overseas before the end of the year? My second question was: How long will Stürmer remain minister of foreign affairs?

Mrs. Tukholka picked up the piece of paper and pressed it to her forehead with one hand while holding my hand with the other. She instructed me to think about the question. Her husband came over, put his hand on her head, and told her to read my thoughts and answer the question. After meditating for a minute or so, she said: "You are wondering whether you'll have to travel abroad before the end of the year. Best not to. You'll have to leave after the new year, anyway, and the circumstances will be far more propitious then. Your job will be good to you." She then closed her eyes and replied to the second question: "Not long." Inquiring whether I wanted a more elaborate answer to the second question, she closed her eyes and fell into a delirium of sorts, saying: "I see a large office, with a large desk full of papers. A tall, fat man with a gray beard walks in and sits at the desk. He occupies an important post. You would like to know how much longer he will continue to occupy it. No, not long. His name is Stürmer."

I have to admit I found this quite impressive. Mrs. Tukholka seemed capable of reading people's thoughts, to the point where she could see what names they were thinking of. She also told me something that made a daunting impression on me. She told me that someone close to me would die in the near future. I did not tell anybody about this when I went back to Moscow, not even my wife. It came to pass—my brother-in-law F. D. Samarin passed away on October 23. Allow me to add that I have decided never to have my future foretold again. I think there is something wrong and even outright sinful in this curiosity to know what fate has decreed.

The first divination came to pass. As for the second, my traveling abroad before the end of the new year, I cannot say as I am writing these lines in January of 1917. I traveled to St. Petersburg once again in mid-December to meet N. N. Pokrovskii, the new minister of foreign affairs. Simple and soft in his approach, he was the complete antithesis of the stuck-up pompous Stürmer. Unlike Stürmer, Pokrovskii did not try to hide the fact he was new to the field of foreign policy; instead, he tried to learn as much as possible about issues that were new to him. He thought it was not worth my while to travel to Corfu but asked me to write a memorandum on war aims. I took on this task in Vasil'evskoe and sent Pokrovskii two letters on the subject.

CONCLUSION

D
ue to a knee injury, I had to cancel my planned trip to St. Petersburg at the beginning of January 1917 and remained in Moscow. I used this opportunity to complete my reminiscences. In conclusion, I would like to give my final impressions from 1916. Before going to my estate, my eldest son, Kostia, and I decided to visit Optina Monastery. I had been thinking about it for a while, and Kostia became interested in the trip after one of his friends described his experience in Optina. We had only two days at our disposal, but these two days in Optina made an indelible impression on both of us. Even upon arrival, I felt a certain peace of mind, which was bound to affect even the most troubled of souls. Everyday worries seemed to vanish at the gates of the monastery. Generations of monks and pilgrims had created an atmosphere of spiritual intensity around these temples and cells.

I went to see Father Anatolii after the midday prayer. He lived in a small white house with columns and a mezzanine. There were plenty of visitors from all walks of life, who were sitting on benches or standing by the inner porch in expectation of the old man's arrival. Only the occasional whispered exchange interrupted the solemn silence.

What faces, what eyes. There was one Russian peasant who made an indelible impression on me. His handsome face was covered by a long Russian beard. His gaze, concentrated and fathomless under heavyset eyebrows, indicated that something weighed heavily on his heart and he was bringing this to the abbot. Next to him stood an officer and a long-haired traveler eating some black bread. An urbane woman, who seemed to know everything about the place, stood by the gate. She had several children with her, including a boy obviously of high school age but very small in stature.

"Last year, Father Varnava gave me an apple every time we visited," he said in a dreamy voice.

"You were still a little boy back then," his mother interjected.

"I expect nothing of the sort this time around," the boy protested with dignity, although it was clear he would not turn down an apple even now.

The door opened with a screeching noise. It was the very Father Varnava, the Abbott's attendant. He had the most humble expression on his face and in his voice. Upon seeing me, he asked who I was and where I had come from. He left, returning shortly. I followed him and eventually came into a small room. The abbot was there. Just as I was about to pay my respects, he turned toward the icons and began saying a prayer, as if inviting me to join him. After he had finished, he bowed, pointed toward a chair, and sat down himself.

The abbot, the venerable Father Anatolii, was hunched and small in stature with a gray beard and wrinkled face. He spoke quickly, mumbling. Although everything he said was simple and straightforward, there was a special aura around him. He suggested that I confess, reading aloud a Church Slavonic confession of sins. I was impressed by his close attention to detail. He seemed to possess finely tuned internal spiritual hearing, which caught the innermost thoughts of people. After I finished my confession, he gave me a few sheets of paper with which he had been fiddling earlier. These contained edifying verses of different value. One of these sheets, which he asked Kostia to give me later, told the story of a man's confession. I was struck by the mood of this confession, which inadvertently seemed to echo my own. The old man seemed to have sensed this and realized I could bene-fit from reading the other man's story. Before I left, the abbot blessed me.

On the next day, he saw Kostia and me separately. I was glad to see how enlightened and tenderly emotional Kostia looked after his talk with the old man. My own second visit left me with even deeper impressions. There is no point in writing down the exact conversation we had, as the ancient's spiritual light and aura are impossible to convey. His eyes, which at first appeared small, seemed to grow bigger and burn with a spiritual fire as he spoke. He could speak to your soul in a spiritual language, and I felt what I had previously felt only rarely in my dreams—an ability to communicate through the soul, without any words. I hope whoever reads these lines will not simply dismiss them as the product of a fanciful imagination.

As I write this, I am trying to convey everything as it really was, to recall and fathom my experience. I feel totally inadequate, however. How can I possibly do justice to this venerable soul with his clear and radiant spiritu-ality, great humility, loving kindness? He was the living image of that very apostolic verse that my mother had written into my copy of the New Testament: "Rejoice in the Lord always: and again I say, rejoice. Let your humility be known unto all men. The Lord is at hand."

The old man's loving spiritual joy was particularly enchanting. The same mood had inspired Dostoevsky to create Old Man Zosima in *The Brothers Karamazov*. Christian moods and Christian deeds are manifold. The monks of Optina Monastery seem to have preserved the joy of this humble loving spirit, which became a great tangible force. It was evident in all the monks with whom I interacted.

The religious service in Optina Monastery was not of the high standard I had come to expect. The war had clearly affected the monastery—150 monks had been drafted into the army, resulting in less magnificent choral singing. We attended a much better service in a nearby chapel in the pine forest. It was nighttime, and the full moon shone on the tall pine trees covered in frost. The white snow on the ground glistened. At midnight, a bell tolled, calling the pilgrims to prayer. It was a scene taken from folk poetry.

In the morning, I saw a gray-bearded, hunched old monk scatter bird seeds by the monastery. Flying pigeons surrounded him like a halo. There were no wars, no politics, no worries here—only peace, quiescence, and a spiritual flame. It is the last image from the troubled year 1916 on which I wish to end my story, as I fall silent before this metaphor of eternal peace and God's quiet.

January 25, 1917.

NOTES

NOTES TO CHAPTER 1

1. N. G. Hartwig (1855–1914) was Russian ambassador to Serbia from 1909 to 1914, a pan-Slavist, and a key figure in the formation of the Balkan League, the union of Bulgaria, Serbia, Greece, and Montenegro in 1912.

2. S. D. Sazonov (1860–1927) was minister of foreign affairs for ten years until 1916.

3. Count F. Pourtalès (1853–1928) was counselor to the German Ministry of Foreign Affairs, 1914–1948, and German ambassador to Russia from 1907–1914.

4. A. A. Neratov (1863–1938) was assistant foreign minister from 1910 to 1917.

5. Wilhelm von Adler (dates unknown).was a banker and financier. In 1913, von Adler propagated a Franco-Austrian acquisition of the western part of the Orient Railway network.

6. A. P. Izvolskii (1856–1919) was foreign minister from 1906 to 1910 and Russian ambassador to France from 1910 to 1916.

7. Count H. L. von Tschirschky (1858–1916) was German ambassador to Austria-Hungary from 1907 to 1914 and supported a hard-line policy against Serbia.

8. Count L. von Berchtold (1863–1942) was the Austro-Hungarian foreign minister in 1914.

9. A. V. Krivoshein (1857–1921) was minister of agriculture.

10. General Count Tatishchev (1868–1918) was Russian attaché to the court of Emperor Wilhelm before the war. He was devoted to the tsar, for which he would later suffer a martyr's death.

11. The Treaty of Portsmouth, September 1905, brought the Russo-Japanese War to an end.

12. V. A. Sukhomlinov (1848–1926), a Russian general and minister of war from 1909 to 1915, was largely responsible for Russia's entry into World War I.

13. The Duma was the legislative assembly first elected in 1906.

14. N. N. L'vov (1867–1944) was a liberal thinker, a writer, and the chairman of the second Duma, and P. B. Struve (1870–1944) was a liberal thinker, an economist, an essayist, and a member of the 1907 Duma. He was involved with Denikin and Wrangel during the civil war.

15. The "Irish Question" refers to the issue of who governs Ireland and to Britain's internal dispute of how to deal with the Irish uprisings and call for independence.

16. Sir N. R. O'Conor (1843–1908) was the ambassador of His Britannic Majesty to the Imperial Russian Court in 1895.

17. Count S. Y. Witte (1849–1915) was first prime minister of Russia in 1905 and chairman of the Council of Ministers.

18. Count V. N. Lamsdorff (1845–1907) was foreign minister from 1900 to 1907.

19. Sir E. Grey (1862–1933) was British foreign secretary 1905 to 1916. He was intelligent but often naïve on foreign affairs, anti-German, and wary of foreign commitments, but more interventionist than most members of the Liberal Party.

20. Count A. K. Benckendorff (1849–1917) was Russian ambassador to the court of St. James in 1914. He helped create the Triple Entente (Allied powers).

21. Count V. N. Kokovtsev (1853–1943), previously minister of finance, was chairman of the Council of Ministers from 1911 to 1914.

22. N. A. Maklakov (1871–1918) was minister of internal affairs—not to be confused with his brother V. A. Maklakov, a "liberal-imperialist" intellectual.

23. B. N. Chicherin (1828–1904) was a philosopher and councillor-at-law. V. V. Solovyov (1853–1900) was a philosopher who pursued the idea of reconciliation and moral unity between the Christian churches. Prince Sergei N. Trubetskoi (1862–1905) was a prominent philosopher and a beloved professor, the first freely elected rector of Moscow University. His funeral spurred large demonstrations and proved an important event in the 1905 revolution.

24. Chervonnaya Rus' (Red Ruthenia) is an area between the Carpathian Mountains and the Dniester River. As of the twelfth century it became known as Galicia.

NOTES TO CHAPTER 2

1. Congress of Berlin (1878) was a summit meeting of Europe's major powers, Russia, and Turkey to reorganize the Balkan countries. The preliminary treaty of San Stefano (also 1878) was a treaty between Russia and Turkey in San Stefano, presently Yesilkoy.

2. Ignatiev was most probably Count N. P. Ignatiev (1832–1908), a Russian military attaché in Paris.

3. Milan, king of Serbia (1854–1901), reigned from 1868 to 1889.

4. The Young Turk Party was a political party founded by Mitkhadom Pasha in the 1870s. Its agenda was to bring European attitudes and social mores to Turkish society. After many years of propaganda, the Young Turks acquired control of the army. In July 1908, there was a military takeover, effectively giving them full control of the government. The main organs of this party were committees loosely translated as "the unified and progressive."

5. The Treaty of Paris (1856) ended the Crimean War.

6. T. Maiorescu (1840–1917) was a writer, a professor, and a minister of education.

7. I. Brătianu (1864–1927) was prime minister five different times. He united the Old Rumanian Kingdom with Transylvania, Bukovina, and Bessarabia.

8. Princess Marie of Rumania (1875–1938) was the wife of Ferdinand I of Rumania and the granddaughter of both Queen Victoria and Emperor Alexander II of Russia.

9. Danev, S. P. (1858–1947) was the chairman of the Bulgarian People's Council. He was given the responsibility of secret diplomatic missions. Traveling around Europe, he initiated discussions, imagining himself a Bulgarian Bismarck.

10. The St. Petersburg Conference (July 17, 1913) was an ambassadors' conference to resolve Rumanian-Bulgarian disputes.

11. Çatalca was a line of defense extending west of Constantinople between the Black Sea and the Sea of Marmara, next to a village of the same name.

12. Adrianople (Edirne) was the capital of the Ottoman Empire from 1361 to 1453.

13. Nikola Pašić (1846–1926) was grand marshal of Serbia and repeatedly the premier. His policy was pro-Russian. He negotiated the union of Serbia, Croatia and Slovenia in 1917. He controlled the country from 1903 until 1926 as Prime Minister of the Kingdom of Serbia and subsequently as Prime Minister of Yugoslavia.

14. E. Venizelos (1864–1936) was a Greek statesman and president of the council from 1910 to 1916. He resisted the pro-German politics of King Constantine. Heading the revolutionary government of Salonika from 1916 to 1918, he made an alliance with the Entente.

15. Rodosto is a port on the Sea of Marmara.

16. A. N. Kuropatkin (1848–1925) was imperial minister of war from 1898 to 1904.

17. V. M. Doroshevich (1864–1922) was at the time a popular humorist, satirist, and distributor of pamphlets.

18. Kavala is a port city in Thrace. Its old name was Neapolis.

19. Trebizond/Trabzon is a port in Asia Minor on the Black Sea.

20. O. Liman von Sanders (1855–1929) was a German general.

21. Scutari (or Ouskoudar or Scutari d'Asie) was the beginning of the Anatolian Railway Line.

22. Count I. I. Vorontsov-Dashkov (1837–1916) was governor of the Caucasus from 1905 to 1916.

23. A dragoman was an interpreter of Turkic and other languages of the Near East.

24. Y. G. Zhilinskii (1853–1919) was chief of general staff from 1911 to 1914 and commander of the Russian northwestern front in 1914. M. N. Giers (1856–1932) was ambassador to Italy in 1915. He is not to be confused with Giers Sr., who was minister of foreign affairs for Alexander III.

25. Livadia was the tsar's summer palace located on the south shore of Crimea.

26. The word *porte* is from the French, meaning "door" or "entrance." It came to be used by diplomats as a metaphor for the Ottoman Empire. In 1536, French diplomats were required to pass under a monumental gate. *Porte* in this case refers to the Turkish government.

27. Bey Enver (1881–1922) was Turkish war minister from January 1914 until 1918. Both reckless and ambitious, he was strongly pro-German.

28. The Bucharest Agreement was the Treaty of Bucharest (1913) ending the second Balkan War. It divided most of Bulgaria's land claims in Macedonia and Thrace between Serbia and Greece.

29. Georges Blondel (1856–1948) was a French historian of Austria and Germany.

30. Enos is a Greek city in Thrace.

31. Take-Ionescu (1858–1922) was prime minister before Brătianu and minister of foreign affairs from 1920 to 1921.

32. A. Marghiloman (1854–1925) was a pro-German politician and leader of the conservative opposition party. He advocated a policy of neutrality. He was prime minister of Rumania for a few months in 1918.

NOTES TO CHAPTER 3

1. Radomir Putnik (1847–1917) was a Serbian field marshal and general chief of staff who was successful against the Austrians in 1914. He served fifty-four years.

2. G. E. L'vov (1861–1925) was chairman of the provisional government in 1917. He resigned over the idea of proclaiming Russia as a republic.

3. Topola is a town and municipality in northern Vojvodina. Crown Prince Alexander (1888–1934) was appointed regent in 1914. He became king in 1921 and was assassinated in Marseilles in 1934 by a Macedonian activist.

4. A konak is a building belonging to an important Turkish official.

5. King Milan Obrenović (1854–1901) was king of Serbia. He was deposed in 1889.

6. Banat district is in the autonomous province of Vojvodina. Vojvodina was partitioned in 1920 between Rumania and Yugoslavia.

7. Sir Arthur H. F. Paget (1851–1932) was a British general. General Paul Pau (1848–1931) was a retired French general. He was the French representative to the imperial Russian army administrative staff (Stavka).

8. Dedeagach is a Thracian port in present-day Greece. It became Bulgarian in 1913.

9. F. Supilo (1870–1917) was a Croatian politician and journalist.

10. Risorgimento, in Italian history, is the period of national unification (ca. 1815–1870).

NOTES TO CHAPTER 4

1. For more details and repertoire, see Faubion Bowers, *Scriabin, a Biography*, 2nd rev. ed. (New York: Dover, 1996), 267.

NOTES TO CHAPTER 5

1. N. A. Kudashev (1868–1925) was a Russian embassy advisor in Vienna.

2. Phanar is a Greek quarter in Constantinople.

3. Pera is a suburb of Constantinople, now part of the Istanbul district of Galata. The Prince Islands are nine islands in the Sea of Marmora, close to Constantinople.

4. Baranovichi is the region of Minsk.

5. A yurt is a rounded Siberian nomadic tent.

NOTES TO CHAPTER 6

1. Sir V. Chirol (1852–1929) was a British journalist, historian, and diplomat.

2. Bačka (Bachka) is in Vojvodina Province. Syrmia is now Sremska Mitrovica, in Vojvodina Province.

3. T. Delcassé (1852–1923) was French minister of foreign affairs in 1913 and previously the French ambassador to Russia. General J. Joffre (1852–1931) was chief of French general staff until 1916.

4. Komitadj, in this case, means an anti-Austrian guerrilla.

5. P. A. Stolypin (1862–1911) was prime minister of imperial Russia from 1906 to 1911. A proponent of land reforms, he was assassinated in Kiev while at an operatic performance.

6. Kadets was the informal name for the Constitutional Democratic Party founded in 1905.

7. K. N. Gulkevich was a diplomat (d. 1935) and ambassador to Norway from 1914 to 1917.

NOTES TO CHAPTER 7

1. Santi Quaranti is presently Saranda, a city in Albania opposite the island of Corfu.

2. Živko Pavlović (1871–1938) was a colonel in the Serbian High Command, and head of operations.

3. General M. P. Sarrail (1856–1929) commanded the French and British division in Salonika.

4. *Arnauts* is the Turkish name for Albanians.

5. Stefan of Dečan (1285–1331) was Stefan Uroš III, king of Serbia from 1322 to 1331. He built Dečani Monastery and was canonized by the Serbian church.

6. The Kmet is a Serbian elder of a village, the mayor.

7. King Stefan Dušan (ca. 1308–1355) was Stefan Uroš IV Dušan. He enforced a universal code of law. Prince Marko (1335–1395) confronted Turkish forces during the earlier period of the Ottoman occupation.

8. Andrejevci is a settlement in the mountains of Montenegro toward Kosovo. The closest center is Ivangrad.

NOTES TO CHAPTER 8

1. San Giovanni di Medua is a port on the Adriatic north of Durazzo and just south of Scutari.

2. Cattaro or Kotor was an important Austrian naval base, which passed to Yugoslavia in 1918.

3. Prince Mirko (1879–1918) was the second son of King Nicholas of Montenegro. Mirko's third son, Michael, became king.

4. Durazzo or Durrës was the second-largest ancient city in Albania and the most important port. Valona was an Adriatic port in the Bay of Valona in southwest Albania.

NOTES TO CHAPTER 9

1. Bizerte was a port in Tunisia on the Mediterranean.

2. Kotliarevskii was an active member of the Muscovite Liberal-Imperialist circles.

3. Lovćen was a mountain national park in southwest Montenegro, extending from the Adriatic Sea. Sandzak was a territory, part of the Serbian state of Raška and Montenegro.

4. Lazar Miušković (1867–1936).

NOTES TO CHAPTER 10

1. The Palestinian Society, founded in 1860 in Russia, guided pilgrims to the Holy Land where it owned properties.

2. Admiral de Guedon. "De Gedon" is Trubetskoi's spelling.

NOTES TO CHAPTER 11

1. J. Cruppi (1855–1933) was a French magistrate and politician. He published remarkable works on reform and judicial organization.

2. K. I. Chukovskii (1882–1969) was an influential literary critic and essayist. The most popular children's poet, he was favored by many generations of children. Wilton was, in fact, most probably Robert Wilton (1868–1925), correspondent of the *London Times* in Russia for seventeen years. He became known as a keen observer of events in Russia during the last years of the tsarist regime. He published an account, *The Last Days of the Romanovs*, in 1920.

NOTES TO CHAPTER 12

1. A. C. Bouteneff (1879–1946) was counselor to the imperial Russian embassy in London.

2. C. M. Onou (1875–1950) was first secretary, later chargé d'affaires in the absence of an ambassador, to the Russian embassy in Washington.

3. The Right Honourable H. Kitchener (1850–1916) was a British field marshal and secretary of state for war in 1914.

4. B. V. Stürmer (1848–1917) was prime minister in January 1916, acting minister of the interior in March, and minister of foreign affairs in July.

Bibliography

Bowers, Faubion. *Scriabin, a Biography*. 2nd rev. ed. New York: Dover, 1996.

Larousse, Pierre. *Larousse universel en 2 volumes: Nouveau dictionnaire encyclopédique, publié sous la direction de Claude Augé*. 2 vols. Paris: Librairie Larousse, 1922–1923.

Lieven, D. C. B. *Russia and the Origins of the First World War*. New York: St. Martin's Press, 1983.

Pavlenkov, F. *Entsiklopedicheskii Slovar'*. 5th ed. St. Petersburg, 1913.

Struve, P. B. *Pamiati Kn. Gr. N. Trubetskogo, Sbornik statei*. Paris: E. Siial'skoi, 1930.

INDEX

Page numbers in bold refer to images.